MARGERY KEMPE'S DISSENTING FICTIONS

MARGERY KEMPE'S DISSENTING FICTIONS

Lynn Staley

The Pennsylvania State University Press
University Park, Pennsylvania

Library of Congress Cataloging-in-Publication Data

Staley, Lynn, 1947–
    Margery Kempe's dissenting fictions / Lynn Staley.

        p.   cm.
    Includes bibliographical references and index.
    ISBN 0-271-01030-4. — ISBN 0-271-01031-2 (pbk.)
    1. Kempe, Margery, b. ca. 1373. Book of Margery Kempe.
2. Christian literature, English (Middle)—History and criticism.
3. Mysticism—England—History—Middle Ages, 600–1500.   4. Christian
women—England—Religious life—History.   5. Dissenters, Religious
—England—History.   6. Fiction—Technique.   I. Title.
PR2007.K4Z75   1994
248'.2'092—dc20
[B]   93-23046
                                                                CIP

Published by The Pennsylvania State University Press,
University Park, PA 16802-1003

For my sister

Contents

"shal never cloc henne be wel crowing cok"

—Bodley MS. 649, fol. 98v;
quoted in Haines,
"Wilde Wittes and Wilfulnes," 152

Introduction and Acknowledgments

The world of Medieval Studies is an exciting and unsettling one right now. In the past few years, we medievalists have been revitalized by the work of scholars in contiguous disciplines and find ourselves considering old problems from new perspectives and confronting both old and new texts in ways we might not have when we first began our careers. *The Book of Margery Kempe* encapsulates the changes in our field during the last twenty years, for, though it was first edited for the Early English Text Society in 1940 and received the attention of distinguished scholars interested in the history of mysticism and in devotional prose, it was never accorded the sort of critical evaluation given to works like *Piers Plowman* or *Sir Gawain and the Green Knight* or *The Canterbury Tales*. Whether the *Book* was marginalized because it was the work of a woman thought of as a religious "hysteric" or because it was seen as a series of memories artlessly dictated and then put into a more acceptable form by a scribe, it nonetheless was, at least in my day, neither featured in graduate seminars nor excerpted in the *Norton Anthology*. Changes in our conceptions of what constitutes the subjects of history and literature have allowed texts like *The Book of Margery Kempe* into the classroom, the conference hall, and the journal. Despite our increased estimate for the *Book,* it has more still to teach us.

The *Book* is an amazing testimony to the social and religious tensions of late medieval urban life. It offers a unique picture of a period in which the traditional and highly ritualized world of late medieval Catholicism was confronted by an inherently radical and modern challenge posed through the Wycliffite system of thought. Where we might tend to reduce and simplify the nature of this ideological confrontation and draw upon oppositional terminology in our efforts to describe it, the *Book* provides us with a more complicated—because more ambiguous—understanding of the apparently contradictory impulses of late medieval social and religious experience. In its accounts of Margery's uneasy relations with others, the *Book* also points up the tensions an individual (particularly a woman) might experience in a world where traditional values are being tested and inevitably altered by social, political, and economic changes. Those issues that are central to any consideration of England during the first half of the fifteenth century—translation, nationality, authority, heterodoxy, community, to name a few—are likewise central to the *Book*. Official pronouncements about the nature of English society focus upon the concept of community, defining the community as an exclusive and homogeneous body bound together by a shared language, set of beliefs, and sense of order. In contrast, though similarly preoccupied by the concept of community, Kempe provides a different model, defining community in terms of what it can include and thus in terms of those individuals who can now be accommodated in this new society whose foundation is love. Through Margery, Kempe translates into her mother tongue, the language of contemporary mercantile exchange, a *vita Christi* in the form of a social gospel that breaks down, rather than erects, boundaries.

As I argue throughout this study, *The Book of Margery Kempe* does not report a world. Margery Kempe, its author, makes a world. Margery Kempe, like Chaucer, with some of whose works I would guess she was familiar, used the literary tradition to which she was heir as well as the world around her to compose fiction. However, that word covers a multitude of sins, of authorial feints and dodges. We are, of course, accustomed to discussing Chaucer or Langland as sensitive to the author's status in the community. We are less accustomed to thinking of medieval women as writers who might also see art as necessitating strategies of indirection and of deception. In the several years I have taught the *Book* to students at Colgate University, talked with colleagues at the many conferences that dot the landscape of Medieval Studies, and tried to keep up with the new information about late medieval culture that constantly enriches (and alters) our knowledge of that world, I have come to view the *Book* with a genuine respect for the intelligence and artistry of its *author,* Margery Kempe. In her, we have a figure who understood the meaning of and thus the need to assert mastery over communal and literary codes. There are times when I have toyed—and only halfway facetiously—with billing the *Book* as the first novel in English.

I now have the pleasure of thanking those who helped me write this book. Franz Bäuml, Sarah Beckwith, Gail McMurray Gibson, and Steven Justice all gave me opportunities to try out ideas in conference sessions sponsored by the Medieval Academy of America, the International Congress on Medieval Studies, and the New Chaucer Society. Parts of Chapter 1 appeared as "The Trope of the Scribe and the Question of Literary Authority in the Works of Julian of Norwich and Margery Kempe," in *Speculum* 66 (1991). Parts of Chapter 2 appeared as "Margery Kempe: Social Critic," in *The Journal of Medieval and Renaissance Studies* 22 (1992). The British Library gave me permission to quote from MS. Additional 41175. The Bodleian Library gave me permission to cite MS. Bodl. 243. The Research Council of Colgate University has generously continued to support my work. I would like to thank Russell A. Peck for reading an earlier draft of Chapter 1 and Linck C. Johnson for reading and commenting on the entire manuscript. I have been blessed by having two of the most knowledgeable scholars of the late Middle Ages as readers for Penn State Press. Both Derek Pearsall and Ralph Hanna III gave my manuscript careful and extraordinarily helpful readings that allowed me to sharpen and, in one case, refocus my argument. Philip Winsor, Senior Editor at Penn State Press, continues to win from me only praises for his rare courtesy and efficiency and for his keen understanding of the needs of presses and authors. My ongoing and gladly assumed debts to my fellows are recorded in the notes throughout this book. My half of the tally stick I have transformed into a list of Works Cited, an account for which there is no recompense. I offer this study as part of the vigorous conversation between the past and the present that is Medieval Studies as it is practiced in the late twentieth century. Finally, I dedicate this book to Kathryn F. Staley, my sister, who has taught me almost as much as Margery Kempe about the art of transgressing boundaries.

1

Authorship and Authority

This book began as a study of the strategies of dissent in late Middle English literature. It has become a contextual study of the strategies of one author, Margery Kempe, whose prose treatise is frequently described as the first autobiography in English.[1] In the distance between those two terms—the one used more generally to describe a literary work that treats of some particular subject, the other to denote a work of self-reflection and self-expression—lies the scope of this book.[2] Those expectations of form and meaning triggered by medieval "autobiographical" texts, expectations that, in the end, serve to define literary kinds or genres, are at once raised and frustrated by *The Book of Margery Kempe*. The *Book* offers itself as the written record of an oral reminiscence that describes the inner development of its subject, beginning with a single moment of despair and recognition. However, it neither makes use of the most obvious of autobiographical techniques, the "I" that is used to signify the shifting identity of the speaker and subject, nor falls into the confessional mode that tended to shape the medieval dialectic of the

1. All quotations from *The Book of Margery Kempe* refer to the EETS (Early English Text Society) edition by Sanford Brown Meech and will be designated in the text by page numbers.
2. I am aware that "autobiography" is a post-Romantic concept. For thoughts on medieval autobiographical texts, see, for example, Ferguson, "Autobiography as Therapy: Guibert de Nogent, Peter Abelard, and the Making of Medieval Autobiography"; Vance, "Augustine's *Confessions* and the Grammar of Selfhood."

self.[3] Instead, the *Book* is cast as a third-person narrative about a life, a narrative that does not follow a chronological progression but describes itself as an account of the random memories of its subject, one Margery Kempe of Lynn in East Anglia. At every juncture, it proclaims itself a collaborative effort between the subject and her "writer" that is intended to capture the spiritual experience or the growth in spiritual understanding of this one woman.

However, as both Gail McMurray Gibson and Karma Lochrie have recently demonstrated, the apparent artlessness of the *Book* conceals a knowledge of the conventions of fifteenth-century piety and of the contemporary literature of devotion, both Latin and vernacular.[4] Although some studies of the *Book* still insist on seeing it as the manifestation of frustration or hysteria, epithets too often linked to the gender of its subject, increasing attention is being paid to the *Book* in relation to the social, spiritual, and cultural trends of the late Middle Ages.[5] My own work on the *Book* has not only convinced me that studies of Kempe's artistry are well justified but that we need to apply to Kempe the complicated series of questions about narrative that we apply to other major authors of the late medieval period. *The Book of Margery Kempe* is not what it appears to be, any more than *The Canterbury Tales* are stories Chaucer heard from "other" pilgrims, or *Piers Plowman* is a tale spun from Langland's tavern-hopping experiences in London. Or it is far more than it appears to be, since it records, often times quite powerfully, Margery's

3. I am drawing here upon Vance's language, see "Augustine's *Confessions* and the Grammar of Selfhood," 3, 5. For a discussion of literary acts of confession, see Patterson, *Chaucer and the Subject of History,* chapter 8, "The Subject of Confession: the Pardoner and the Rhetoric of Penance."

4. Gibson, *The Theater of Devotion: East Anglian Drama and Society in the Late Middle Ages,* chapter 3; Lochrie, *Margery Kempe and Translations of the Flesh.* For another study of the artistry of the *Book,* see Mueller, "Autobiography of a New 'Creatur': Female Spirituality, Selfhood, and Authorship in *The Book of Margery Kempe.*"

5. For studies that define *The Book* as evincing a certain amount of hysteria or frustration, see Hirsch, *The Revelations of Margery Kempe: Paramystical Practices in Late Medieval England;* Knowles, *The English Mystical Tradition,* chapter 8; Partner, "Reading the Book of Margery Kempe." For other studies linking the *Book* to contemporary social and cultural conventions, see Aers, "Rewriting the Middle Ages: Some Suggestions"; idem, *Community, Gender and Individual Identity: English Writing 1360–1430,* 73–116; Atkinson, *Mystic and Pilgrim: The Book and the World of Margery Kempe;* Beckwith, "A Very Material Mysticism: The Medieval Mysticism of Margery Kempe"; Dickman, "Margery Kempe and the English Devotional Tradition"; idem, "Margery Kempe and the Continental Tradition of the Pious Woman"; Goodman, "The Piety of John Brunham's Daughter of Lynn"; Wallace, "Mystics and Followers in Sienna and East Anglia: A Study in Taxonomy, Class and Cultural Mediation."

growing ability to assert authority over her self and to trust the strength of her private experience of the nature of the divine.[6]

Just as we commonly distinguish between Will, the layabout, and Langland, the author, or between the pilgrim Geoffrey and the poet Chaucer, so in this study I draw a distinction between Margery, the subject, and Kempe her author. Like Julian of Norwich, whose ardent admirers are for the most part committed to the picture of a "Mother Julian," whose serene faith can easily be accommodated within the bosom of the Church, readers of Kempe frequently assume that Margery's lack of serenity reflects her author's insecurity and victimization.[7] Since Julian of Norwich and Margery Kempe are two of the major prose writers of England's late medieval period, it seems grudging to define their achievements in terms of the stereotypes of gender: placidity, on the one hand, and hysteria, on the other. As this chapter will demonstrate, both writers evince their awareness of the need for strategies to conceal or disguise their strongly original and, in some cases, destabilizing, insights into systems of theological or communal ordering. The unwillingness to grant them the full measure of their achievement suggests our inability to confront women writers as fully enfranchised by their art. For example, Kempe's first chapter, which describes Margery's early crisis of faith, is often written off to postpartum depression. In contrast, how often do we ascribe the melodies of *Go Down Moses* to *bourbon*? Were the *Book* attributed to Geoffrey Chaucer or William Langland or even to Joyce Cary or William Faulkner, we would pay a good deal more attention to its narrative strategies, to its voices, and to its decidedly irreverent approach to the hallowed verities of contemporary life. Implicitly, however, Kempe's achievement is undervalued precisely because, before we even begin to talk about that achievement, we define the *Book* in terms of its author's gender and so circumscribe our response to it by assuming an absolute equation between the *Book*'s author and its subject.[8]

In so doing, we signal our baffled reaction to what is *designed* to be a

---

6. For studies focusing on Margery's growth in authority, see Beckwith, "Problems of Authority in Late Medieval English Mysticism: Language, Agency, and Authority in *The Book of Margery Kempe*"; Feinberg, "Thematics of Value in *The Book of Margery Kempe*."

7. On Julian, see, for example, Pelphrey, *Love Was His Meaning: The Theology and Mysticism of Julian of Norwich*. Pelphrey is not only committed to Julian's serenity, but to her relative lack of education.

8. On this subject, see Nina Baym, "The Madwoman and Her Language: Why I Don't Do Feminist Literary Theory."

disturbing and difficult reading experience. The *Book* not only resists our efforts to grow comfortable in it; its protagonist also seems to belie any preconceived notions we might have of the status and expectations of medieval women, and perhaps of women in general. There are times when the *Book* appears a wickedly ironic and highly literate "answer" to the questions posed by Chaucer through the Wife of Bath, dominant among them, "What *is* it women want most?"[9] But where the Wife talks, Margery acts. In relation to the Wife of Bath and her finally empty rhetoric of social change, Margery's life traces a truly revolutionary spiral. Kempe uses what are the "normative" elements of female experience, such as Margery's relations with her husband and her children, to express or clarify the nature of her true preoccupation, her vocation. Thus the very few details Kempe gives of domestic life serve only to highlight Margery's increasing committment to a life whose very devotedness marks her disengagement from the interests and activities of her contemporaries. At the *Book*'s end, Kempe makes no attempt to depict Margery as seeking to reestablish a species of domestic or communal harmony. Rather, she offers us a picture of a woman in her sixties, whose husband and oldest son are dead and barely mourned, whose other thirteen children are never mentioned, and whose physical circumstances and future are left unspecified. Like Chaucer or Langland, who were willing to end their poems with incidents that defy our conventional notions of closure, Kempe denies us the comfort inherent in circular form. What resolution Kempe provides has nothing to do with Margery's reintegration into her community, but, instead, depends upon our acceptance of her achieved status as a singular figure.

The *Book* is finally the work of an author whose narrative demonstrates her ability to use the conventions of sacred biography and devotional prose that she inherited as the means of scrutinizing the very foundations of community. In so doing, she demonstrates a keen sense of the ways in which what we might call generic categories can be expanded. Kempe, like other medieval women writers, inevitably faced constrictions that reflected the status of women in a hierarchical and patriarchal community.

9. My suggestion is not a spurious one. For suggestions about the fifteenth-century audience for key fourteenth-century texts, see Middleton, "The Audience and Public of *Piers Plowman*"; Patterson, "Ambiguity and Interpretation: A Fifteenth-Century Reading of *Troilus and Criseyde*"; Strohm, "Chaucer's Fifteenth-Century Audience and the Narrowing of the Chaucer Tradition." For an early reading of Margery Kempe in relation to the Wife of Bath, see Delany, "Sexual Economics, Chaucer's Wife of Bath and *The Book of Margery Kempe*."

Most women authors acknowledged these in their prefatory remarks, seeking authorization for female speech in divine inspiration or in some other communally acceptable activity such as the transmission of foreign or ancient matter.[10] Since the convent, and in some cases, the court, were the likeliest places where women could acquire an education, the bulk of medieval women's writing was devotional. Thus, where male authors theoretically had available to them a wide range of literary conventions— to some extent reflecting the wide range of activities in which they might engage—women's literature reflected their general social, ideological, and economic restriction. Such exigencies are necessarily evinced in Kempe's *Book* and testify to her understanding of what in a later age we would call the literary marketplace, as well as to her willingness as a writer to take risks. Thus, though the *Book* is cast into a communally sanctioned "female" form, Kempe uses the very conventions that tended to define that form to test its outer limits. In producing a text whose apparatus locates it in a communal context, she signals her grasp of the relationship between genre and public, but her underlying technique works to dissolve the very community she thereby constitutes. In so doing, she creates a work that is open to radically opposed readings.

For example, Kempe's description of Margery's trial before the Archbishop of York can be seen either as an instance of Margery's successful rebuttal of charges of heresy or as a slyly subversive commentary upon the English church (see 125–28). The episode itself dramatizes some of the major issues associated with the Lollard heresy in the fifteenth century. Kempe first describes Margery's distinctive dress and outspoken moral views as threatening communal values and hence order. When she is called to account for her nonconformity and the Archbishop quizzes her about the Articles of the Faith, Margery acquits herself well, thus verifying her orthodoxy. However, he then asks her to swear not to "techyn ne chalengyn" the people in his diocese, something that Margery cannot do. She not only refuses to so swear (thus dangerously aligning herself with the Lollards, who were known to disapprove of swearing), but insists that she must rebuke those who themselves swear "gret othys." She then implicitly compounds her dilemma by citing the Gospel as precedent for her mission, since the Lollards, who frequently described themselves as "Bible men," persistently rooted their arguments about church reform in

10. For a discussion of one aspect of this topic, see N. Z. Davis, "Gender and Genre: Women as Historical Writers, 1400–1820."

Scripture, which they saw as the only true authority. Margery cites Christ as her final authority, saying that in Luke he authorized anyone, man or woman, to speak of God.[11] The Archbishop's clerks are suspicious of her use of Scripture, saying, "sche hath a deuyl wyth-inne hir, for sche spekyth of þe Gospel" (126). Another clerk cites Saint Paul's disapproval of women preachers and chastizes her for preaching. Kempe insists that she does not preach but only uses "communication" and "good words." Another comes and accuses her of telling the worst tale he ever heard about priests. The Archbishop asks for the tale, which Margery tells and the Archbishop praises.

The tale is about a priest who goes wandering in the woods and, when night falls, takes refuge in a fair garden which contains a beautiful pear tree:

> al floreschyd wyth flowerys & belschyd, and blomys ful delectabil to hys syght, wher cam a bere, gret & boistows, hogely to be-heldyn, schakyng þe pertre & fellyng down þe flowerys. Gredily þis greuows best ete & deuowryd þo fayr flowerys. &, whan he had etyn hem, turnyng hys tayl-ende in þe prestys presens, voydyd hem owt ageyn at þe hymyr party.

The priest is bothered (filled with "gret drede & heuynes") by the sight of the bear defiling the flowers, seeing the episode's loathsomeness as exter-nal to himself. However, a palmer disabuses him, telling him that he is the pear tree, whose fair flowers are his sacramental activities, flowers he then reduces to excrement by his heedlessness and worldliness, by his lack of contrition, and by his devotion to the pleasures of his own flesh. He is thus both the "lothly ber" and the pear tree: "þu deuowryst & destroist þe flowerys & blomys of vertuows leuyng to thyn endles dampnacyon & many mannys hyndryng lesse þan þu haue grace of repentawns & amendyng" (127). The Archbishop's clerk is particularly "smitten" by Margery's tale, asking her to pray for him. Though the Archbishop him-self likes the tale, he nonetheless wishes Margery to leave his diocese. She then passes through York, where she "was receyued of mech pepil & of ful worthy clerkys, whech enioyed in owr Lord þat had ȝouyn hir not lettryd witte & wisdom to answeryn so many lernyd men wyth-owtyn velani or blame" (128).

Kempe's account of this episode is richly—and strategically—inconsis-

11. For further discussion of this passage, see below, pages 119–21.

tent. Ostensibly, it stages a confrontation between Margery and Henry Bowet, the actively anti-Lollard Archbishop of York, and becomes one more piece of evidence we can use to illustrate Margery Kempe's difficulties in establishing her orthodoxy in a community hostile toward the pious but outspoken woman. If we take the *Book* simply as a memoir whose veracity can be ascertained by reference to ecclesiastical records, then we may be justified in taking the incident at face value. However, if we look more closely at the texture and technique of the episode, ultimately at its fiction, we can begin to see it as raising (but not laying) some of the most important and more inflammatory issues of the day. Unlicensed preaching was, of course, forbidden and punishable; preaching by women was even more reprehensible, since the Lollards were commonly accused of encouraging women to preach and even to administer the sacraments.[12] Whether or not the accusations were true, they reveal the degree to which Lollardy was associated with fears of dislocation and disorder. Kempe's straightforward approach to this issue is somewhat disingenuous, for Margery answers the charge by saying she comes "in no pulpytt" but only communicates and "uses" good words. As Lochrie has pointed out, Margery quite rightly draws a distinction between preaching and teaching, justifying herself in terms Kempe's public would recognize.[13] The situation thus points up Kempe's awareness of what is at stake here, as well as her highly self-conscious handling of what were, finally, issues of law.

There is, however, more to the incident than Kempe's awareness of legal or ecclesiastical precedent; for, though it purports to acquit Margery of charges of Lollardy, it refuses to silence the very questions it raises. The accusation of the clerk that Margery must have a devil because she quotes Scripture Kempe leaves hanging in the air, no doubt fully aware that Lollards accused the Church of being of the devil's party because they did *not* read Scripture to the people. The tale Margery tells is similarly designed as a signifier of Margery's orthodoxy, for Lollards were well known for their dislike of "fables."[14] By putting a tale in Margery's mouth, Kempe

---

12. See Aston, *Lollards and Reformers: Images and Literacy in Late Medieval Religion*, chapter 2; Cross, " 'Great Reasoners in Scripture': the Activities of Women Lollards"; Hudson, *The Premature Reformation*, 326.

13. For an extended discussion of this entire passage in relation to Lollard arguments for women preaching, see Lochrie, *Margery Kempe and Translations of the Flesh*, 107–13.

14. These are issues, of course, that Chaucer deliberately raises through the Parson, who not only dislikes swearing, but who stoutly and pointedly refuses to participate in the game of tale-telling on the way to Canterbury.

locates Margery in the bosom of mother Church. But Margery's tale of a bear who eats the fair flowers and voids them out his "hymer" part is all too like Lollard attacks on the doctrine of transubstantiation. Wyclif, following the lead of thinkers like Berengar of Tours, had insisted that the elements of the Mass were both substance and accident; substance could not be changed without also altering accident (that is, taste and appearance).[15] His argument, which was cast in the learned Latin of academic polemic and which ultimately concerned the nature of the corporal world, emphasized the spiritual, rather than the physical, change that occurs during the Mass. Though Wyclif certainly was not the first to pry into the mystery of sacramental change, his unwillingness to accept the doctrine of transubstantiation was taken up by his followers and appeared in Lollard rebuttals of sacramental efficacy; many of these discussions focused on the physical process of defecation.[16] Thus Margery Baxter, a Norfolk Lollard (and no university-trained divine) tried in a diocesan court in 1429 in Norwich, was accused of having heretical views about the sacrament. Joanna Clyfland, who bore witness against Margery Baxter, reported her as using an argument from analogy that, by that time, had become a standard Lollard trope for sacramental change. Margery Baxter was accused of saying that if, in fact, the Host is God and the true Body of Christ, then there are as many Gods as Hosts, which are made by thousands of priests each day and thereafter consumed, and, eaten, are discharged through their rears into filthy stinking privies ("quia mille sacerdotes et plures omni die conficiunt mille tales deos et postea tales deos comedunt et commestos emittunt per posteriora in sepibus turpiter fetentibus").[17] Baxter's reply goes beyond recognizing that what is eaten is then voided, for she "discharges" the fair unity of the *corpus Christi* into foul multiplicity, thereby questioning not only the doctrine of the Eucharist itself but its social and cultural manifesta-

15. Rubin, *Corpus Christi,* 14–35; Keen, "Wyclif, the Bible, and Transubstantiation."

16. I realize the exact relationship between Wyclif and the Lollards is still an open question.

17. For the entire deposition, see Tanner, ed., *Heresy Trials in the Diocese of Norwich, 1421–31,* 41–51; the passage above is on 45. A reading of this deposition formed the core of a paper given by Rita Copeland ("Lollardy, Literalism, and the Vernacular: Margery Baxter's Deposition in the Norwich Heresy Trials") at the 27th International Congress on Medieval Studies. For a discussion of the trial that is focused on the relationship between vernacular texts and the female voice (Baxter's words are reported by another, then translated into the Latin of the ecclesiastical courts), see Copeland, "Why Women Can't Read: Medieval Hermeneutics, Statute Law, and the Lollard Trials." For a provocative discussion of this deposition in relation to the broader problems posed by Lollardy, see Hanna, "The Difficulty of Ricardian Prose Translation: The Case of the Lollards," 331–38. For discussions of the coarseness that accompanied either Protestant or proto-Protestant iconoclasm, see Thomas, *Religion and the Decline of Magic,* 51–77.

tions.[18] The sacral and unified body that was invoked in the medieval celebrations of the Feast of Corpus Christi and imaged in the civic processions that marked the day, Baxter dissolves into fragments no more mysterious than any other element of nature.

Whether or not Kempe intends the unusual word "hymyr" (disgraceful)[19] to suggest the unseemliness likewise connoted by "posteriora" and "turpiter," her use of the fable as an ostensible defense of Margery's orthodoxy would implicitly have suggested two key Lollard issues. The first, the nature of the sacrament, as we have seen, was frequently linked to accounts of the process of digestion. The second is inherent in the palmer's exposition of the priest's experience, for the worldly priest is disclosed as both the pear tree and the bear who defiles it, to his own harm and to "many mannys hyndryng." Kempe stops short of linking sacramental efficacy to priestly virtue, but the tale nonetheless emphasizes what was a common topic of Lollard reproach of the contemporary Church. Furthermore, many Lollards, following Wyclif's theory of dominion felt that spiritual authority should be vested only in the virtuous, that the sinful priest had nullified his spiritual powers. Kempe takes care to contain the effect of Margery's tale by having the Archbishop himself approve it, but she refuses to sanitize completely either the tale or Margery's actions. The final sentence, wherein the people of York laud Margery for her God-given ability to answer the learned with her unlettered wisdom, leaves the chapter poised delicately somewhere between irony and criticism: Kempe may present Margery as unlettered, but the sources for her maker's invention go well beyond the scraps of learning tossed to inquisitive wives by sympathetic clergy. By investing this incident with a series of unresolved or explained inconsistencies, Kempe suggests more than a method of narration. She underlines, or gives dramatic form to, some of the unresolved conflicts and tensions she perceives in her own age. She does not report a persistent reality; she composes a reality that evinces cracks and fissures that belie by their existence the unity of the English body politic.

Perhaps the most pronounced, or most denounced, crack in communal harmony during the early fifteenth century was the Lollard heresy.

18. On these, see Rubin, *Corpus Christi*, 233–68. See also my Conclusion.

19. Though Meech thinks *hymyr* is a miswriting of *hyndyr*, *hymyr* appears plainly in the manuscript. I am inclined to accept it and to think that *hymyr* is a variation of *himmere*, a word whose roots the editors of the *Middle English Dictionary* question, but conjecture as meaning inglorious or miserable.

To some extent, I have chosen to beg the question of Kempe's orthodoxy. I have done so for several reasons. First, the *Book* itself, as the
"fable" of the bear and the pear tree illustrates, deliberately negotiates a
space for itself somewhere between institutional faith and outright heresy. Thus, Kempe applies to Margery what sounds like a Lollard epithet,
"thys creature"; describes her as unalterably opposed to swearing, to the
wealth and worldliness of the church; and dramatizes her movement
away from parochial control. Furthermore, she consistently applies the
adjective "good" to nouns like *man, lady,* or *priest* as a way not only of
indicating their manner toward Margery and her needs, but of designat-
ing their spiritual status. Kempe uses "good" eight times alone in chapter 52, which contains the account of her trial in York and the fable of
the bear and the pear tree, prefixing the adjective to nouns like "clerk,"
"preacher," "man," or "prior." While "good" is an innocent-enough
word, Kempe's use of it forms a kind of pattern, suggesting that it
functions in ways similar to such Lollard codes as "trew man" or
"known man."[20] As part of the *Book*'s private vocabulary, "good," unlike
terms like "worshipful," links men and women of all circumstances and
stations in a network of simplicity and charity. On the other hand, if
there are times when Margery resembles a Protestant more than she does
a medieval Catholic, she nonetheless also goes on pilgrimages, worships
at the sites of relics, reveres the sacrament, and generally inhabits the
world of communal ritual and symbol that describes to some extent late
medieval religion.[21] The *Book,* like the fable of the bear and the pear tree
inserted into it, resists any single reading and proclaims Kempe's determi-
nation to refuse strict definition in either social or theological terms.
Here, I think, Kempe has much to teach us about the nature of
fifteenth-century thought and the *shapes* that heterodoxy might take. For
where we can compartmentalize many late medieval works as polemic,
we cannot reduce all works to one of two rubrics. Kempe's deft handling
of the issues of early fifteenth-century England suggests that she was not
only aware of the social and religious tensions and needs of her age but
had also considered the ways in which she might present these as in-

---

20. See Hudson, "A Lollard Sect Vocabulary," in *Lollards and Their Books,* 166–73; Mc-
Farlane, *Lancastrian Kings and Lollard Knights,* 210. Though it is not strictly relevant to Kempe,
as Ladurie points out in *Montaillou,* the Cathars used the term "good man" to indicate the
perfecti.

21. Gibson's *Theater of Devotion* is an eloquent testimonial to the imagistic richness of this
world.

forming a fiction that, in turn, constitutes the age in fictional terms. Because Kempe refuses to be programmatic, I have hesitated to apply to her work the cruder techniques that she herself eschewed. On the other hand, it is extremely hard to understand her techniques or what she might have expected a reader to respond to if we do not seek to understand the terms of fifteenth-century conversation. The outlines of that conversation—or, at least, the written evidence for that conversation— can be found in the network of roughly contemporary texts that concern the subject of the Lollard heresy and the state of the communal body.

One of Kempe's most important means of achieving her scrutiny of contemporary institutions is her deployment of the individual, Margery, as both a foil for and a representative of the community that she adumbrates in the numerous episodes that compose the *Book*. Like other medieval authors, Kempe at once constructs and effaces the self that is inscribed in the text. Just as "Long Will" shadows the text of *Piers Plowman,* so Kempe calls herself by her Christian name throughout the *Book,* and, at moments of peril, identifies herself by her town, by her surname, by her father's status, by her married name—or simply as a wife—and, on one occasion, as the mother of fourteen children.[22] The limpidity and conventionality of Margery's terms of self-definition deflect our attention from Kempe herself, who employs a series of screens to downplay her own agency in the making of her book. If the *Book,* as has been argued, describes Margery as fashioning an identity for herself or as struggling to articulate a subjectivity seen as threatening the community, we must not forget that it is Kempe who so describes Margery's progress toward spiritual and rhetorical authority. The uncertainty we assign to Margery should not be mistaken for Kempe's timidity, but rather should be taken as a sign of her awareness that truth-telling demands some form of authorial fashioning, what I will call a strategy of dissent. One of her most carefully contrived strategies concerns the act by which Margery's life comes to be written; a key part of the *Book*'s fiction is its subject's illiteracy and holiness, two conditions that demand a third party, the scribe who can transcribe the life God himself has inscribed.

The subject of medieval scribes is bound up with the question of textual authority. Scribes not only left their marks upon the manuscripts they copied; they also functioned as interpreters, editing and consequently

---

22. For an essay discussing the process of composing a literary identity, see Middleton, "William Langland's 'Kynde Name': Authorial Signature and Social Identity in Late Fourteenth-Century England."

altering the meaning of texts. Writers, however, did not simply employ scribes as copyists; they elaborated upon the figurative language associated with the book as a symbol and put scribes to another use by incorporating them into their texts as tropes.[23] Such "ghostly scribes" provided authors with figures through which they could project authorial personas, indicate what we would call generic categories, express a sense of community, or guide a reader's responses to a text. Though a writer like Chaucer employed scribal metaphors to signal his relative powerlessness, thereby indicating the outlines of a carefully conceived and concealed persona, women writers such as Hildegard of Bingen or Christine de Pisan exploited those same metaphors to signal both their sense of authority and their awareness of the social constraints placed upon it. Both Julian of Norwich and Margery Kempe seem especially aware of the ways in which the deployment of a scribe could be used strategically, as a means of maintaining control over texts they profess neither to control nor to aspire to control.

Chaucer's poem to Adam, his scribe, suggests ways in which scribes, both literally and figuratively, might impinge upon authorial control. Through Adam, the scribe, Chaucer not only addresses the insecurities of the medieval author and the fear of being miswritten, but indicates ways in which an author might use a scribe as a trope linking language to meaning:

> Adam scriveyn, if ever it thee bifalle
> Boece or Troylus for to wryten newe,
> Under thy long lokkes thou most have the scalle,
> But after my makyng thow wryte more trewe;
> So ofte adaye I mot thy werk renewe,
> It to correcte and eke to rubbe and scrape,
> And al is thorugh thy negligence and rape.[24]

Chaucer describes a relationship between scribe and author in which a writer's truth (whether translated or invented) is at the mercy of another's carelessness and haste. Both Robert E. Kaske and Russell A. Peck have suggested that by referring to his scribe as "Adam," Chaucer acknowl-

---

23. For a discussion of the book as a symbol throughout classical and medieval times, see Curtius, *European Literature and the Latin Middle Ages*, 302–47.

24. "Chaucers Wordes Unto Adam, His Owne Scriveyn," in *The Riverside Chaucer*, 650.

edges the broader problem of semantic inaccuracy brought upon us by the sin of our forefather.[25] As Adam debased language, using it to misrepresent reality, so Chaucer's Adam mars his master's efforts, creating texts in which deformities must be scraped away by the author who must now both create and renew his own creation.[26]

Chaucer's words also seem to underline his tendency to link the problem of transmission of texts with the broader subject of mutability or instability. In *Troilus and Criseyde,* for example, he emphasizes the instabilities of the very medium in which he works:

> Ye knowe ek that in forme of speche is chaunge
> Withinne a thousand yeer, and wordes tho
> That hadden pris, now wonder nyce and straunge
> Us thinketh hem, and yet thei spake hem so,
> And spedde as wel in love as men now do . . .
>
> (II, 22–26)

In the closing stanzas of the poem, he echoes this description of a semantics of mutability by recognizing the fundamental instability of his own mother tongue:

> And for ther is so gret diversite
> In Englissh and in writyng of oure tonge,
> So prey I God that non myswrite the,
> Ne the mysmetre for defaute of tonge;
> And red wherso thow be, or elles songe,
> That thow be understonde, God I biseche!
>
> (V, 1793–98)

Chaucer thus identifies the problem of scribal transmission of texts as a threat to his control over his own words, meter, and meaning. A scribe's "defaute of tonge" might spoil his careful composition, scrambling a poem that Chaucer wished to be understood in a certain way. Chaucer's scribal references seem to disavow final control over his works

---

25. Kaske, " 'Clericus Adam' and Chaucer's 'Adam Scriveyn' "; Peck, "Public Dreams and Private Myths: Perspectives in Middle English Literature." See also Dinshaw, *Chaucer's Sexual Politics,* 3–5, for another look at the figurative possibilities of the poem.

26. For medieval language theory, see Colish, *The Mirror of Language.*

and to serve as one of the many screens Chaucer imposes between himself and a reader. His interest in disclaiming his authorial control seems curious only if we ignore the other elements of a carefully composed Chaucerian persona, whereby Chaucer styles himself as merely a reporter or recorder (*Canterbury Tales*), an inept lover (*Troilus and Criseyde*), a bookworm (*Parliament of Fowles*), or a failed courtier (*Legend of Good Women*). Each of these guises allows Chaucer a means of distancing himself from his writing, thus affording him the freedom only a marginal figure can have.[27]

Chaucer's references to scribes point up the degree to which authorship was bound up with the subject of authority. His comments also suggest ways in which the scribe might serve as a *topos* for a certain type of authority or for the tension a medieval writer might feel concerning his or her relationship to a text. From depictions of God dictating the book of the world, through representations of biblical authors taking down heavenly dictation, to literary metaphors characterizing authors as mediators between divine inspiration and earthly readers or *auditores,* the men and women of the Middle Ages gave ample evidence of their interest in the process of composition, a process in which a writer was dependent in some sense upon the person who took down or copied his or her text. Since a scribe could play a major role in textual disemination, the scribe exerted a good deal of control over a text and its position in a community that increasingly vested authority in literacy.[28] The scribe's—or, more accurately, a secretary's—role was even more pronounced in the early and High Middle Ages, since many authors used dictation to compose texts. As Paul Saenger has noted, by the tenth century *dictare* had supplanted *scribere* as the standard synonym for composition. Secretaries would take down summaries, which were expanded and then read back to the author.[29] With the development of a Gothic cursive in the thirteenth cen-

27. On this issue, see, for example, Bynum, "Women's Stories, Women's Symbols: A Critique of Victor Turner's Theory of Liminality."

28. On the shift in perceptions of authority from oral to written, see Bäuml, "Medieval Texts and the Two Theories of Oral Formulaic Composition: A Proposal for a Third Theory"; Clanchy, "Looking Back from the Invention of Printing"; Stock, *The Implications of Literacy.*

29. See Saenger, "Silent Reading: Its Impact on Late Medieval Script and Society." For references to scribal roles, see also Brown, *Augustine of Hippo,* 272–73; Curtius, *European Literature and the Latin Middle Ages,* 314; Gurenvich, "Oral and Written Culture of the Middle Ages: Two 'Peasant Visions' of the Late Twelfth–Early Thirteenth Centuries"; Parkes, "The Influence of the Concepts of *Ordinatio* and *Compilatio* on the Development of the Book"; Stock, "Medieval Literacy, Linguistic Theory, and Social Organization."

tury, authors increasingly could compose silently and write their works with their own hand, thus exerting a good deal more control over their texts. More important yet, as Saenger points out, the new mode of composition began subtly to affect the view of the reader as someone who might make private use of a book. The shift from public *lectio* to private reading was not complete by Chaucer's lifetime, and his works suggest his awareness that literature was both performance and text.

The fact that a text had to be mediated by both a scribe and an audience presented an author with a set of problems—and necessitated a range of strategies—ultimately related to the degree of authorial control he or she might wish to exert, or to be perceived to exert, over a work. We can sense the frustrations an author might experience in Hildegard of Bingen's complicated description of Volmar, her secretary / scribe. Speaking of herself in the third person, she ascribes her description of Volmar to the "living light" who has inspired her with the gift of prophecy:

> Then she considered in her mind, where she could find some one in My love who would run in the way of salvation. And she found such an one and loved him, recognizing what a faithful man he was, like to herself in that part of his work which concerned Me. And holding fast to him, she laboured together with him in all these matters, in the high and earnest endeavour that My hidden miracles should be revealed.
>
> And this man did not exalt himself above her, but yielded to her with many sighs in the height of that humility which he obtained, and in the intention of a good will. Thou, therefore, oh man, who receivest these things not in the inquietude of deception, but in the straightforward purity of simplicity, for the manifestation of hidden things, write what thou seest and hearest.[30]

---

30. Hildegard of Bingen, *Scivias*, trans. Steele, in *Medieval Women's Visionary Literature*, ed. Petroff, 154. The tenderness of Hildegard's Latin conveys the sense of married concord between herself and Volmar: "Unde in amore meo scrutatus est in animo suo, ubi illum inveniret qui viam salutis curreret. Et quemdam invenit et eum amavit, agnoscens quod fidelis homo esset et similis sibi in aliqua parte laboris illius qui ad me tendit, tenensque eum simul eum illo in omnibus his per supernum studium contendit, ut absconsa miracula mea revelarentur. Et idem homo super semetipsum se non extulit, sed ad illum in ascensionem humilitatis et in intentione bonae voluntatis quem invenit, se in multis suspiriis indinevit. Tu ergo, o homo, qui haec non in inquietudine deceptionis, sed in puritate simplicitatis accipis ad manifestationem absconditorum directa, scribe quae vides et audis." (*Scivias* 1, col. 385.)

Through the Living Light, who speaks in the first person, Hildegard describes her relationship with the monk Volmar as a kind of marriage, in which Volmar displays all the fidelity, industry, and humility of a pre-lapsarian Eve. He labors with Hildegard; he yields not only his stylus but his will to her; he becomes the perfect partner in the Lord's work. Finally, the Living Light addresses Hildegard, the seer, in the final sentence, directing her ("oh man") to write what she has received from God. As recipient of the vision, Hildegard is herself a scribe or mediator of divine truth. Such perfect mediation is possible because Hildegard receives "these things" in simplicity of spirit and passes them on to Volmar, whose simplicity is likewise assured. Hildegard thus underlines her authority as both author and seer, an authority manifested through Volmar, who does not attempt to impose his will upon her words. That same authority became an issue after Volmar's death, when Hildegard had to petition the pope for another scribe. The third and last of her secretaries, Guibert of Gembloux, was far less yielding; after some controversy, Hildegard allowed him to polish her idiosyncratic style. As Barbara Newman remarks, he polished her last works beyond all recognition, and students of Hildegard are grateful that their association began very late in her career.[31] The frontispiece to Newman's study of Hildegard captures the relationship Hildegard perceived between her authorship and her authority. The miniature, from a thirteenth-century manuscript of Hildegard's *De operatione Dei,* depicts Hildegard receiving fire from *Caritas.* Hildegard transcribes this vision onto a wax tablet, while in the smaller left portion of the miniature Volmar copies Hildegard's vision into a book. Hildegard is thus portrayed as a prophetic figure who receives her inspiration from above; Volmar receives his inspiration from Hildegard. The distinction is captured by the composition of the figures: Hildegard looks upward as she writes; Volmar's look is horizontal, toward the page he is copying.

Both the miniature and Hildegard's account of Volmar seem to hint that an author's authority is in some measure enhanced by the presence of a scribe. Hildegard's quarrel with the monks of Saint Disibod, who would not give her a replacement for Volmar, suggests that Hildegard's own perception of her status in the religious community was verified by having

---

31. On the relationships between Hildegard and her scribes, see Newman, *Sister of Wisdom,* 13–14, 22–24. On Hildegard's Latin style, see Dronke, *Women Writers of the Middle Ages,* 148, 193–95.

a scribe who would take down those words she herself received from the Living Light. Since Saint Augustine, Saint Gregory, and Saint Bernard had composed "through" a secretary, Hildegard explicitly claimed her right to compose and asserted her status as an author. This authority she traces directly to divine inspiration, which allowed an "unlearned" woman to understand exegetical and theological matters for which she was not trained.[32] Hildegard's special understanding is then further verified by the scribe who transcribes in a more permanent form the wax tablets he receives from the author.

That same awareness that a description of the circumstances of composition might serve to define the nature of an author's authority is apparent in Christine de Pisan's opening remarks in *The Book of the City of Ladies*. The portrait she offers of herself suggests that she linked her authority as a writer to her mastery of a cultural tradition adumbrated in the first chapter and elaborated upon in the remainder of her book. Christine de Pisan locates herself in her library, where she is alone and engaged in "literary studies."[33] Her inspiration to write comes from a trinity of beings, Reason, Rectitude, and Justice, whose origin is celestial but whose habitation is the well-trained mind. The architectural or structural metaphor Christine employs to describe the act of writing the book is a strategic and arresting one for a woman, for it allows her to insist on the labor involved in writing a book. She thus describes herself as readying a field, as laying a foundation, as building walls, towers, and houses, and as populating the city. She continues the metaphorical association between her stylus and an instrument of labor in the opening to *The Treasure of the City of Ladies,* where Reason, Rectitude, and Justice ask her why she is now idle: "What my studious daughter, have you already put away the tool of your intelligence and consigned it to silence? Have you let your ink dry and abandoned your pen and the labour of your right hand . . . ?"[34] By defining her stylus as the tool of her intelligence, Christine links it to the tongue, to the instrument through which language is articulated. By laboring with this tool, Christine becomes a type of redeemed Adam, whose work seeks to ameliorate the linguistic disarray resulting from the first Adam's sin.

32. In the Preface to the *Scivias,* Hildegard describes herself as suddenly transfused by a fiery light and just as suddenly comprehending the meaning of the Scriptures.
33. Christine de Pisan, *The Book of the City of Ladies,* 3. For a reading of this opening, as well as a discussion of the ways in which Christine inscribes herself upon her text, see Quilligan, *The Allegory of Female Authority,* chapter 1, "The Name of the Author."
34. Christine de Pisan, *The Treasure of the City of Ladies,* 31.

Since Christine serves as her own scribe, she implicitly depicts herself as her own figure of authority and responsibility.

Christine de Pisan, in fact, elegantly "re-genders" a metaphor more often linked to male responsibility and power. The word for pen, *stilus* (stylus), was also the word for a pointed agricultural implement used for cultivating and for a plow.[35] Chaucer exploits the pun early in *The Canterbury Tales,* where the Knight employs it as a species of the "modesty *topos*" and describes his duties as narrator, or author, in terms of his sense of himself as a dutiful laborer: "I have, God woot, a large feeld to ere, / And wayke been the oxen in my plough" (I[A] 886–87). He thus explains his unwillingness to add extra details to an already long tale by suggesting that his strength as a plowman is limited by the weakness of his oxen. The Miller picks up and transforms the Knight's reference to himself as a plowman / writer into a bawdy reference to his own sexual powers and their limits. For the Miller, the "field" is, not the tale, but his wife: "I have a wyf, pardee, as wel as thow; / Yet nolde I, for the oxen in my plogh, / Take upon me moore than ynogh . . ." (I[A] 3158–60). Where the Knight labors as a faithful Adam and the Miller as a carnal, Christine, by her employment of the metaphor, emphasizes her capacity to labor as an educated woman and a writer, thus maintaining control over her work. On the other hand, her description of herself as reading or studying alone suggests that she viewed books as objects having private uses, uses that would inevitably vary with each reader. In other words, the implicit control over the meaning of a text provided by the public *lectio* is altered once that text becomes a token of private thought and study.[36]

Texts could then become flexible to a degree unsettling to any author. An author could certainly try to establish personal control over his or her text, particularly in the later Middle Ages when books and copyists were less associated with monasteries and monastic libraries.[37] In England, for example, there is increasing evidence of literacy from the late fourteenth century on, particularly after the Statute of Artificers in 1406, which allowed "every Man or Woman, of what Estate or Condition that he be, shall be free to set their Son or Daughter to take learning at any manner

35. For examples of Latin wordplay with *stilus,* see Curtius, *European Literature and the Latin Middle Ages,* 313; Gellrich, *The Idea of the Book in the Middle Ages: Language, Theory, Mythology, and Fiction,* 34.

36. See Saenger, "Silent Reading," 399.

37. For an account of monastic libraries and scriptoria, see de Roover, "The Scriptorium."

School that pleaseth them within the Realm."[38] Michael Clanchy's argument that printing emerged from a complex culture that gave "extraordinary prestige to the written word" seems to be borne out by accounts of London in the later Middle Ages, when the city became a center for the copying and dispersal of texts.[39] Chaucer clearly is one author who attempted to maintain the accuracy of his own text, checking the work he had hired Adam to do. The numerous revisions in works by writers like Gower and Langland certainly indicate their continued care for their own works. From what we know of Christine de Pisan's writing practices, or her business acumen, she sought to maintain an equally great degree of control over her work.[40] Peter Lucas has argued that John Capgrave functioned as his own "publisher," revising every copy of his work before it was distributed and adding his own trefoil to the revised and corrected manuscript as a sign that it went out with its author's approval.[41] Capgrave presumably sought to offset not only the incidence of scribal error but the too-frequent habit of scribes editing the texts they were intended merely to copy.[42] For example, some of the fifteenth-century scribes who copied Chaucer's works are now described as his first critics or readers. In the case of the fifteenth-century translation of Margaret Porete's *Mirror of Simple Souls,* a text that shed its heretical author and thus enjoyed a wide circulation throughout the fourteenth and fifteenth centuries, the Middle English translator or scribe functioned as a theological

---

38. *Statutes of the Realm,* 158. The statute is also noted in Davies, *Teaching Reading in Early England,* 45, 51. On the literacy of the English upper and middle classes, see Denley, "Elementary Teaching Techniques and Middle English Religious Didactic Writing"; Moran, *The Growth of English Schooling, 1340–1548: Learning, Literacy, and Laicization in Pre-Reformation York Diocese;* Thompson, *The Literacy of the Laity in the Middle Ages;* Thrupp, *The Merchant Class of Medieval London, 1300–1500.*

39. See Clanchy, "Looking Back from the Invention of Printing." See also Bennett, "The Production and Dissemination of Vernacular Manuscripts in the Fifteenth Century"; Griffiths and Pearsall, *Book Production and Publishing in Britain, 1375–1475;* Hanna, "Sir Thomas Berkeley and His Patronage"; Parkes and Watson, eds., *Medieval Scribes, Manuscripts, and Libraries: Essays Presented to N. R. Ker.*

40. For a discussion of medieval bookmaking and of Christine de Pisan's degree of involvement with the production of her own books, see Hindman, *Christine de Pizan's "Epistre Othéa": Painting and Politics at the Court of Charles VI,* 63–77, 98. For the suggestion that Christine functioned as a scribe early in her career, see Willard, *Christine de Pizan. Her Life and Works,* 45.

41. Lucas, "John Capgrave, O.S.A. (1393–1464), Scribe and 'Publisher.'"

42. Scribal editing has been the focus of much attention lately. See Blake, *The Textual Tradition of the Canterbury Tales;* Kennedy, "The Scribe as Editor"; Windeatt, "The Scribes as Chaucer's Early Critics."

censor, guaranteeing the inherent orthodoxy of what might have appeared to be—and what often were—heterodox ideas.[43]

Authorial efforts to control texts were even more difficult for little-known figures or for women such as Julian of Norwich and Margery Kempe. Both of these women give evidence of seeking control over their texts and consequently deployed the scribe in ways that illuminate their senses of themselves as authors. The image each projects is carefully designed to elicit certain responses in a reader. Unlike Hildegard of Bingen, Chaucer, and Christine de Pisan, Julian of Norwich and Margery Kempe are not authorized to speak as representatives of official culture. Hildegard, who was from a respected Benedictine house and was "licensed" to speak and write by the pope, rhetorically allied herself with the voice of the Old Testament prophets and thus spoke with a power and a directness she could ascribe to the force of the God who inspired her. Similarly, Christine de Pisan and Chaucer buttressed their works with the weight of traditional culture and evolved ways of speaking from within the confines and inevitable constrictions of that culture.

In contrast, both Julian of Norwich and Margery Kempe inherited a tradition whereby the female text—whether that text was written word or the life of a holy woman—was mediated and thus verified by a male author or scribe. Thus, the writings of Catherine of Siena and Catherine of Genoa were dictated to male confessors; the autobiography of Beatrice of Nazareth was translated from its original Flemish into Latin by an anonymous confessor; the revelations of Bridget of Sweden were transcribed into Latin by her confessor; and *The Mirror of Simple Souls* lost its female author and, desexed and anonymous, was treated as an orthodox and valuable work of mystical theology by its male translators and glossers.[44] In addition, the majority of late medieval holy women had male biographers. Writers like Thomas of Cantimpré and Jacques de Vitry used the examples of holy women to shame their more secular contemporaries.[45] Officials of the church assumed positions of authority over these

---

43. See Colledge and Guarnieri, "The Glosses by 'M.N.' and Richard Methley to 'The Mirror of Simple Souls.' "

44. See Bynum, *Holy Feast and Holy Fast*, 21–23; Colledge and Guarnieri, "The Glosses by 'M.N.' and Richard Methley to 'The Mirror of Simple Souls'"; Ellis, ed., *The Liber Celestis of St. Bridget of Sweden*, 367; Kieckhefer, *Unquiet Souls*, introduction; Riehle, *The Middle English Mystics*. Figures such as Gertrude the Great and Hadewijch are, of course, exceptions to this tendency to female illiteracy.

45. See Baldwin, *Masters, Princes and Merchants: The Social Views of Peter the Chanter and His Circle*, 72ff., 110; Bynum, *Holy Feast*, 229; Kieckhefer, *Unquiet Souls*, 31–33. For a provocative

women by serving as their confessors and by writing their lives, thereby using holy women such as Mary of Oignies and Christina Mirabilis as goads to contemporaries presumably in need of such "texts." Behavior and views that might appear to subvert the official culture were organized by and integrated into it through the voice of the scribe who testified, mediated, and verified.[46]

In addition, from the last part of the fourteenth century on, there were increasing constraints in England on theological writing.[47] Although it was not until the drafting of the *Constitutions* of Archbishop Arundel in 1407 that those constraints became official, from 1378, when the pope censured John Wyclif for his views on temporalities, there was growing unease with heterodoxy.[48] That unease, of course, did not preclude the literature of dissent, but it is nonetheless important to recognize that, at the same time that literacy and the tendency toward private devotion were beginning to increase, an official distrust of both was also on the rise. This distrust finally became explicit in the Lollard trials of the early fifteenth century, when book ownership might well arouse suspicion of heterodox views. By that time, Lollardy was also linked to political dissent, so the charge was more serious than it would have been in Chaucer's time. The very books that were seen as tokens of reverence and authority were also seen as potentially threatening to authorities.[49] The works of both Julian

---

discussion of the ways in which in the medieval West men told women's stories and women told their own, see Caroline W. Bynum, "Women's Stories."

46. For further thoughts on this tendency, see Bynum, *Holy Feast,* 230ff.; idem, "Women Mystics and Eucharistic Devotion in the Thirteenth Century"; Goodich, "The Contours of Female Piety in Later Medieval Hagiography"; Martin, "Character as Emblem: Generic Transformations in the Middle English Saint's Life."

47. On this subject, see Simpson, "The Constraints of Satire in 'Piers Plowman' and 'Mum and the Sothsegger' "; Wawn, "Truth-telling and the Tradition of *Mum and the Sothsegger."*

48. For ecclesiastical legislation in this period, see Wilkins, ed., *Concilia Magnae Britanniae et Hiberniae,* vol. 3. For evidence of official concern with heterodoxy, see 123, 157, 158–65, 159, 166–72, 176, 204, 208, 210, 211, 221–22, 225, 247–49, 252–54, 254–63, 265, 270, 282. For Arundel's Constitutions, see 314–19. For studies of this issue, see Coleman, *Medieval Readers and Writers, 1350–1400,* 213ff.; Hudson, ed., *Selections from English Wycliffite Writings,* introduction; McFarlane, *John Wycliffe and the Beginnings of English Nonconformity,* 89ff.; McKisack, *The Fourteenth Century, 1307–1399,* 290; McNiven, *Heresy and Politics in the Reign of Henry IV,* 11ff.; Peck, "Social Conscience and the Poets"; Robertson, *Chaucer's London,* 133–35.

49. See Aers, *Community, Gender, and Individual Identity: English Writing 1360–1430,* introduction; Aston, *England's Iconoclasts;* idem, *Lollards and Reformers: Images and Literacy in Late Medieval Religion;* Hudson, *The Premature Reformation: Wycliffite Texts and Lollard History;* Hughes, *Pastors and Visionaries: Religion and Secular Life in Late Medieval Yorkshire;* Tanner, ed., *Heresy Trials in the Diocese of Norwich, 1428–31.*

of Norwich and Margery Kempe suggest that both women were aware of the possible constraints on a female devotional writer. However, their works also suggest that they nonetheless thought of themselves as authors and consequently sought to create texts that are not simply annals of spiritual experience but narratives intended to give a particular form or meaning to experience.[50] They thus found it necessary to evolve narrative strategies that establish a certain textual authority; for both, this authority is bound up with a scribal presence.[51]

In both the long and the short text of the *Showings* by Julian of Norwich we have evidence of a highly self-conscious author.[52] We owe our knowledge of her authorial care to her own precision about the dates of her vision and of her composition of the two accounts of her vision. On 13 May 1373 she experienced the series of visions that she soon thereafter recorded in what is known as the Short Text of the *Showings*. She says that she meditated on the meaning of these visions for fifteen or more years and then wrote a second text, which once seems to have existed in two versions. The second version of the Long Text, which contained the full exposition of her important allegory of the Lord and the Servant, was apparently composed around 1393; so we can surmise that from about 1388 to 1393, she rewrote her original work. When considering Julian, it is important to keep in mind that she never had any more visions: all versions of the *Showings* are accounts of those she experienced in 1373, when, by her own account, she was thirty and a half years old. Thus, though she was certainly a recluse and a mystic, she was also a writer, one who sought to clarify and to represent experience, which she locates in time, through a narrative, which she likewise anchors in time. Such references point to the process of composition, or to her sense of her own authority as a visionary and as a writer or interpreter. Like Chaucer, Gower, and Langland, Julian's acts of revision suggest that she is attentive to the ways in which her text was read and understood.

The types of revisions she made hint at her desire to control the mean-

---

50. On this distinction, see White, "The Value of Narrativity in the Representation of Reality," in *The Content of the Form: Narrative Discourse and Historical Representation,* 1–25.

51. For thoughtful considerations of the functions of literacy, see Bäuml, "Varieties and Consequences of Medieval Literacy and Illiteracy"; idem, "Medieval Texts and the Two Theories of Oral Formulaic Composition: A Proposal for a Third Theory."

52. For important studies of Julian's artistry see the introduction to Edmund Colledge and James Walsh's edition, *A Book of Showings to the Anchoress Julian of Norwich,* and Barry Windeatt's article, "Julian of Norwich and Her Audience." All quotations from the *Showings* refer to the above edition and will be cited by page number in the text.

ing of her text by projecting a persona whose shifting relationship to a scribal presence underlines her growing understanding of the art of narrative and, perhaps, of her ability to "constitute" the public whom she addresses in her text.[53] The Short Text of the *Showings* is, for the most part, a record of the visions themselves and reads like a testimony of a singular experience. It seems designed to locate its authority as a devotional text in that it bears witness to an extraordinary experience. Thus, its authorial voice seems less authoritative than the one we encounter in the Long Text. The opening sentence of the Short Text presents Julian through the eyes of another, presumably a scribe: "Here es a visionn schewed be the goodenes of god to a deuoute womann, and hir name es Julyan, that is recluse atte Norwyche and ȝitt ys onn lyfe, anno domini millesimo CCCC xiij; in the whilke visyonn er fulle many comfortabylle wordes and gretly styrrande to alle thaye that desires to be Crystes looverse." This opening frames Julian in a highly specific way. It identifies her by gender, by vocation, by geographic location, and by chronology. The final clause designates the way in which we are to take this vision: it will stir up devotion in those who desire to be Christ's lovers. Julian is thereby insinuated into the circle of Richard Rolle and others who were linked to the fervent and mystical love of Christ. Julian's Short Text, which was clearly still circulating in 1413, was not only assimilated into an emotive or affective framework; it was also assigned a genre and thus a range of expectations.[54]

Later, in chapter 6, Julian pauses to focus on the problems of authority inherent in her gender. After emphasizing that love and vision shall teach and comfort the person who needs comfort (221), she says:

> Botte god for bede that ȝe schulde saye or take it so that I am a techere, for I meene nouȝt soo, no I mente nevere so; for I am a womann, leued, febille and freylle. Botte I wate wele, this that I saye, I hafe it of the schewynge of hym tha(t) es soucraync techare. . . . Botte for I am a womann, schulde I therfore leve that I schulde nouȝt telle ȝowe the goodenes of god, syne that I sawe in that same tyme that is his wille, that it be knawenn? (222)

53. The phrase is Bäuml's. See "Varieties," 253.

54. I am employing generic terminology here in a way that links any understanding of genre to an understanding of historical and social context. For a fuller exposition of this, see Jauss, *Toward an Aesthetic of Reception.*

As Kempe has Margery do when threatened by the clerks who surround the Archbishop of York, Julian here draws a distinction between teaching and telling. She certainly is not teaching (and thereby possibly incurring ecclesiastical censure) *because* she is a woman, but should she condemn herself to silence *simply* because she is a woman? She defines her authority as issuing from God, or from the visions she has experienced. However, lest she be accused of too much "singularity," she ends the chapter by stressing her allegiance to the teachings of the Church: "bot in alle thynge I lyeve as haly kyrke techis, for in alle thynge, this blyssede schewynge of oure lorde, I be helde it as ane in god syght, and I vndyrstode neuer nathynge þer yn that stoneȝ me ne lettes me of the trewe techynge of halye kyrke" (223). Julian's strategy here suggests her own awareness of the tension between her identity as a daughter of Holy Church and as a recluse and author of private visions. She uses the weakness implicit in her gender to a particular end, since only the writings of holy women, whose holiness had been verified by others, circulated with such authority.

Near the end of the Short Text, in chapter 23, Julian seems to project such an image by conjuring up the presence of a scribe who listens to and thus verifies her account of her visions:

> Alle the blissede techynge of oure lorde god was schewed to me be thre partyes, as I hafe sayde before, that es to saye be the bodely sight, and be worde formed in mynn vndyrstandynge, and by gastelye syght. For the bodely sight, I haffe sayde as I sawe, als trewlye as I cann. And for the wordes fourmed, I hafe sayde thamm ryght as oure lorde schewed me thame. (272–73)

Her language in this passage is designed to depict a specific scene in which the visionary dictates what she has seen through "bodily" and "ghostly" sight. The fact that these "sayings" now appear in the form of a book bears witness to the authoritative nature of the visions and hence of the book in which they now appear. Julian thus sketches in a familiar triune relationship, in which the seer (in this case a female visionary) is authenticated by God, who inscribes teachings upon the spiritual eye of the visionary, and by the scribe, who inscribes that vision (or the visionary) upon parchment.

In the Long Text, Julian seems to be striving for a different kind of authority. The Long Text opens merely with "Here begynneth the first chapter. This is a reuelation of loue that Jhesu Christ our endles blisse

made in xvi shewynges" (281). Not only are the specifics of the first
sentence of the Short Text omitted, but what follows is a summary of the
content of each vision recorded in the book. Such tables of contents
emerged from the university world of the thirteenth century and the new
attitude toward books as objects meant for private study and use. Although they tended to be added onto texts by the scribes, Colledge and
Walsh feel that this one was the work of Julian herself.[55] If so, she clearly
foresaw a particular type of reader for her book, which she sought to
inscribe with an opening that at once enhanced its usefulness as a spiritual
guide and suggested its authority as a book designed for serious thought.
This first chapter also prepares us for a representation of visionary experience, containing not only accounts of the visions themselves but the
author's glosses upon that experience. To this end, the Long Text, which
is indeed much longer, is more concerned to explain the meaning of the
visions and is thus more theologically inclined than the Short Text.

In the Long Text, Julian is also interested in projecting a different type
of persona. First, she omitted the references to her gender that occur in
the Short Text.[56] Since by drawing on the "unlearned, feeble, and frail
woman" topos, Julian had earlier categorized her work as experiential,
emotive, and perhaps prophetic, she may have perceived the inherent
constrictions that topos imposed on her as a writer. She spoke neither as a
prophet nor as a saint, but as a person who had had a series of revelations,
the meaning of which had continued to preoccupy her for a number of
years. Thus, her life was not the text that authorized her written text; she
spoke as a thoughtful, intelligent Christian. Second, she may have felt that
her authority as a theological writer was implicitly compromised by her
gender and therefore chose a persona that linked her to countless other
authors whose employment of the "humility topos" was quickly belied by
the rhetorical polish of their works. After the first chapter, a summary of
the content of each vision, chapter 2 begins: "This reuelation was made to
a symple creature vnlettyrde leving in deadly flesh, the yer of our lord a
thousannde and three hundered and lxxiij, the xiij daie of May, which
creature desyred before thre gyftes by the grace of god" (285). The ironies
of this sentence would have been apparent to any alert and educated

55. See Saenger, "Silent Reading"; Colledge and Walsh, *Showings*, 284 n. 51. In the prologue
to his life of Mary of Oignies, Jacques de Vitry explains that he has provided chapter headings so
a reader can find what he is looking for; he thus indicates his own expectations that a reading of
the life might well be a private devotional experience.
56. See also Bynum, *Holy Feast*, 418 n. 49; Colledge and Walsh, *Showings*, 222 n. 40.

reader, for the *Showings* demonstrates Julian's mastery of rhetorical figures, of the Latin of the Vulgate, and, as Colledge and Walsh point out, of
the Western monastic traditions of *lectio divina*.[57] In fact, one of the
differences between the two texts of the *Showings* is the rhetorical sophisti-
cation of the Long Text, suggesting that Julian spent the fifteen years not
only thinking about her visions but also mastering the conventions of
classical rhetoric.

Despite the subtlety of the Long Text, it appears at once less individualistic and more authoritative than the Short. In omitting details that are
not central to her point, she trims some things that make the Short Text a
more personal work.[58] In the Short Text, for example, she says her desire
for three spiritual wounds was inspired by a reading in church of the story
of Saint Cecilia (204–6). That personal and immediate reference, which
links her desire to her own experience, is transformed in the Long Text to
a more generally accessible statement: "by the grace of god and teeching
of holie church I conceiued a mightie desyre to receive thre woundes in
my life" (288). Just as the "teaching of Holy Church" replaces an account
of personal experience, so, as Colledge and Walsh remark, Julian tends to
replace the singular pronouns of the Short Text with the plural pronouns
of the Long Text.[59] The unlearned and feeble woman has become a voice
aligned with the community of the Church (as the oft-repeated phrase
"my evyn cristen" implies) and speaking with the authority of the seer and
the teacher. Although Julian retained the passage in which she describes
herself as dictating her visions, its position in the Long Text (666) miti-
gates its force. Rather than appearing two short chapters from the end, as
it does in the Short Text, it occurs in chapter 73 of a book of 86 chapters.
In fact, in the final chapter of the Long Text, she emphasizes the number
of years she has devoted to trying to understand "oure lords menyng"
(732). The answer she offers is worthy of quoting in full:

> Wytt it wele, loue was his menyng. Who shewyth it the? Loue.
> [What shewid he the? Love.] Wherfore shewyth he it the? For
> loue. Holde the therin, thou shalt wytt more in the same. But thou
> schalt nevyr witt therin other withoutyn ende.

57. See Colledge and Walsh, *Showings*, 45–47 and their appendix to the *Showings*, "Rhetorical Figures Employed by Julian," 735–48. For a discussion of humility formulas to be found in
Latin prefaces, see Janson, *Latin Prose Prefaces: Studies in Literary Conventions*, 120ff.

58. In "Julian of Norwich and Her Audience," Windeatt also makes this point.

59. Colledge and Walsh, *Showings*, 285 n. 11.

> Thus was I lernyd, þat loue is oure lordes menyng. And I sawe fulle
> surely in this and in alle that or god made vs he lovyd vs, whych loue
> was nevyr slekyd ne nevyr shalle. And in this loue he hath done alle
> his werkes, and in this loue he hath made alle thynges profytable to
> vs, and in this loue oure lyfe is evyr lastyng. In oure makyng we had
> begynnyng, but the loue wher in he made vs was in hym fro with
> out begynnyng. In whych loue we haue oure begynnyng, and alle
> this shalle we see in god with outyn ende. (733–34)

This statement issues from no frail figure, but is magisterial and full-
voiced. That Julian's assumption of authority may well have troubled a
scribe is borne out by a scribal epilogue that appears in two of the manuscripts of the Long Text warning the reader not to take only the part of
the work that seems pleasing ("after thy affection"), "for that is the condition of an heretique."[60]

The Long Text is the work of a writer, not a seer. It presents experience
mediated by time, literary craft, intelligence, and study. I do not deny that
Julian was and saw herself as a visionary, but the Long Text testifies to her
growing understanding of her role as a writer. In effect, she becomes her
own secretary or scribe. She apparently provided the text with its introduc-
tory apparatus. She depersonalizes the text and thus does not need to
explain why she, a woman, is writing a book like this. She makes every
attempt to link herself with the community of Christ, seeking to avoid the
charge of "singularity" and of presumption. She derives her authority in
the Long Text not only from her visionary experience, but from her years
of meditation and study. Finally, in the opening sentence of the last chapter, she affirms her book as a text for a life: "This boke is begonne by
goddys gyfte and his grace, but it is nott yett performyd, as to my syght"
(731).[61] The book's "performance" will be the life lived in the knowledge
and love of God. The book, then, stands as a text whose authority is
derived from God and manifested in the life of prayer. Its author has
become our mediator and our guide for this still-unfinished text. She thus
suggests, not that we should read her book because she is a holy woman,
but that her book might be used as a guide to the holy. She thereby adopts
the persona of the author who inscribes a text, not of the saint whose life
is inscribed upon a text.

60. Colledge and Walsh, *Showings*, 734 n. 29.
61. In "Julian of Norwich and Her Audience," Windeatt also considers this sentence.

To some extent, her strategies may be read as manifesting her awareness of her own, perhaps dangerous, theological speculation and originality. As Colledge and Walsh note, in the Long Text of the *Showings*, she deliberately repressed any suggestion that the text was directed at a primarily cloistered public.[62] If Julian indeed saw herself as at once expanding upon her original insights and addressing a broader public in the Long Text, she may well have been more concerned to underline her fundamental orthodoxy. Although I am not suggesting that the *Showings* contains heretical passages, the book nonetheless evinces a certain tension in Julian herself between her revelations and the teachings of Holy Church. This is particularly the case when she discusses topics like sin and judgment. Julian, like Margery after her, is far less interested in manifestations of divine wrath as they are figured in the doctrines of hell and purgatory than she is in seeking to understand the mercy and grace of the divine nature. In fact, even the most cursory reading of the *Showings* reveals the outlines of a theologian who is most concerned to understand the divine as it exists apart from human nature but dwells in human nature.[63] What no reader will take from the *Showings* is a reminder of divine or paternal wrath. While maintaining her own line of argument and of theological exposition, Julian nonetheless signals her uneasiness with the distance between her own emphasis upon mercy and grace and more official doctrines of sin in passages like the following,

> The furst dome, whych is of goddes ryghtfulnes, and that is of his owne hygh endlesse loue, and that is that feyer swete dome that was shewed in alle the feyer revelation in whych I saw hym assign(e) to vs no maner of blame. And though theyse were swete and delectable, ȝytt only in the beholdyng of this I culde nott be fulle esyd, and that was for the dome of holy chyrch, whych I had before vnderstondyn and was contynually in my syght. And therfore by this dome me thought that me behovyth nedys to know my selfe a synner. And by the same dome I vnderstode that synners be sometyme wurthy blame and wrath, and theyse two culde I nott see in god. And therfore my desyer was more than I can or may

62. Colledge and Walsh, eds., introduction, *Showings,* 137.

63. I can only send a reader to the long introduction by Colledge and Walsh in their edition of the *Showings*. They take great pains to demonstrate Julian's familiarity with a long and thoroughly orthodox tradition of primarily monastic theologians. Their exposition of Julian's theology is especially full.

telle, for the hygher dome god shewed hym selfe in the same tyme, and therfore (m)e behovyd nedys to take it. And the lower dome was lernyd me before tyme in holy chyrche, and therfore I myght nott by no weye leue the lower dome. (487–88)

The tension displayed in this passage is enormous. Julian juxtaposes two judgments, the first a "feyer swete dome," that presents God's endless love as the extension of his justice and equity ("ryghtfulnes"). This judgment Julian herself "beholds" in her private visions. However, she is uncomfortable with this revelation because it seems to contravene the judgment of Holy Church, which formed the basis for her previous understanding of the nature of God. Under the terms of this second judgment, she knows herself a sinner and knows that sinners are sometimes "worthy" of blame and wrath. She is at first unable to reconcile the Church's definition of heavenly justice (worthy of . . .) with that vouchsafed to her, which is "swete and delectable." The adjectives with which she qualifies the two "domes," higher and lower, however, underline her fundamental belief in the veracity of the visions she has had. In this chapter she defers the need to resolve the conflict between what has been taught to her and what she has experienced by going on to say that the "mervelous example" of a lord and a servant that she has tried so long to penetrate contains the answer to her need to "see" how the teachings of Holy Church are true, how both judgments might be worshipful to God and "*ryght wey to me*" (488; emphasis added). This same urgent need to reconcile private revelation with public doctrine reappears in chapter 50, where Julian presents them as "two contraryes." She says that she knows by the teachings of the Church and by her own feelings that the blame of sin hangs over us, but she "saw" God show us no more blame than if we were angels in heaven. Since she cannot find the "truth" of sin in her sight of God, she is caught between two versions of what truth, in fact, is.[64] Then, in the next chapter Julian launches into the mysterious and arresting story, which she insists on calling an *example,* thereby alluding to its parabolic function, of the Lord and the Servant.

The story of the Lord and the Servant, like her magnificent exposition of the motherhood of God, focuses upon sin as a manifestation of frailty, as, perhaps, an originally laudable impulse gone wrong. Rather than emphasize God's anger with us for failures of will and action, Julian

64. See Colledge and Walsh, *Showings,* 511–12.

chooses to emphasize God's might and love. As she expresses it, sin is catalytic, inspiring the creative mercy that she identifies with the divine nature to shelter, to soothe, and to correct the human child. She identifies God's goodness with his very nature and hence with the supreme expression of nature ("goodnesse that is kynd, it is god"), asserting that we are bound to God through both grace and nature. Julian goes on to suggest the ways by which we may seek God: "Her may we see that vs nedyth nott gretly to seke ferre out to know sondry kyndys, but to holy church into oure moders brest, that is to sey in to oure owne soule, wher oure lord dwellyth" (612–13). On the one hand, the sentence attempts to resolve some of the difficulties that underlie Julian's efforts to understand and thus to explain sin and judgment, for she implies that both Holy Church and the soul are sites of entry into our mother's breast, which is God. However, the sentence also begs the more fundamental question of contraries by suggesting that Holy Church and the soul are the same place, when her fear that they are not has formed the core of her troubles over the doctrine of sin and punishment. Julian's continual care to align herself with Holy Church and to stress her ties with her fellow Christians in some measure defines the surface of some of her arguments, allowing her to maintain views that, while not heretical, nonetheless give primacy to a theology whose dominant notes are those of mercy, love, forgiveness, and likeness. There are, in fact, times when her avowals of obedience seem designed to function as screens for her own strongly original and oftentimes bold cast of thought.[65] Her tactics suggest her keen sense of community and her grasp of the ways in which literary texts at once express communal views and test the outer limits of community by expanding upon existing traditions.

If Julian of Norwich employs strategies that seem to authorize her pen as an instrument of the communal "body of Christ," Kempe uses techniques designed to verify the value of her book by stressing the holiness and singularity of Margery's life. Where Julian draws a reformulation of theology from her recollection of experience, Kempe presents experience as the very point she wishes to make. Nonetheless, despite what may appear to be simply a random account of one woman's experience, Kempe

---

65. My examples here are drawn from the matter of the fourteenth revelation, which Julian vastly expanded from one chapter in the Short Text to twenty-three in the Long Text. But the entire Long Text of the *Showings* seems to me to suggest Julian's recognition that her writings might well be open to "mis-interpretation."

is an author as self-conscious and highly skilled as Julian herself. Her keen ear for language and acute sense of literary strategy combine to create a persona as vivid as any of Chaucer's characters, one whose "experiential veracity" is rooted in a culture of the book, and, hence, of the scribe. Kempe's scribes are integral to her purpose as a writer. Just as the phrase "my euen cristen" serves Julian as a signifier of communal solidarity, so Kempe's deployment of the figure of the scribe links her text to the community of the faithful.

The Book of Margery Kempe is a book of witnesses. It bears witness to the holiness of the "creatur" whose story it is and the book does so by and through the scribes who serve as amanuenses for this English "holy woman."[66] The Book begins with a proem that locates Margery in a community in which books serve as tokens of permanency and authority. The proem, which is described as the work of Margery's scribe, who adds it "to expressyn mor openly þan doth þe next folwyng, whech was wretyn er þan þis" (5), serves as a scribal testimonial that underlines Margery's holiness by stressing the scribe's own "conversion." Directly following is a one-paragraph proem that is also focused on the actual composition of the Book. Taken together, the two proems serve to emphasize the authority of the record they introduce. The writer thus describes how the book came to be written:

> Summe of these worthy & worshepful clerkys tokyn it in perel of her sowle and as þei wold answer to God þat þis creatur was inspyred wyth þe Holy Gost and bodyn hyr þat sche schuld don hym wryten & maken a booke of hyr felyngys & hir reuelacyons. Sum proferyd hir to wryten hyr felyngys wyth her owen handys, & sche wold not consentyn in no wey, for sche was comawndyd in hir sowle þat sche schuld not wrytyn so soone. (3)

Only after another twenty or so years after her first mystical experience does God command her to write down her feelings so that "hys goodnesse myth be knowyn to alle þe world" (4). Kempe carefully positions Margery between the learned clerks on the one hand and God on the other. Once Margery knows that God intends to use her words to

---

66. For discussions of Kempe's scribes, see Atkinson, Mystic and Pilgrim; Ellis, "Margery Kempe's Scribe and the Miraculous Books"; Hirsch, The Revelations of Margery Kempe, all of whom see the scribes as shaping the text in various ways.

manifest his goodness, she needs to find a writer who can inscribe her experience for her and thereby give "credens to hir felingys" (4). Kempe persistently describes Margery as part of a community that values the written word, or the written life. Though he is at first offended by her copious weeping, one priest becomes her supporter *because* he reads the life of Mary of Oignies (152–53). The abbot of Leicester wishes to "record" her conversations with him for the benefit of the bishop at Lincoln (117). Margery herself feels more comfortable about her salvation when she has a vision of her name inscribed in the Book of Life (206–7).

Although she describes a community that derives authority from its books, Kempe's persistent emphasis upon Margery's illiteracy is a key part of her persona. Her description of herself as one of "owyr Lordys owyn secretarijs" (71) points us to her life as the text she "writes," not to an actual book. Notwithstanding the fact that by the first quarter of the fifteenth century it was fairly common for women of her social status to read and not unusual for them to write, Kempe insists that Margery reads and writes only with the aid of a clerk or a scribe. The proem to the *Book* therefore depicts Margery as a holy woman who is scorned by her worldly contemporaries but cherished by some members of the clergy. Those who recognize her sanctity offer to write down her story "wyth her owen handys" (3), thereby verifying God's presence in Margery by helping her to "make a book" out of her feelings and visions. The vignette provides a highly specific focus upon the life before us by locating Margery within both the conventions of sacred biography and the sanctions of Holy Church. Categorized generically and stamped with orthodoxy, the intricately woven fictions of the *Book* are spun between the poles of a holy *accessus* and an even holier "epilogue," the prayers that complete the volume. Kempe also describes one priest who read to Margery over a period of seven or eight years (143); a little child who must point out her name in the Book of Life because she cannot recognize her own name (206–7); a master of divinity who wrote a letter for her (45); as well as the various scribes she engages in the writing of the *Book* (4–5, 216, 220–21). Her presentation of Margery as illiterate may reflect contemporary distrust for those who possessed or could read religious books. Margery's remark that one priest read her "þe Bybyl wyth doctowrys þer-up-on" (143), underlines her devotion to the Scriptures and signals her orthodoxy. In a world where owning or reading a Bible, particularly a copy of the Bible in the vernacular, could be construed as an act of religious and political dissent,

Margery's remark that her knowledge of Scripture was mediated through a priest locates her in the bosom of Holy Church. However, Kempe's emphasis upon illiteracy may also indicate her sure understanding of the conventions of spiritual writings by or about women.

In such writings the scribe was an essential component of the authority of the life itself. In this sense, it is less important to ascertain whether Kempe was actually illiterate and therefore dictated her book to a scribe than to seek to understand what function the scribe serves in her book. Since Kempe stresses the amount of time Margery spent with her scribe (216), it is likely she exerted a good deal of control over the text itself: either she wrote it herself and created a fictional scribe, or she had it read back to her and was aware of exactly what was in the text. In other notable accounts of holy women, the scribe tends to lend his authority to the life. Jacques de Vitry in the prologue to his life of Mary of Oignies speaks as a preacher, castigating the spiritual weaknesses of the clergy of his own time and dedicating his work to the bishop of Toulouse in the hopes that the life of this woman may kindle religious fervor in others. Thomas of Cantimpré identifies himself as writing in the tradition of Jacques de Vitry, implicitly justifying his life of Christina Mirabilis by underlining his own veracity as a witness. Philip of Clairvaux describes himself as a witness to the life of Elizabeth of Spalbeck.[67] In a longish proem, Osbern Bokenham explains that he is turning into English verse the collection of female saints' lives he offers as his "legends" in order to excite men's affections.[68] The writer thus frequently adopts the role of the preacher who verifies the significance of the life he recounts by linking the example of the holy woman to the perceived inadequacies of the present age.[69]

Similarly, the scribes who figure in *The Book of Margery Kempe* function as witnesses to her holiness and singularity. However, like such figures of doubt in medieval mystery plays as the Midwives who attend Christ's birth and Thomas who doubts the Resurrection, Kempe's scribes need to be convinced that they have witnessed the miraculous. She describes Margery's second scribe as a priest who is initially willing to correct the errors

---

67. For Middle English versions, see Horstmann, ed., *Prosalegenden*. Though the translator does not translate Jacques de Vitry's Prologue, he is careful to identify him. See Jacques de Vitry, *Vita Maria Oigniacensis*. See also Kurtz, "Mary of Oignies, Christine the Marvelous, and Medieval Heresy."

68. Osbern Bokenham, *Legendys of Hooly Wummen*. See also the much later *Lives of Women Saints*, ed. Horstmann, 1–10.

69. On this point, see also Bynum, *Holy Feast*, 229.

created by her first scribe (4), but who then refuses, saying he cannot read the manuscript of the first scribe. Margery says that it is her reputation in the community that makes him unwilling to appear to sponsor her, observing that cowardice made him fear to be associated with her and her copious weeping. He consequently sends her to a third scribe, who cannot transcribe the foul manuscript she presents to him. Finally the priest, or the second scribe, "was vexyd in his consciens" (4) and agrees to have another try at what looked like an unreadable manuscript. Margery prays for him, and a minor miracle occurs: he is suddenly able to read the broken English of her first scribe and to do the work he had at first agreed to do. At the end of the long first book, Kempe notes that here ends the work of the first scribe, corrected by the priest (220). The short second book begins with yet another scribal testimonial:

> Afftyr þat owr Souereyn Sauyowr had take þe persone whech wrot first þe tretys aforn-seyd to hys many-fold mercy, and þe preiste of whom is be-forn-wretyn had copijd þe same tretys aftyr hys sympyl cunnyng, he held it expedient to honowr of þe blisful Trinite þat hys holy werkys xulde be notifyid & declaryd to þe pepil, whan it plesyd hym, to þe worschip of hys holy name. And þan he gan to writyn in þe ȝer of owr Lord m.cccc.xxxviij in þe fest of Seynt Vital Martyr sweche grace as owr Lord wrowt in hys sympyl creatur ȝerys þat sche leuyd aftyr, not alle but summe of hem, aftyr hyr owyn tunge. (221)

Having earlier sought to distance himself from her, this priest has become a true witness to the Lord's grace as it is manifested through the life of Margery Kempe. He therefore adds a second book, written two years after the first (see 5 and 221), concluding this second book with a selection of Kempe's prayers (248–54).

Kempe underlines the important function the scribe fulfills by suggesting that the act of writing is a form of penitential prayer. In answer to Margery's worry that the time spent "in hir chamber wyth hir writer" took time away from prayer in church, God says to her:

> "Drede þe not, dowtyr, for as many bedys as þu woldist seyin I accepte hem as þow þu seydist hem, & þi stody þat þu stodiist for to do writyn þe grace þat I haue schewyd to þe plesith me ryght meche & he þat writith boþe. . . . ȝet xulde ȝe not plesyn me mor

þan ʒe don wyth ʒowr writyng, for dowtyr, be þis boke many a
man xal be turnyd to me & beleuyn þerin." (216)

Both Margery and her scribe are described as sanctified through their
labors; in fact, the scribe, like the holy woman whose words he transcribes, is blessed with the gift of tears during the time they worked on the
book (219).[70] Finally, Christ, Mary, and many of the saints come into
Kempe's soul to thank her for the writing of the book (219). Kempe's
references to scribes and to the process of writing ultimately relate to her
emphasis upon the process involved in making a book, a process that, in
turn, focuses attention upon the subject of that book, the holy woman.

Just as Kempe uses the voice of God as a screen for the social criticism
inherent in many of her descriptions, so the scribe serves to shift attention
from her role as a social critic to Margery's status as a holy woman. For
example, during her time in the Holy Land, God tells her of her special
position: " 'Dowtyr, I xal makyn al þe werld to wondryn of þe, & many man
& many woman xal spekyn of me for lofe of þe & worshepyn me in þe' "
(73). Kempe follows God's praise for Margery as a singular vessel of his
glory with an account of her fellow pilgrims, who do not wish her to
accompany them to the River Jordan. By juxtaposing their dislike of her
behavior with God's approbation for it, Kempe highlights the disbelief, the
spiritual tepidity, of the contemporary English. However, her narrative
strategy shields her from charges that she functions as a voice of social and
religious criticism. First, God (as he does throughout the *Book*) speaks to
Margery directly, using first- and second-person pronouns, thereby giving
us the impression that we are eavesdropping on a private conversation.
Moreover, Margery's experience is described by an omniscient, third-
person narrator, presumably the scribe, whose ability to recount both
God's intimate speeches to her, as well as the experience of Margery herself
renders him a powerful "witness" to her life. By emphasizing her singularity, the scribe isolates Margery and gives her the freedom, the flexibility, the
safety, if you will, to speak against the spiritual laxities of her own age.
Kempe does not directly address the reader; she addresses the reader
through the scribe. Only God speaks directly, and he does so only to

70. Atkinson remarks (*Mystic and Pilgrim,* 164) that Brother Arnold, who transcribed the
visions of Angela of Foligno experienced "in the very act of writing a spiritual and new grace."
This is not to deny Kempe's priest his tears but to suggest that the detail is one more in a strand
linking *The Book of Margery Kempe* to a highly self-conscious culture of the book.

Margery herself. Where Julian of Norwich becomes her own scribe and speaks with the authority of the seer and thinker, Kempe embodies authority and thus freedom in the scribe who writes Margery's life.

The very presence of a scribe at certain points in the *Book* heightens its bookish quality. With its allusions to other books of spiritual counsel, its attention to its own veracity as a written text, and its careful delineation of the chronological relationship between experience and transcription, it seems to insist upon its own literary authority.[71] In part, this authority rests upon the presence of a scribe whose fear, skepticism, service, and emotive recognition duplicates perhaps any man or woman's reaction to the carefully conceived protagonist of *The Book of Margery Kempe*. I would like to be able to say that the scribe never existed, that Kempe created him, but I can say that, in terms of the shape and function of the *Book*, its author needs a scribe, even a succession of scribes, as witnesses and mediators who authorize the text. Lacking a scribe, we would be left with one woman of forty-something (that age, thought of as postmenopausal and thus less "female,"[72] in which so many medieval women say they began to write), who sits down to record a series of visions and adventures that occurred some years before. How would we class such a work? Would it be it picaresque narrative? Satire? Chaucerian imitation? Heresy? From the very beginning, the scribe mediates, guiding our response to this extraordinary text. If control is one of the issues most pertinent to the subject of scribes, Kempe, like Chaucer, found a way to control scribes by writing them into a work, where they function as keys to authorial strategy and design.

Though scribes obviously existed throughout the Middle Ages, that fact should not prevent us from questioning an author's reasons for employing scribal metaphors within a work. Since the scribe served as a

71. Considering the care Julian of Norwich takes to indicate similar matters of chronology as they relate to her own authority, it is tempting to speculate that Margery had not only read and thought about the technique of some version of the *Showings,* but consciously sought to insert herself into a particular authorial company by her own references to time and place.

72. See Anderson and Zinsser, *A History of Their Own,* 1:105. See also the very pertinent comments of Peter Brown on the status of widows in the early church and the ways in which a woman who was in some way "de-feminized" attained a flexibility and a freedom she did not have as a sexual being (*The Body and Society,* 144–45). In book 5 of *The Republic,* Plato defines a woman's childbearing years as ending at forty. After menopause, women were supposed to become more male, freer, healthier. The fact that so many women say they begin to write at about this time in their lives, suggests that the age itself functioned as a trope of female authorship and thus authority.

mediator, the relationship adumbrated through a scribe is social or communal. The uses to which authors like Chaucer, Hildegard of Bingen, Christine de Pisan, Julian of Norwich, and Margery Kempe put scribes not only underline the authors' awareness of their relationships to their communities, but suggest how a stylus might be trimmed to suit individual needs, needs that were frequently related to gender. An author might use the scribe as a literary trope to suggest both the public and private aspects of his or her vocation. Sometimes the scribe served as a screen between the author and the reader and was deliberately used to mask intent, particularly when the author intended to criticize either civil or ecclesiastical institutions. The scribe, or the scribe's ghostly presence, was at other times used to legitimate the author and verify the import of the work. Since the question of authority would have been particularly pressing to a woman author, a figure such as a scribe or secretary could be used as a signifier of vocation. All of these ways of employing the scribe as a figure of speech relate to the author's perception of the act of producing literature, or of the relationship between author, scribe, and audience. Ultimately, the scribe can be described as a code that at once conferred authority and denied it, indicated scope and delimited it.

Kempe's use of the trope of the scribe indicates her fundamental understanding of the terms of the genre in which she worked. What she offers is best understood, not as an autobiography, but as a biography, a "treatise," written by someone about an exemplary person. As the following chapter will demonstrate, the precise type of biography to which Kempe's *Book* can be assimilated is sacred biography, a form increasingly translated into vernacular languages throughout the late Middle Ages.[73] The work of Kempe's fellow East Anglians Osbern Bokenham and John Capgrave provides strong evidence of the growing public for such vernacular lives. By using Margery's life as a means of scrutinizing not only the foundations of English society but also the nature of ecclesiastical and political authority, Kempe develops what was nascent in the traditions of sacred biography she would have inherited from Latin and Continental models. She also reveals her shrewd grasp of the ways in which the issues and the language of her day could be used to signify more fundamental truths about societies; like Chaucer and Langland, she is able to convey a world

73. On the need to situate genre historically, see Cohen, "History of Genre"; Jauss, "Literary History as a Challenge to Literary Theory," in *Toward an Aesthetic of Reception*, 3–45. See also De Mann's introduction to the volume.

whose immediacy only appears a reflection of reality. In terms of the *Book*'s function, the scribe is an integral component of the fiction, for by his very existence *in the text* he testifies to the local eminence of the holy, the exemplary. Written in English about an English "saint," *The Book of Margery Kempe* dramatizes the weaknesses of the social and ecclesiastical institutions of an age whose need for such sanctity is acute. Through her scribe, Kempe can speak of the unspeakable, can raise issues best left alone, can detail the process by which Margery threatens a community that exacts a heavy price for nonconformity, and can finally question the very process by which we invest authority in communal bodies. Kempe uses her scribe at once to contain the effect and to underline the urgency of questions she poses through Margery and her extraordinary life.

2

Sacred Biography and Social Criticism

If Margery Kempe is to be seen as a writer and not a reporter, we must acknowledge her ability to use, or to exploit, the literary traditions to which she was heir. By exploit, here, I mean to emphasize her fundamental understanding of traditional materials and her corresponding willingness to recast and thus reinvent forms and modes. A refusal to acknowledge Kempe's agency leaves us trying to negotiate between the claims of either victimized or hysterical femininity and to establish the credibility of a text (classed as reminiscence) whose form we owe to the superior intelligence and literary artistry of a scribe.[1] However, like Chaucer and Langland, Kempe employs techniques and strategies that enable her to construct a context or background for the narrative of the self she also creates. Thus, although Kempe uses autobiographical apparatus to shape an account of Margery as a representative type, she uses those details as a screen for an analysis of communal values and practices. It is her composition of the background for her narrative that most concerns me here, for through it she suggests a keen interest in the idea of community and of the interplay between "saint" and community that establishes her as a major commentator upon the quality of life and of

1. For an urgent discussion of agency and authority in *The Book of Margery Kempe,* see Beckwith, "Problems of Authority in Late Medieval English Mysticism: Language, Agency, and Authority in *The Book of Margery Kempe*," especially 199–200.

social relations in the late Middle Ages. When Kempe's portrait of her community is compared with what we are coming to understand of the period, it becomes clear that she provides a highly selective vision of a social reality that is designed to reinforce Margery's centrality in that community. In so doing, she dramatizes that conflict between internally perceived and externally imposed codes that lies at the heart of the late medieval literature of social and religious dissent.

Consequently, in this chapter, I am less interested in the *Book* as a record of personal experience than in Kempe's carefully controlled depiction of the relationship between Margery and the community. Kempe introduces her narrative by sketching Margery's relatively rapid movement from communal integration to liminality: directly following her conversion and for most of the narrative, Margery inhabits two worlds. The one, which is invisible save to the eye of her mind, confers spiritual authority upon her. The other world rejects her for the very values and practices that serve to signify her acceptance by her spiritual guides. It is the tension Margery experiences between the demands of these two worlds that Kempe uses as the subject for the numerous minidramas that compose the *Book*.² In Margery, Kempe creates a figure who so thoroughly occupies the foreground of the narrative that she distracts from Kempe's characterization of her community as stifling, conformist, mercantile, violent, and superficial.

Kempe avails herself of the freedom of the social critic by drawing upon the conventional elements of female sacred biography. In so doing, Kempe suggests how well she understood the strategies of the sacred biographer. By deliberately placing themselves on the margins of society, the holy men and women of the Middle Ages dramatized the nature of their spiritual quest for perfection in terms of their separation from conventional modes of life. As Peter Brown has reiterated, these figures and the written accounts of their lives must be understood within the

---

2. Rather than the marginality that most scholars assign to Margery, I see Kempe as creating a figure whose liminal status is ultimately resolved, not by reintegration into the community, but by her rejection of its demands and practices. My emphasis is thus upon Kempe's staging of Margery's achieved status, not upon her ability to cope with a state that is thrust upon her by the community. For a fine discussion of the subject of marginality, see Lochrie, "*The Book of Margery Kempe:* The Marginal Woman's Quest for Literary Authority." For two cogent applications of the concept of liminality as Victor Turner uses it to describe social drama, see Bynum, "Women's Stories. Women's Symbols"; MacAloon, *Rite, Drama, Festival, Spectacle: Rehearsals toward a Theory of Cultural Performance,* introduction.

context of the societies from which they dissociated themselves.[3] Accounts of the pillar saints offer a commentary upon the values and culture of the eastern Roman Empire of the fourth and fifth centuries; studies of the group of third-century Christians that surrounded Justin Martyr offer a view of the tensions experienced by a community of men and women uprooted from Asia Minor and dwelling in Rome; and accounts of martyrs like Saint Perpetua are intended to redefine heroism in terms that make light of the crude heroics of the public arena. That the lives of the desert fathers and the stories of the martyrs of the early Church continued to play a prominent part in the imaginative lives of later medieval Christians says much about the Church's perception of the uses of such examples.[4] Furthermore, as Thomas Heffernan has most recently pointed out, sacred biography is a fiction meant to shape a reader's understanding of what constitutes holiness.[5] The continued literary existence of such singular figures reveals not only a society's need for what is spiritually exemplary but also testifies to a biographer's ability to image the holy in ways that speak to the social conditions of a public.

For example, the twelfth-century life of Christina of Markyate is a text designed as both sacred *exempla* and social commentary.[6] While Christina of Markyate actually existed and even founded an abbey at Markyate, those facts should not prevent us from seeing her biography as a fiction exemplifying the strategies appropriate to the various sorts of lessons embodied within it. On one level, the biographer recounts what is a classic struggle of female spirituality: Christina, like so many women in the annals of the holy, must struggle against her family and her society for the right to pursue her spiritual vocation. By carefully pitting earthly against spiritual society, the biographer indicates his awareness of the conventional dynamics of this struggle. He therefore depicts Chistina's mother as a virago, whose desire to maintain through her daughter the conventionalities of worldly wealth and status manifests itself in acts of fury and cruelty against Christina. To the unnatural natural mother, he counterposes the Blessed Virgin, who offers the young woman counsel,

---

3. P. Brown, *The Making of Late Antiquity;* idem, *Society and the Holy in Late Antiquity.*

4. John Cassian was one of the major transmitters of such exemplary lives; see his *Conferences.* See also Heffernan, *Sacred Biography,* 197.

5. See Heffernan, *Sacred Biography.*

6. For the text, see Talbot, ed. and trans., *The Life of Christina of Markyate: A Twelfth Century Recluse.* For excerpts from this text, along with some important comments on it, see Petroff, *Medieval Women's Visionary Literature,* 136–38; 144–50.

love, nurture, and hope for her future. Where Christina's mother wishes to define her daughter in sexual terms—even going so far as to urge Burthred, to whom Christina's parents had betrothed her against her will, to rape Christina since he cannot persuade her to marry him—the Virgin provides her with an identity unfettered by gender roles. The "world" Christina flees is that of her parents, which is described in terms of stately homes, large estates, lavish hospitality, and networks of power. The order of this world is based upon the power and authority vested in prestige and wealth. Thus, Christina's father, complaining to the Prior of Saint Mary's in Huntingdon of his daughter's rebelliousness, says that if she is allowed to resist parental "authority," they will earn the contempt of their neighbors, and Christina's life of poverty will bring the nobility into disrepute. He says finally, in despair, "Let her marry in the Lord."[7] However, rather than the life of conventional Christian marriage her parents envision for her (or for themselves), Christina chooses the strictures of a hermit's cell. As the narrative makes plain, the physical privations Christina endures as an anchorite are ultimately richer and more comfortable to her than the spacious quarters, luxurious clothes, and ample food of her parents' world. The authority she wins over her own body translates eventually into a growth in spiritual authority, then into a singular status among the powerful figures of the twelfth-century English church.

What I have epitomized here is a tale that is repeated throughout the pages of female sacred biography, from earliest times to the present. As Thomas Heffernan describes female sacred biography, its mode is at once ironic and utopian, since it is based upon the renunciation of social and sexual mores rooted in the family. In choosing to pursue her spiritual vocation, the woman inevitably opposes herself to those orthodox ideas of family, sexuality, and male authority sanctioned by the *civitas hominis;* in exchange she reaps the benefits of a series of relationships under the aegis of faith, not under the rule of law.[8] Thus Christina's biographer locates her in a new kinship system: the Virgin Mary becomes her true mother, and those who sympathize with her calling are closer to her than any brothers or sisters. Moreover, Roger, the old hermit, with whom she shares a living space for more than four years, serves as a foil to Burthred, who has only actual marriage to offer her. Rather than the disruptive physical passion with which Burthred threatens Christina, she and Roger

7. Talbot, *Life of Christina of Markyate,* 58–59.
8. Heffernan, *Sacred Biography,* 188, 191–92.

experience a passion for their mutual love, Christ: "Nempe calor qui succensus fuit Dei spiritu ardebat in singulis . . . unde facti cor unum et anima una in caritate et in castitate in Christo."[9] Similarly, the biographer describes Christina as commonly referring to Geoffrey, the Abbot of Saint Albans, as her "beloved" ("dilectum suum. ex hinc enim sic eum vocare solebat").[10] By using the language of physical desire to describe chaste love, the biographer signals his belief that the life he defines is one based upon polarities, that the goods of the spirit are in opposition to and supercede those of the world.

The potency of such narratives owes as much to the biographer's ability to describe the world from which the saint escapes as it does to the empathy evoked by the saint herself. The biographer of Christina of Markyate suggests his own grasp of the exigencies of sacred biography in his complicated handling of the social setting for the life he recounts. For example, as C. H. Talbot points out, all of Christina's connections appear to be Anglo-Saxon, and, even apart from Christina and her circle, almost all the names of those connected to the hermit movement in England are Anglo-Saxons. Talbot speculates that the undercurrent of national feeling in the *Life* provides hints of the contemporary tensions experienced by those who perhaps saw themselves as pressed between those who led the simple lives of the holy and those who administered the institutional church.[11] Indeed, the picture of the episcopacy that emerges from the *Life* is hardly different from that of the world of Christina's parents: both are dominated by secular concerns, by the desire for status, for the good opinion of neighbors, and for wealth. Since the author of the *Life* was probably a monk of Saint Albans and Christina herself went from the eremetical life to the conventual, founding an abbey and functioning as a figure of genuine power in her own day, it is likely that her biographer found more than simple sanctity in her exemplary life. The very lack of physical power or authority that is implicit in her gender allows him to use her to comment upon those prelates who seem hardly distinguishable from rich and powerful magnates. Thus, the lack of sympathy for Christina's calling that her mother displays is shared by some members of the Church; nor is Burthred alone in seeking to violate her chastity, for she is

9. Talbot, *Life of Christina of Markyate*, 102.

10. Talbot, *Life of Christina of Markyate*, 144–45.

11. I am extending Talbot's speculations here. See Talbot, *Life of Christina of Markyate*, introduction, 12.

threatened less violently but more seductively by a prominent member of the institutional Church.

On the other hand, the effect of social and ecclesiastical criticism is contained by the *Life* itself. Though Christina flees from her parents' home and its various networks of secular and ecclesiastical power to the hidden closet in Roger's hermitage, finally inheriting the hermitage itself on his death, she goes from there to a more conventional community. In other words, though we may wish to see the *Life* as a medieval version of *A Room of One's Own,* Christina neither remains on the margins of her society nor struggles for individual autonomy; instead she founds an abbey where she lives a life almost as socially involved (or as socially fettered) as the one she left. The criticism of the Church that we sense in the first part of the *Life* is not allowed to stand, but is rather channeled into a more positive picture of the spiritual community to be found in monastic foundations. What is potentially radical about the *Life* is finally subsumed into a text that should be seen in the context of the struggle for hegemony among the various power groups of twelfth-century England.[12]

Similarly, churchmen like Jacques de Vitry and Thomas of Cantimpré use the lives of Mary of Oignies and Christina Mirabilis to chastize their contemporaries and to direct popular devotion toward the channels of grace offered by the institutional Church.[13] Jacques de Vitry's Prologue to his *Life of Marie d'Oignies* establishes a perspective upon the life he intends to recount by outlining the ways in which he thinks the life of such a figure ought to be used. He first emphasizes the nutritive value of the lives of the holy, comparing them to crumbs gathered after a meal that can then sustain the faith of the weak. He than describes the holy women to be found in early thirteenth-century Liège as shining examples of faith in the midst of heresy. He especially emphasizes their veneration for the sacraments of the Church. Throughout the prologue, he goes on to play upon the contrast between these women and contemporary heretics and nonbelievers. The latter, in particular, he compares to mad dogs or to Jews, since

12. Heffernan speculates that the Church intended works like those in the early thirteenth-century *Katherine*-group to provide approved versions of a type of asceticism available to women. See Heffernan, *Sacred Biography,* 298.

13. For the lives, see *Vita Christinae Mirabilis* in *Acta Sanctorum* (24 July) 5, pp. 637–60; *Vita Maria Oigniacensis* in *Acta Sanctorum* (23 June) 5, pp. 542–72. For Middle English translations, see Horstmann, "Prosalegenden: die Legenden des Ms. Douce 14." For modern English translations, see Thomas of Cantimpré, *The Life of Christina of Saint Trond* and Jacques de Vitry, *The Life of Marie d'Oignies.*

they do not comprehend the nature of the holy within their midst. Of these women who serve God in chastity and eucharistic devotion while surrounded by violence and disbelief Mary stands out for her purity and faith. Like the author of the *Life of Christina Markyate,* Jacques de Vitry and Thomas of Cantimpré describe their protagonists in terms of their confrontations with their families, friends, or neighbors. In so doing, they reveal their awareness of the social function of the biographer's art, for the lives themselves seem, at times, intended to deflect attention from the incisive commentary upon contemporary mores they inevitably provide.

For example, Thomas of Cantimpré's account of Christina Mirabilis, which he himself admits contains fabulous elements, provides a stunning commentary upon the fundamental skepticism or hostility to spiritual devotion that characterizes the citizen of the early modern town. From the beginning of his *Life,* Thomas insists upon a social context for Christina herself: she is born of respectable ("honestis") parents in the town of Saint Trond. After her death and miraculous rebirth, she flees the world of respectable men and women, unable to bear proximity to her own kind. Her behavior is so strange that her fellow townspeople react to her continual flight from ordinary life by binding her with a heavy yoke, seeking to enchain her spirit by harnessing her body to an ox's yoke (see sec. 19). Along with this and other depictions of contemporary Christians as not recognizing the Christ-like example among them, Thomas includes details of the wars and social disruptions of the early thirteenth century. The broader picture of Europe, like the more intimate one of the town of Saint Trond, underlines the fragmented and spiritually needy quality of contemporary life. Christina, like her divine exemplar, offers a picture of the possible to a world fixed in the actual. Thus, such obviously fabulous details as her ability to survive hot ovens, to sustain herself on milk from her own virginal breasts, and to live under the waters of the Meuse River for as long as six days at a time emphasize not only the relation between the divine and the marvelous, but also dramatize our reaction to the divine when it appears among us. Rather than locate Christina in a faraway place or in another time, Thomas situates her in the town, a federation of persons held together by networks of economic exchange, by practical considerations, and by shared values and customs. That such a body is by its nature unwilling to accommodate Christina, who sees herself as willingly enduring penitential suffering for their sins while she lives among those very citizens who reject her, points toward Thomas's understanding of the mode in which he wrote. Rather than overtly castigate the spiritual tepidity of an age of commerce, he presents a drama in which we ourselves are the likely persecutors of the one who is unlike us but nonetheless lives in our midst.

What both Thomas of Cantimpré and Jacques de Vitry affirm is the power of the sacramental church to provide a Europe fragmented by heresy, economic and social changes, and political tensions with a means of achieving a transcendent unity. Their focus on the eucharistic devotion of the early Beguines is designed to promote the sacrament as a symbol of the oneness possible in Christ, the body broken and joined again each time the Mass was celebrated.[14] The Mass was, of course, celebrated neither by laymen nor by holy women, but by members of a priesthood striving to achieve and to maintain standards by which the Church itself could be united in a whole. However, these holy women—with their single-minded devotion to the sacrament, their celibacy, their ability to live in the world and remain pure, and their apparent freedom from the constrictions of the flesh, such as hunger and pain—are presented as answers to a situation of increasing complexity and ambiguity. In place of the purity and simplicity of the "goodmen" of the Albigensians, who offered a sharp rebuke to a wealthy and elaborate ecclesiastical hierarchy, Jacques de Vitry presents Mary of Oignies, the simplest and gentlest of Christians, who nonetheless remains closely attached to the foundations and representatives of the organized church.[15] Rather than debate again the troubling and complicated issue of clerical celibacy, a subject more suited to the academic circle around Peter the Chanter in Paris, writers could affirm the superiority of the celibate life through the fictions of a Christina Mirabilis, whose virginity was all-sustaining and nurturing, or a Mary of Oignies, whose life of married chastity bore everlasting spiritual fruit.[16]

In their exploitation of the figure of the holy woman, they evince their awareness of the possibilities encoded in the feminine. Even women of authority and power like the twelfth-century visionaries Hildegard of Bingen and Saint Elizabeth of Schönau explicitly refer to gender in ways

14. See Kurtz, "Mary of Oignies, Christine the Marvelous, and Medieval Heresy." On the early shaping of eucharistic theology, see Rubin, *Corpus Christi,* 12–13.

15. On the Albigensians, see Ladurie, *Montaillou;* Strayer, *The Albigensians,* chapter 2. For an account of some of the social (and hence, moral) complexities of the period, see Little, *Religious Poverty and the Profit Economy in Medieval Europe.*

16. On contemporary debates over clerical celibacy, see Baldwin, *Masters, Princes, and Merchants,* 338.

that suggest its use as an indicator of public morality. Ekbert of Schönau, the brother who took down Elizabeth of Schönau's visions, compares the times to those of ancient Israel, when God raised up women like Deborah, Judith, and Jael because the men were too sluggish ("quando viris socordie deditis") to prophecy, to govern, or to triumph over Israel's enemies.[17] Jacques de Vitry's presentation of Mary of Oignies as an example of firmness, fortitude, and leadership is similarly intended to point up the torpor and flaccidity of those whose gender has fitted them for responsibilities they will not assume. Thus, by her very presence in history, the holy woman proclaims the inadequacies of an age which she, in turn, can rejoin in the harmony of the corporal body restored to itself through the channels of the sacramental Church. The monopoly of power that is adumbrated here is one that depends on the recognition that the tales of the holy are fictions every bit as powerful and as meaningful as any worked out between London and Canterbury.

Like other key texts in the tradition of sacred biography, *The Book of Margery Kempe* displays its author's keen sense of the uses of the holy. The proem to the *Book* establishes polarities that allow Kempe to write about her world by describing the experience of a self whose fictive identity is social.[18] The proem describes Margery's conversion as a turning away from the values of her community:

> Her werdly goodys, whech wer plentyuows & abundawnt at þat day, in lytyl whyle after wer ful bareyn & bare. Þan was pompe & pryde cast down & leyd on syde. Þei þat be-forn had worshepd her sythen ful scharply repreuyd her; her kynred & þei that had ben frendys wer now hyr most enmys. (2)

Her loss of communal status is described as offset by her gains in heavenly. The copious tears, which turn people against her, are signs of God's merciful acceptance of her penitential devotion. Those who believe in her, such as the priest who first agrees to help her write her book, are subject to the same acrimony that Margery herself experiences and must

17. For Elizabeth of Schönau, see *Die Visionen der hl. Elisabeth*, 40. For a discussion of Hildegard of Bingen's "anti-feminism," see Newman, *Sister of Wisdom*, 238.
18. For an important discussion of Chaucer's attempt to construct through Criseyde a psychology intended to reflect the relationship between the individual and society, see Aers, "Criseyde: Woman in Medieval Society."

overcome their fear of social ostracism and choose another, spiritual, community.

But where the description in the proem is cast in the stylized language of conversion narratives, Kempe's actual account of Margery's turn from the world reveals her interest in the nature of communal codes. Like Chaucer or Langland, both of whom provide vivid pictures of sins in terms of their manifestations in the community, Kempe describes such potentially abstract ideas as pride or avarice by referring to contemporary trends. Though she is hardly original in using women's fashions to exemplify the sin of pride, her account of Margery, with her "daggyd" cloaks and her gold wires in her headdress, does more than image female vanity.[19] Kempe explicitly states that Margery's obsession with dress reflects her appraisal of communal status. Thus, Margery arrays herself so she "schuld be þe more staryng to mennys sygth and hir-self þe mor ben worshepd." Not only is she sensitive about her social status ("hir fadyr was sum-tyme meyr of þe town N."), but she is envious of those "neybowrs" who are arrayed as well as she. As Kempe says, "Alle hir desyr was for to be worshepd of þe pepul" (9). Her disastrous business ventures, which suggest the ways in which the early fifteenth century offered a certain amount of economic opportunity for women, are undertaken in an effort to maintain a style of life that guarantees her a position in the community.[20] Since she is successful neither as an alewife nor as a mill-owner, her neighbors scorn her and chastize her for her worldliness. Shortly thereafter, Margery begins to focus on her inner self and to begin to discount the "worshepys of þe world."

What Kempe outlines here is at once stereotypical and analytical. The language she uses makes liberal use of the tropes of spiritual conversion. Terms like "þe world," phrases like "forsake hir pride," and scenes like the ones describing her unsuccessful attempt to harness the stubborn elements of nature, men, or beasts to her desire for gain deliberately provoke our recognition that the world is indeed to be fled, pride is to be shunned, and women who seek to manipulate the world around them deserve to be disappointed. But unlike Chaucer, whose portrait of another business-woman, Alison of Bath, focuses upon issues of authority that are ex-

19. See Owst, *Literature and Pulpit in Medieval England,* 96, 222, 390–411. See also the remarks of Chaucer's Parson.
20. On late medieval women and work, see Abram, "Women Traders in Medieval London"; J. M. Bennett, *Women in the Medieval English Countryside,* 196ff.; Hilton, "Women Traders in Medieval England."

pressed in the language of gender, Kempe uses these details as a means of expressing more broadly social concerns. For implicit in the chapter is a picture of "the world" as held together by communal values that, in the end, are oriented around profit.[21] The world Margery flees is the world in which Kempe lives, where success is valued as highly as failure is scorned. Margery's world, the East Anglia of the early fifteenth century, was dominated by mercantile interests and, correspondingly, by the values of a prosperous mercantile community. The great "wool churches" that dotted the landscape, the comfortable and carefully composed groupings of the Holy Family that looked out on and blessed the tradesmen of East Anglian towns, the concern for family relations and inheritances evinced in documents like the Paston Letters, bear witness to the contemporary concern for gain.[22] What Margery then rejects is the notion of material profit, thereby eliciting a communal scorn greater even than that reserved for the failure of a business venture.

That Margery's spiritual status rests upon her nonconformity suggests ways in which Kempe uses her to signify the demands and pressures of the community; she defines Margery in terms of her frequently oppositional relationship to others. Kempe presents Margery as diverging from the communal standards encoded in rituals involving food, clothing, and marriage. Margery's desire to fast, to wear clothes that signify her vocation, and to live chastely with her husband are conventional enough in relation to the literature of medieval piety; but Kempe handles these desires by relating each to the community's unwillingness to accept Margery's singularity.[23] Furthermore, she uses such instances of conflict to suggest that a complex series of tensions underlies the very idea of community.

For example, Kempe's treatment of the subject of food describes a society whose demands for conformity seem to stifle individual percep-

21. In her essay, "Sexual Economics, Chaucer's Wife of Bath, and *The Book of Margery Kempe*," Sheila Delany has, of course, rightly noted the relationship between the two figures. I suggest that that relationship is intentional because it is literary, and that Kempe alludes to Chaucer as a way of locating Margery in a stereotypical realm. Those stereotypes, in turn, deflect our attention from a more trenchant analysis of the codes of her day.

22. See the essays collected in Ashley and Sheingorn, *Interpreting Cultural Symbols*; Gibson, *Theater of Devotion*, chapter 2; Rosenthal, *The Purchase of Paradise*.

23. For discussions of the conventions of medieval female piety, see: Bynum, *Holy Feast and Holy Fast*, 13–30; idem, *Jesus as Mother*, 170–262; idem, "Women Mystics and Eucharistic Devotion in the Thirteenth Century"; Heffernan, *Sacred Biography*, 187–97, 261ff.; Kieckhefer, *Unquiet Souls*.

tions and needs. Considering the extraordinary attention many devotional writers and biographers paid to the subject of food when describing female piety, *The Book of Margery Kempe* is surprisingly free of what can seem a morbid fascination with physicality.[24] Margery does not reject food or become ill when she smells or sees it; nor does she become wraithlike from fasting. In fact, Kempe's handling of the subject of food or of corporality contrasts sharply to that found in other lives of holy women. Jacques de Vitry and Thomas of Cantimpré use the subject of food to define the triumphant physicality of Mary of Oignies and Christina Mirabilis. Where the spiritual food of the Eucharist refreshes and sustains the holy woman, the physical food she is forced to eat repels and sickens her. In such treatments, fasting, which to us is deprivation, is refreshment for the holy woman, since it is through her body that she manifests her freedom from constrictions imposed by sexuality, society, and family. For Thomas of Cantimpré, Christina Mirabilis's body is a sign of her ability to transcend the boundaries of the flesh. Primarily sustained by the Eucharist and by what little food she receives from begging, she can, when necessary, nourish herself from her own breasts. Her body has also an extraordinary agility: it bends into hoops, flies into the tops of trees, walks on waters, or enters Saint Trond by passing swiftly over the ground. Like Christ, Christina breaks the bounds of the natural world, doing what reason tells us cannot be done. Jacques de Vitry describes Mary of Oignies as capable of fasting for periods of eight, eleven, or even thirty-five days and as remaining free from pain and as effective in work on the last day of a fast as on the first.[25] On her death, he describes her corpse as an icon of the holy life: "When her tiny body was washed after death, it was found to be so small and shrivelled by her illness and fasting that her spine touched her belly and the bones of her back seemed to lie under the skin of her stomach as if under a thin linen cloth."[26] Her flesh, then, like the cloth covering the elements of the Mass on the altar, serves as a thin veil for the sanctified body whose waste testifies to God's plenty.

Rather than focus upon fasting as a token of Margery's otherworldliness, Kempe uses food as a signifier of both Margery's private and public

24. The classic study of food in relation to female piety is Bynum's *Holy Feast and Holy Fast*.
25. See sections 23, 24, 25 of her *Life*.
26. King, trans., *The Life of Marie d'Oignies*, 103. "Cum autem a morte lavaretur ejus sacrum corpusculum, inventa est ita attenuata et infirmitate jejuniisque confecta, quod dorsi ejus spina ventri ejus contingua erat; et quasi sub tenui panno lineo, sub ventris ejus pellicula ossa dorsi ejus apparebant" (*Vita Maria Oigniacensis*, 572).

communities. Kempe signals Margery's allegiance to a community of the spirit by describing her adherence to a private rule for living. With the exception of her early effort at fasting (11), it is in private conversations with Jesus that she develops rules governing food. He commands that she give up meat (17), fast on Fridays (21), and, later, give up her Friday fasts (24–25). Much later, Christ allows her to eat flesh again and to refrain from fasting once a week (161). Margery indicates the degree of her intimacy with the Virgin Mary by making her a warm drink to comfort her after the burial: "Than þe creatur thowt, whan owr Lady was comyn hom & was leyd down on a bed, þan sche mad for owr Lady a good cawdel & browt it hir to comfortyn hir" (195).[27] Though Mary refuses it, saying that she wants only spiritual food ("no mete but myn owyn childe"), Kempe describes Margery as lingering in the Virgin's home, in the inner core of Jesus' followers.

Of even more interest is Kempe's use of food to indicate the nature of the contemporary English community, which thrusts Margery from its midst because her eating practices are different. In the Middle Ages, eating was a far more communal act than it is now.[28] A medieval table would have probably been covered with a cloth but would have contained few signs of the individuals who would eat there; cutlery or even plates would have been rare. Instead, dishes were served on common platters and the diner either conveyed what he wished to eat to a large slice of bread before him or directly to his mouth. Fingers, rather than forks were the common utensils. In other words, the act of eating served, in John Bossy's phrase, as a "ritual of participation."[29] Margery's unwillingness to share the eating practices of her fellows has a significance that goes well beyond her wish to abstain from certain foods; by her abstinence, she marks her distance from communal values. However, in what is ostensibly an account of Margery's eating habits, Kempe, in fact, describes a community that seems to fear what is not immediately capable of assimilation. Margery is initially "slandered" for her early attempts at fasting (12) and, later, on the trip to Jerusalem, ostracized by her fellow pilgrims for her lack of camaraderie at mealtimes.

Kempe's description of the behavior of these pilgrims suggests the iro-

---

27. On Kempe's use of a suggestion from the influential devotional treatise, the *Meditationes* as the source for what appears an artless, housewifely detail, see Gibson, *Theater of Devotion*, 51.
28. Cosman, *Fabulous Feasts*, 16–17; Bossy, *Christianity in the West, 1400–1700*, chapter 4.
29. Bossy, *Christianity in the West, 1400–1700*, 59. In "Holiness and Society," 136, Bossy underlines the importance of eating as a sign of *convivium*, a possible synonym for fraternity.

nies inherent in social structures. Supposedly bound together by shared religious values, these pilgrims reject Margery for her unwillingness to abandon her private rule and join their more earthly community. Food becomes an issue at an early stage of the pilgrimage to Jerusalem. Margery's confessor first enjoins her to resume eating flesh and drinking wine, something she had not done for four years (61). Margery asks to be allowed to follow her own conscience on this matter, thereby displeasing both her confessor and her fellow pilgrims. Thereafter, when the company forsakes her, a man who "louyd hir wel" enjoins her to "go to hys felaws & mekyn hir on-to hem & preyn hem þat sche myth go stylle in her cumpany tyl sche come at Constawns" (62). Though Margery performs this act of social negotiation and is supposedly reintegrated into the company, she remains a figure on the threshold of the fellowship. They signal their attitude toward her with what are rituals of social humiliation: they cut her gown so short that she appears a fool, and they make her sit "at þe tabelys ende be-nethyn alle oþer þat sche durst ful euyl spekyn a word" (62). Like her fool's clothing, her place at the table signifies her provisional status in the pilgrim community, a status that is ameliorated by the "good man" who houses them at one point and by the papal legate they meet in Constance, whom the company invites to dinner. After a dinner in which Margery occupies her usual lowly position, the company asks the legate to command Margery "to etyn flesch as þei dedyn & levyn hir wepyng & þat sche xulde not speke so mech of holynes" (63–64). When the legate refuses, the company casts her out, so that she must find another guide to Jerusalem.

What has been a minidrama of community rejection, negotiation, partial acceptance, and further rejection becomes a more pointed commentary about the nature of social contracts when Margery rejoins the company in Bologne. There, she is invited to see if the fellowship will receive her once again. What follows is a social drama about mealtime demeanor that Kempe casts in legal language:

> '3yf 3e wyl gon in owyr felawshep, 3e must makyn a new comnawnt, & þat is þis, 3e schal not [speke] of þe Gospel wher we come, but 3e schal syttyn stylle & makyn mery, as we don, boþin at mete & at soper.' Sche consentyd & was receyued a-geyn in-to hir felawshep. (65)

This passage suggests a complicated social dynamic. First, the group signals its sense of cohesiveness by using the first-person plural pronoun to describe itself; Kempe consistently describes it with the singular nouns "company" or "fellowship." "Company" was a term commonly used for guild, so Kempe's employment of it here underlines the exclusivity of this particular group.[30] Both the pronoun, "we," and the nouns define the group as a collective mentality, one that is opposed to Margery because she separates herself from it by following her conscience. Kempe maintains this distinction between collective and individual identities by distinguishing those few persons who come to Margery's aid— an innkeeper, a papal legate, and a William Weaver from Devonshire (64), who leads her to Bologne. Where the group is faceless and nameless, these persons have occupations, locales, and, in once case, a name. Moreover, Kempe implies that words commonly used to define social entities can also be used to identify groups that are held together by spurious or sham values. The very company or fellowship that goes to worship in the lands of Jesus' ministry describes itself as bound together by mealtime rituals that exclude any talk of Jesus. They insist that Margery agree to a covenant signifying her willingness to comport herself "as we don." If such covenants bind pilgrims in fellowship, by what rules do we bind ourselves in societies?[31] Do such societies have room for the individuals who wish to differ from common practice? That Kempe is aware of the force of this scene is clear from Margery's speech in Venice, where she declares her intention of breaking the bad covenant she had made. After being reprimanded for speaking of the Gospel at a meal, she says: "3a, serys, forsoþe I may no lengar hold 3ow comenawnt, for I must nedys speke of my Lord Ihesu Crist þow al þis world had forbodyn it me" (66). Through Margery, Kempe hints at the link between social bonds and intention: Margery here chooses to break one covenant in order to maintain her fidelity to her vocation. She thus implicitly shifts from one group with its rituals to another fellowship. She follows her statement with an explicit move away from such fellowship: "& þan sche toke hir chawmbre & ete a-lone vj wokys" (66). Moving from the threshold to the margin of the group, she now chooses an isolation—and, significantly, one linked to eating practices—that had at first been the punishment the group used as a threat to circumscribe her actions.

30. On "company," see F. R. H. Du Boulay, *The England of "Piers Plowman,"* 62.

31. On the importance of the idea of contract and of contractual relation, see Black, *Guilds and Civil Society in European Political Thought,* 35ff.

Kempe also uses the issue of clothing to express the hostility aroused by Margery's nonconformity. Her clothing reflects her obedience to Christ's private rule for her; as a sign of her love for him, he commands her, first, to wear white clothing (32); then to change into black (84); and, finally, to wear white again, which she does for the rest of her life (91–92). To what is a matter of individual allegiance and choice, Kempe counterposes the public's reaction to Margery's clothing. In a crude inversion of medieval sumptuary preoccupations with overelaborate or costly clothing, the English respond harshly to Margery's humble manner of dressing.[32] In Leicester, where she is put under house arrest for suspicion of Lollardy (111ff.), the Mayor is particularly incensed by her white clothing: "I wil wetyn why þow gost in white clothys, for I trowe þow art comyn hedyr to han a-wey owr wyuys fro us & ledyn hem wyth þe" (116). By linking the two clauses with the conjunction, "for," Kempe points up the social irony inherent in Margery's situation. In terms of late medieval society, she is in a particularly vulnerable situation, alone, female, and without any kinship group to defend her integrity; and yet the Mayor, the local representative of authority and degree, sees Margery's white clothing as a sign that she intends to upset those hegemonies upon which late medieval society was supposedly based and lead away "our wives."[33] A little later, at York, her clothing again arouses public comment:

> & also sche had many enmyis whech slawndryd hir, scornyd hir, & despysed hir, of whech o prest cam to hir whil sche was in þe seyd Mynster &, takyng hir be þe coler of þe gowne, seyd, "þu wolf, what is þis cloth þat þu hast on?" (120)

The accusation that she is a wolf in sheep's clothing is followed up by the Archbishop of York's more explicit query of heresy:

> "Why gost þu in white? Art þu a mayden?" Sche, knelyng on hir knes be-for hym, seyd, "Nay, ser, I am no mayden; I am a wife." He commawndyd hys mene to fettyn a peyr of feterys & seyd sche xulde ben feteryd, for sche was a fals heretyke. (124)

32. The medieval concern for dress was ultimately directed at the idea of order or degree. For contemporary remarks about the potentially disorderly effect of women's dress, see Owst, *Literature and Pulpit in Medieval England*, 390–411. For the expression of more social concerns, see *Statutes of the Realm*, 1, 37 Edward III (1363), 380–82.

33. Aers ("Rewriting the Middle Ages," 238) also remarks on this line.

By presenting the Archbishop as capable of understanding virginity only in physical terms and completely misunderstanding the spiritual state signified by her clothing, Kempe stresses the crude literalism of the very man who should be able to understand more than one level of reality. It is a literalism that the Church too often shares with the burgher community.

Kempe draws together these twin signs of food and clothing in chapter 9 of the second part of the *Book,* when Margery arrives in London after her trip to the Continent.[34] Whereas, years before on her trip to Jerusalem, her fellow pilgrims had forced her to wear white canvas "in maner of a sekkyn gelle" (62), now she wears the same rough sackcloth as a sign of her pilgrim's poverty, disguising herself until she can borrow money for more appropriate clothing. She is, however, recognized as Margery Kempe of Lynn and accused of hypocrisy. Significantly enough, this accusation is expressed in terms of her attitude toward food, for she is accused of being the notorious hypocrite who once passed up less tasty herring for "good pyke" (243). In this sequence, Kempe describes London as a sort of echo-chamber where the taunt, "A, þu fals flesch, þu xalt no good mete etyn" (243) mocks Margery wherever she goes. Finally Margery confounds her tormentors by asserting both her innocence and her charity for them despite their civic mischief, going on to speak "boldly & mytily wher-so sche cam in London a-geyn swerars, bannars, lyars & swech oþer viciows pepil, a-geyn þe pompows aray boþin of men & of women" (245). Kempe's handling of this chapter is masterly; in describing the merging of Margery's private vocation with her assumption of a public role as preacher and intercessor,[35] Kempe also offers a characterization of contemporary London for which Margery's figure serves as a kind of screen. The chapter can thus be read two ways, as a crucial moment in the spiritual development of Margery, or as a trenchant commentary upon the stifling and conformist atmosphere of fifteenth-century London. What is in a sense fantastic about the account—the whispering campaign against Margery, her bold preaching, wherein she spares neither civic nor ecclesiastical authorities—deflects the force of Kempe's diagnosis of Londoners as petty, worldly, malicious bullies, who are cowed and then won over by Margery, who is now unwilling to be their victim.

34. The very fact that the manuscript of the *Book* has chapter divisions suggests its inherent structure, or bookishness. See Parkes, "The Influence of the Concepts of *Ordinatio* and *Compilatio* on the Development of the Book."

35. On the subject of Margery as a "preacher," see Lochrie, *"The Book of Margery Kempe:* The Marginal Woman's Quest for Literary Authority," 42–47.

If the contemporary model for community was founded on the idea of unity, Kempe offers a picture of society as fragmented by tensions that cannot be so easily resolved by the act of naming.[36] Her methods of analysis are indicative both of her unwillingness to fall back upon the stock-in-trade of the pulpit castigator and her recognition that the society she contemplates is not so easily assimilated to a neat and orderly model. For example, her composition of contemporary society is far more ambiguously poised than that provided by an earlier observer, Thomas Wimbledon, whose influential English sermon, "Redde racionem villicacionis tue," preached at Paul's Cross in 1388, was seen as providing important insights into the reasons for contemporary social unrest.[37] What Wimbledon defines is a social body, which he identifies with the Church, that should but does not function as a unified whole. He therefore employs estates' theory as a means of urging all to work for a common good. Since by 1388, the tripartite scheme of priests, knights, and laborers was hopelessly anachronistic, Wimbledon indicates his awareness of a more complex social body: "It is nede þat summe beþ acremen, summe laboreris, summe makeris of cloþ, and summe marchaundis to fecche þat þat o lond fauteþ from anoþer þer it is plente. And certis þis shulde be o cause why euery staat shul loue oþer, and men of o craft shulde neiþer hate ne despise men of anoþer craft, siþ þey beþ so nedeful euerych to oþer. And ofte þilke craftis þat semen most vnhonest myȝthen worst be forbore."[38] Wimbledon goes on to remind all—laborers, "crafti" men, servants, merchants, knights, justices, priests—to work faithfully in whatever "astaat" God has called them. While Wimbledon certainly admits the possibility of the social tensions that result from the conflicts of certain interest groups, he nonetheless seeks to remind his hearers that the many competing parts of the social body can be fitted together again. He therefore devotes the bulk of his sermon to the questions Christ will ask

36. On the contemporary tension between the ideal model for society and the actuality, see Mills, "Religious Drama and Civic Ceremonial"; Reynolds, *Kingdoms and Communities in Western Europe, 900–1300,* chapter 8; Rubin, "Corpus Christi Fraternities and Late Medieval Piety," "Small Groups: Identity and Solidarity in the Late Middle Ages"; Pythian-Adams, "Ceremony and the Citizen: The Communal Year at Coventry, 1450–1550."

37. For the text of Wimbledon's sermon, see Owen, "Thomas Wimbledon's Sermon: 'Redde racionem villicacionis tue.' " For speculations about Wimbledon's identity, see Owen, "Thomas Wimbledon." For the sermons, many of them directed at social ills, of Thomas Brinton, see the edition of Mary Acquinas Devlin. Owst's *Literature and Pulpit in Medieval England* is, of course, a gold mine of information about medieval sermons and their social relevance.

38. Owen, "Thomas Wimbledon's Sermon," 179. For a searching examination of the origins and social and political uses of the idea of the three orders, see Duby, *The Three Orders: Feudal Society Imagined.*

each member of society on the Last Day, suggesting that Apocalypse may serve as the catalyst for individual change and, hence, for social rejoining. The continued popularity of this sermon well into the sixteenth century bears witness to Wimbledon's ability to appeal to the ideal of social unity despite what could seem overwhelming evidence of actual division.[39] It also suggests his deft handling of the techniques of estates' satire, which provided a language for addressing the ills of the age but that was, despite its topical relevance, general enough to apply for some two hundred years.[40]

The social ideals, or myths, of the Middle Ages are likewise apparent in such documents as the sermon that forms a prologue to the Book of Ordinances of the York Corpus Christi Guild, the largest and most important religious fraternity in the city.[41] Dated 1408, the sermon describes the fraternity as, by its very nature, ameliorating the divisions among people that resulted from the Fall. The sermon thus stands as an important testimony to the late medieval attempt to construct a social ideal that matched, or justified, a social institution. Since the sermon celebrates the founding of the Corpus Christi guild, it is fittingly organized around the metaphor of the body—Adam's infected ("infectam") body, the figurative body of humanity split through the original act of disobedience, but remedied through the sacrifice and resurrection of Christ's sacred flesh, which is reenacted as a memorial of intercession and as a token of the unity available through Christ's Passion. The sermon then links the founding of the fraternity itself with the sacral act: "For which reason, beloved, since our fraternity for the veneration of this same precious sacrament has been begun by rule, gathered together in the faith of the Church in peaceful unity, we will be a homogeneous part of the mystical body of Christ through our prayers, devotions, and acts of charity. The unity and concord of our brotherhood are rooted in love, which is one in its root and sevenfold in the carrying out of works of mercy."[42] The idea of unity

39. See Johnson, "*The Shepheardes Calender*": *An Introduction,* 62n.

40. Mann, *Chaucer and Medieval Estates Satire,* 3–16.

41. For texts of this sermon, see Skaife, ed., *The Register of the Guild of Corpus Christi in the City of York,* 1–9; Lozar, "The 'Prologue' to the Ordinances of the York Corpus Christi Guild." Lozar's is both a reedition and a translation. For a provocative analysis of the challenges posed by this prologue, see Colletti, "Reading REED," 275–77.

42. Lozar, 104–5. "Quapropter carissimi cum nostra fraternitas in veneracione istius preciosi sacramenti sit regulariter incepta. erimus in fidei ecclesiae / vnitate pacifice congregati velut corporis Christi mistici in precibus votis et actionibus elemosinariis pars homogenia. cuius fraternitatis vnitis et concordia in caritate radicatur que est vna in radice et septiplex in operum miseriarum execucione."

dominates the sermon. The images themselves—of a body with its separate organs and limbs, of a vine with various branches, of the rays of the sun, of tributaries issuing from one fountain—insist that what appears diverse is, in fact, unified in its function and essence. The notion of brotherhood, or community, that is worked out in the sermon is one in which division is seen as a manifestation of sin, and oneness as a sign of redemptive love. By disallowing the possibility of division within members of a single body, the sermon proclaims a social unity that is a manifestation of unity through the faith. What draws all together is, of course, the sacred, divided, and reconstituted body of Christ, imaged in the guild itself that took its identity from that body.

The theory of brotherhood articulated by the sermon must, however, be situated within the context of the late Middle Ages and the role played by parish fraternities in the lives of medieval citizens. Although both the craft guilds and the religious fraternities promulgated notions of social solidarity, friendship, and mutual aid, the craft guilds were explicitly rooted in the mercantile life of the town. Divided according to crafts, the guilds enforced standards of craftsmanship and promoted justice and fraternity among guild members.[43] The parish fraternities, on the other hand, ostensibly served less worldly ends. First, they described themselves as representing an overarching affinity, for they drew their membership from all "worthy" persons in a given city. Since they were composed of people from both sexes and of many trades, they primarily functioned as mutual aid societies, helping out brothers in need and presiding over the deaths, burials, and commemoratory masses of members. They also usually helped maintain parish churches and met at least once a year to elect wardens and to feast together and several times a year to pray for the souls of their dead.[44] The fraternities served as a sort of compensatory "family," providing stability in a world where economic change seemed the dominant mode.[45] As Miri Rubin has pointed out, not only did the fraternities employ the language of kinship, they practiced the types of rituals we

43. For discussions of guilds, see Black, *Guilds and Civil Society in European Political Thought;* Green, *Town Life in the Fifteenth Century,* 55–149; James, "Ritual Drama and Social Body in the Late Medieval English Town."

44. I am drawing my remarks from the York Pater Noster Guild Return, 1388–89 in Johnston and Rogerson, eds., *York,* 2:863–66.

45. On the economic instabilities of late medieval life, see Thrupp, *The Merchant Class of Medieval London, 1300–1500,* 191–233. For other remarks on parish fraternities, see McRee, "Religious Gilds and Civic Order: The Case of Norwich in the Late Middle Ages."

associate with families: members ate and drank together, prayed together, and oversaw the details of death, burial, memorial masses, as well as more practical issues like wills and inheritances.[46] They also served to regulate communal behavior: the ordinances of many fraternities penalized, and therefore checked, behavior that might have been socially or politically damaging for the community.[47] Despite language suggesting the inclusive nature of the parish fraternity, however, the fraternities themselves were as hierarchical as the society out of which they grew. Power was concentrated in the same patrician class that ruled the separate craft guilds, and the order celebrated by these fraternities was, in fact, the uneasy order of the medieval town itself.[48]

Kempe's depiction of contemporary society strongly suggests her awareness that there was more to communal life than homogeneity. If official documents can state, "Unity is cause for rejoicing, and division by sin greatly to be lamented," Kempe presents an image of community that severely questions the shared values and activities by which corporate entities define themselves.[49] The simple equation between division and sin does not adequately describe the complexities of the world in which Margery lives. Thus Kempe's accounts of the hostility raised by Margery's clothing and eating practices are designed to point up the ways in which "unity" can become conformity, thereby splitting into separate parts what is not allowed to be diversely one. Kempe persistently describes Margery as offending her contemporaries' sense of community by acts that apparently threaten its own myths of brotherhood, myths that Kempe suggests are ultimately founded upon falsely imposed hierarchies. Her treatment of what we might think of as Margery's private relationships are rarely removed from a communal context.

For example, Margery's marital status arouses a good deal of public comment. In contrast to the binding public agreement to a chaste marriage that Margery initially asks of her husband, their marital relations remain a private matter between the two of them. Neither the Bishop of

46. Rubin, "Small Group Identity and Solidarity in the Late Middle Ages," 140.

47. See McRee, "Religious Gilds and Regulation of Behavior in Late Medieval Towns," in *People, Politics, and Community in the Later Middle Ages,* ed. Rosenthal and Richmond. For example, McRee notes that men were warned not to wander the street at night or to play games of chance; women were cautioned to avoid the company of suspicious men (108–9).

48. This realization has formed the core of much recent work on medieval fraternal organizations. See, for example, the work of McRee and Rubin cited above, notes 45–47.

49. The sentence is from the York Corpus Christi sermon, Lozar, 107–9.

Lincoln nor the Archbishop of Canterbury is willing to invest her with
the mantle and the ring of married widowhood and so to give public
sanction to the private ceremony celebrated between Margery and John
Kempe on Midsummer's Eve on the road from York (see 23–25). Their
mutual vow of chastity, for which Margery gives up her Friday fasts and
agrees to have dinner with John Kempe each Friday, never seems to have
been a matter of public record.[50] Although they continue to see one
another, and John travels a good deal with Margery, their relationship
ceases to be a sexual one. Kempe handles this aspect of Margery's story
by focusing upon the ways in which the public impinges upon the
private life of the nonconformist. Margery is not only frequently called
to account for her marital status; Kempe also suggests that, for the
public, her identity is a social one. Wherever she goes in England, she is
John Burnham's daughter, John Kempe's wife, and the mother of fourteen children. Such tags, of course, reflect the interdependent networks
of late medieval society, which was at once astonishingly mobile and
firmly local.[51]

It is, however, in her treatment of John Kempe's final illness that Kempe
reveals her interest in the relationship between these private and public
spheres. When, as a man past sixty, John Kempe falls down the stairs of his
house and hits his head, Margery is called to take care of him. Kempe
compresses the events of several years into one tightly written chapter that
underlines the public significance of Margery's marital nonconformity.
First, the account makes clear just how thin were the walls of medieval
houses: "&, as God wold, it was knowyn to summe of hys neybowrys how
he was fallyn downe of þe gresys, perauentur thorw þe dene & þe luschyng

50. For a study of the Church's regulation of private devotional impulses, see Davis, "The
Rule of St. Paul, the First Hermit, in Late Medieval England." Davis remarks that private
clothings, such as the one Margery desires, would have been made matters of ecclesiastical
record. Here, as elsewhere in the *Book*, Kempe's account cannot be verified by official registers. In
his notes to *The Book of Margery Kempe*, Meech remarks (274 n. 33) that he had the register of
Philip Repingdon, the bishop of Lincoln, searched for mention of his interview with Margery
and her request for clothing, but found nothing. I, too, have looked closely at that register and
found nothing that might be linked to interviews between Repingdon and Margery. Rather than
speculate about lost records, we might begin to turn our attention to Kempe herself, whose
fictions are meant as commentaries upon the official institutions of her day.

51. For studies of ways in which mainly aristocratic networks operated see, for example,
Bennett, *Community, Class and Careerism;* Given-Wilson, *The English Nobility in the Late Middle
Ages;* Hanna, "Sir Thomas Berkeley and His Patronage." Though these studies concern magnate
culture, they nonetheless illustrate ways in which medieval persons were at once rooted in their
particular locales and pledged to a life of motion.

of hys fallyng" (179).⁵² After this fall, he is sick for a long time, and the people turn on Margery, blaming her for not taking care of him:

> And þan þe pepil seyd, ȝyf he deyd, hys wyfe was worthy to ben hangyn for hys deth, for-as-meche as sche myth a kept hym & dede not. They dwellyd not to-gedyr, ne þei lay not to-gedyr, for as is wretyn be-forn, þei bothyn wyth on assent & wyth fre wil of her eiþyr haddyn mad avow to leuyn chast. & þerfor to enchewyn alle perellys þei dwellyd & soiowryd in diuers placys wher no sus-picyon xulde ben had of her incontinens, for first þei dwellyd togedir aftyr þat þei had mad her vow, & þan þe pepil slawndryd hem & seyd þei vsyd her lust & her likyng as þei dedyn be-forn her vow makyng. (179–80)

Kempe here skillfully weaves together an account of the Kempes' pri-vate relations with a richly ironic account of the ways in which the public edges its way into the bedroom. John and Margery Kempe live separately because the public will not let them work out a more idiosyncratic arrange-ment. If they share the same house, Margery is slandered for sexual hypoc-risy. Their living arrangements, therefore, reflect their appraisal of their neighbors' low estimate of human nature:

> They, hauyng knowlach how prone þe pepil was to demyn euyl of hem, desiryng to avoydyn al occasyon, in as mech as þei myth goodly, be her good wil & her boþins consentyng, þei partyd a-sundyr as towchyng to her boord & to her chambrys, & wentyn to boord in diuers placys. (180)

On the other hand, if John Kempe were to die from his fall, the people make it clear that Margery will have to answer for his death. She is released from the straits of one problematic situation into another; though Christ assures her that John Kempe shall not die this year, her spiritual husband bids her take her earthly husband back into her home and nurse him back to health. Margery is thus presented with a solution to her problem with her community that limits the time she will be able to

---

52. For remarks about the domestic architecture of the town of Lynn, see Parker, *The Making of King's Lynn*. See also Dyer, *Standards of Living in the Later Middle Ages*, chapter 7, "Urban Standards of Living."

spend alone in contemplation. However, she accepts her former husband as a part of her new vocation, caring for him for many years, until as a senile and incontinent old man he can only function as a symbol of her former delight in the pleasures of the flesh (181).

By bringing the marriage of John and Margery Kempe full circle, so to speak, Kempe refigures the medieval concept of the marriage debt in a way that suggests a view of her society as inherently tension-bound and inevitably constrictive. Kempe's justly famous and Norton-anthologized account of that original bargain struck between John and Margery on Midsummer's Eve captures the ways in which the concept of marriage was infused with the metaphors of the marketplace.[53] Drawing upon Saint Paul's notion of marriage whereby both husband and wife exchange "authority" over their bodies, theologians placed the idea of debt in the center of any discussion of sexual relations in marriage. Kempe not only organizes this scene around the idea of debt, she locates marriage and marital relations in the public sphere. Thus, though the conversation between husband and wife on the road from York is a private one, the subject of their conversation is not. In exchange for releasing her from her sexual debt, John Kempe asks that she not sever her ties to community: "My fyrst desyr is þat we xal lyn stylle to-gedyr in o bed as we han do befor; þe secunde þat ȝe schal pay my dettys er ȝe go to Iherusalem; & þe thrydde þat ȝe schal etyn & drynkyn wyth me on þe Fryday as ȝe wer wont to don" (24). John Kempe here seems to suggest that marriage may be reformulated in terms of a different notion of community, the creature comfort of sharing a bed and a weekly meal.[54] John's words are intended

---

53. For discussions of the concept of the marriage debt, see Flandrin, "Sex in Married Life in the Early Middle Ages: The Church's Teaching and Behavioral Reality"; Heffernan, *Sacred Biography,* 187. For discussions of the ways in which marriage was linked to emotional, rather than sexual, aspects of relationship, to consent, rather than simply to *coitus,* by later theorists, see Brundage, *Law, Sex, and Christian Society in Medieval Europe,* 175, 223, 274; Duby, *Medieval Marriage,* chapter 1; Goody, *The Development of the Family and Marriage in Europe,* 66. For two discussions of this scene in relation to Kempe's portrait of a world governed by economic relationships, see Aers, "Rewriting the Middle Ages," 237; Delany, "Sexual Economics, Chaucer's Wife of Bath and *The Book of Margery Kempe.*"

54. In a conversation David Benson reminded me of how fundamentally sympathetic a figure John Kempe is and how we do both him and Kempe, his "author," a disservice if we simply see him as the villain of the piece. I agree; Kempe provides evidence that John is neither monstrous nor stupid. He faithfully accompanies Margery on many of her trips around England, standing by her when her neighbors turn against her. Kempe has also given John the greatest gift of all, the gift of irony. Witness his remarks to Margery on closing their "marriage bargain," when he wishes "As fre mot yowr body ben to God as it hath ben to me" (25).

to do more than reiterate Kempe's awareness of her society's mercantilist ethic of marriage. Through John, Kempe suggests those rituals of social involvement by which individuals are at once linked and tied, debts that can be interpreted metaphorically or literally. John's words suggest that Margery can discharge her figurative debt by paying his actual debts, but her willingness to do so also signifies her identity as a creature bound to him and, through him, to the greater community. Margery eventually agrees to his terms, buying back authority over her own body. Later, as John Kempe lingers into senescence, Margery reenters into relationship with him, giving up her solitude in exchange for community approval. Her reward for this second bargain is likewise a spiritual one, for she learns to serve him and help him "as hir thowt, as sche wolde a don Crist hym-self" (181).

Through her depiction of the marriage of John and Margery, Kempe seems to hint at a conception of Christian community that has its foundations in her recognition that, for better or worse, we are bound to one another. First, she never questions the realities of social bonds. Margery and John owe one another their bodies whenever the other wishes it or until they release each other from debt. Once they agree to live chastely, they attempt to work out a public relationship that reflects the state of their private relations. Their community, however, rejects any but the most literal interpretation of marriage, driving them to separate establishments, since their neighbors refuse to accept that those who live together do not also engage in sexual relations. To this rigid concept of marriage as physical union, Kempe juxtaposes a different way of thinking about intimacy. Margery abandons physical union with John for spiritual marriage to the Godhead, while nonetheless maintaining her ties to John, her legal husband. Despite her mobility and her sense of vocation, she thus continues to identify herself as John Kempe's wife. Furthermore, his neighbors have no difficulty locating her or hesitation in calling upon her when John is hurt. By taking John into her home during his last years, Margery creates a household whose similarity to the original establishment is more apparent than real. First, it is her house, and she is the authority figure and the caregiver; she offers John the security, the aid, and the companionship that serve as the basis for a different type of social unit. She, in effect, creates a community whose foundation is the brotherhood that binds people together through love of Christ. That this remains only a minor incident in the conflict-ridden narrative of Margery's life says much about Kempe's view of the limitations of her own community. Where through John and Margery, Kempe hints at ways in which individuals can reinterpret social rules, through her characterization of contemporary society, she figures the noose that convention can throw over those same individuals.

In the accounts of individuals who are kind to Margery, Kempe provides the outlines of an alternate society, a society whose ideals can ultimately be traced to Christ's apocalyptic description in Matthew 25 of the community of his new kingdom. There, he describes the blessed as giving food, drink, shelter, clothing, and comfort to the stranger, pilgrim, or prisoner in their midst. The passage, of course, had a wide currency in the Middle Ages, for it was the *locus* for the concept of the seven works of mercy.[55] Kempe uses the passage as an informing principle in her image of a community that stands in sharp contrast to the contemporary society that rejects Margery for the discomfort she arouses in others. Whereas Margery's vociferous crying, her eating habits, her clothing, and her style of life arouse frequently violent reactions in most people, Kempe sprinkles the *Book* with cameo portraits of more charitable individuals. During Margery's time in the Holy Land, for example, the Grey Friars invite her to dine with them (73), and the Saracens lead her to holy places when her fellow Christians desert her (74–75). Later, in Rome, when she is in great poverty, a Dame Margaret Florentyn feeds her three days a week, a man called Marcelle feeds her two days, and "an holy mayden" gives her food on Wednesdays; in addition, the Master of the Hospital of Saint Thomas holds her in high esteem and offers her hospitality (92–94). When she returns to England, "a worshepful man in Norwich" gives her the white clothing she wishes to wear (103–4). Much later, when she returns to Dover from her final trip to Germany, "a good woman" takes her into her home, washes her, and gives her a new smock (241). She is also offered comfort during various moments of distress: in Leicester, where she is accused of Lollardy, the jailor takes her home for his wife to care for, serves her at his own table, comforts her, and lets her go to church when she wishes (112); during her difficult stay in London, despite the hostility of so many, she is offered "mete and drynke" by a "worshepful woman" and is "hily cheryd" in many places in London "in owyr Lordys name" (244).

Kempe casts each of these acts of kindness in the form of those social rituals by which communities establish their identities. These are signs

---

55. The clearest expression of the meaning this passage had can be found in the Doomsday pageants of the mystery plays.

that she consistently uses to signal Margery's liminal relationship with her contemporary society; by using them to point up the outlines of a new group, she seems deliberately to offer the possibility of an alternate society. Kempe indicates the significance attached to such instances of community when, in Lynn, a "worschepful doctour" invites Margery to dine: "Þer was a dyner of gret joy & gladnes, meche mor gostly þan bodily, for it was sawcyd & sawryd wyth talys of Holy Scriptur" (170). Kempe's description of Margery's dinner with the doctor plays upon the multiple associations she establishes that concern eating, communing, and community, and the ways in which such rituals adumbrate the true natures of social groupings. Her wording also implicitly links the concept of community with that of communion.[56] Using the rituals that for the guilds and confraternities embodied their shared interests as signifiers of a fellowship where charity has less to do with trade, Kempe frequently indicates the affinity between Margery and someone sympathetic to her by saying that the person invites Margery to dine. Kempe thus employs those very aspects of Margery's life-style that set her apart from contemporary society as tokens of a new society governed by none except spiritual law, whose citizens are bound together by a new, and scriptural, authority.[57] By depicting them as better defined than those who despise Margery, Kempe distinguishes the members of what is a society predestined for blessedness (see Matthew 25:34). She typically describes Margery's detractors using nouns and pronouns that identify them only in relation to their group. On the other hand, those individuals who offer kindness to Margery, are more likely to have names or epithets that set them apart (a holy maiden, a worshipful doctor) and serve to hint at an identity rooted in personal belief. Through these individuals, Kempe adumbrates a potential for community that remains unrealized in the world imaged in her *Book*.

In fact, Kempe's primary focus upon the social discomfort Margery's behavior occasions helps to blunt the effect of what is a sharp critique of the contemporary world. In a literary fiction where Margery's life seems a

56. See the *MED* for the various associations of community and fellowship (both secular and sacred) that had accrued around the word by the late Middle Ages.

57. The outlines of Kempe's new society would have seemed dangerously heterodox if she had stated them explicitly. See, for example, the summary provided by Deanesly, in *The Significance of the Lollard Bible*. For a sense of the official fear of Lollardy, see *Statutes of the Realm*, 2, 2 Henry IV (1400–1401), XV, pp. 126–28; 2 Henry V (1414), VII, pp. 181–84. In both statutes, the link between books and sedition is stressed, and, in 1414, Statute VII, against Lollardy, is followed by Statute VIII, against riots.

reenactment of the Passion of Christ or of the persecution of the early martyrs, her neighbors play the part of the hostile, crucifying, tormenting crowd that sought to destroy Christ and his Church. From sermons, pageants, and devotional writing, Kempe would have known that this crowd was typically characterized as malicious, gossipy, literal-minded, violent, and conformist.[58] From depictions of the midwives attending the Virgin birth, to those of stock villains like Herod and Christ's execution- ers, to the ironic accounts of Noah and Joseph, the "crowd," with its literalist and therefore limited expectations, figured strongly in medieval attempts to image the divine. In this sense, Kempe's portrait of the public is conventional, since it is based on the attributes commonly ascribed to the citizens of the city of man, or to the lineage of Cain. However, in her treatment of her world Kempe not only seems to draw upon such charac- terizations, she also reveals herself as more than capable of mingling in a single treatment what she would probably have described as various levels of reality. Kempe particularizes what we might be tempted to ascribe solely to exegetical sources in ways that suggest her attempt to understand and to analyze the world in which she lived. Kempe, like Chaucer, Langland, and the authors of the mystery plays, presents us with an opportunity to understand some of the tensions of the late medieval world.

For example, like the authors of the mystery plays, Kempe would have known the conventions linking the citizens of the city of man to violence, especially to the sort of violence that underlies civic disorder. In depicting the people who are Margery's antagonists, however, Kempe does not draw so simply upon the attributes of Cain's kin. Instead, she focuses our attention upon Margery and stresses her vulnerability, establishing an implicit link between the mythic violence of the human city and the actual conditions of her own, frequently violent, world.[59] She thus emphasizes

58. See Gibson, *Theater of Devotion,* for a study of the devotional climate of East Anglia. See also Nelson, "On Recovering the Lost Norwich Corpus Christi Cycle."

59. On the dangers of gang rape to women living without explicit communal protection in late medieval French towns, see Rossiaud, "Prostitution, Sex and Society in French Towns in the Fifteenth Century," 84–86. Rossiaud notes that the objects of such rapes were maidservants, daughters of the impoverished working class, or widows, or women living by themselves. The "crime" committed by the woman living alone was the implicit attack on the settled life repre- sented by her style of life. For discussions of the violence of late medieval life, see Bellamy, *Crime and Public Order in the Later Middle Ages;* Sir John Fortescue, *The Governance of England,* introduction; Putnam, ed., *Proceedings before the Justices of the Peace in the Fourteenth and Fifteenth Centuries;* Rossiaud, *Medieval Prostitution;* idem, "Prostitution, Sex and Society in French Towns

the dangers an individual might encounter once ties to the group were severed. Margery's fears, which are understandable, especially given what we know about the tensions of late medieval society, are cast in the form of her sense of her vulnerability to physical attack. As a woman traveling alone, whose status is therefore unclear, she realistically fears rape whenever she travels. On her journey from Constans to Bologne, Kempe stresses the safety Margery finds with William Weaver as her guide by saying that no man they met said an evil word to Margery and "þe good wyvys þer þei weryn at inne leyden hir in her owyn beddys for Goddys lofe in many placys þer þei come" (65). In Leicester, the Steward of Leicester, who is supposedly a "steward" of civic order or a representative of the very social hierarchy that inspires order, threatens his female prisoner with "fowyl rebawdy wordys," to which Margery replies, "Ser, for þe reuerens of al-mythy God, sparyth me, for I am a mannys wife" (113). Her boldness seems to excite him, and Kempe describes him as struggling with her, "schewyng vn-clene tokenys & vngoodly cuntenawns" (113). As an old woman, on her way home through France from Germany, she is most afraid at night: "Sche durst trustyn on no man; whedir sche had cawse er non, sche was euyr a-ferd. Sche durst ful euyl slepyn any nyth, for sche wend men wolde a defylyd hir. Þerfor sche went to bedde gladlich no nyth les þan sche had a woman er tweyn wyth hir" (241; see also 236).

Kempe suggests the provisional status of women by playing upon Margery's fears of sexual violation. She also dramatizes a more incipient violence that is only partially checked by the social contracts that serve as the basis for community. In her depiction of Christendom, Kempe underlines the very real threat that thieves posed to travelers (see 99–100, 234, 239). She frequently characterizes the people as given to violence against the isolated individual. Kempe describes Margery as threatened with a heretic's death at the stake in Canterbury (28) and as publicly scorned for her supposed Lollardy in Beverly (134–35). On her final trip, she is warned not to spend the night in a certain town, whose citizens are described as a "perlyows pepil" (240). Kempe also implies that the tendency to violence does not simply manifest itself in public unrest when Margery notes that she weeps if she sees a man or beast with a wound or "ȝyf a man bett a childe be-for hir er smet an hors er an-oþer best wyth a

---

in the Fifteenth Century." For the contemporary distrust for the individual who took to the roads, see *Statutes of the Realm*, 2, 12 Richard II (1388), pp. 56, 58.

whippe, ȝyf sche myth sen it er heryn it, hir thowt sche saw owyr Lord be betyn er wowndyd lyk as sche saw in þe man er in þe best, as wel in þe feld as in þe town, & be hir-selfe [a]lone as wel as a-mong þe pepyl" (69). The sentence briefly opens a window upon the sort of casual domestic violence that must have been a common feature of life in a late medieval community. What Kempe thus hints at in these vignettes is a network of abuse, linking men to women, traveler to thief, man to child or beast in a grim parody of the hierarchical ordering of society. The weak appear to have little recourse because they are isolated by gender, status, or age and must, like Christ, suffer the consequences of the greed and frustration of others.

Kempe's focus upon the nature or foundations of community may be one reason, for instance, for the startling anti-Jewish comments near the end of the first part of the *Book*. I say startling because the *Book* is free from the sort of distasteful anti-Judaism that we frequently encounter in medieval treatments of New Testament subjects. The N-Town cycle, which has an East Anglian provenance, certainly contains a number of episodes that depict the Jews as unalterably opposed to Christ and his followers and therefore as chicanerous and malicious. East Anglian towns, including Norwich and Lynn, had had respectable Jewish communities in the twelfth and thirteenth centuries, but they were also the locations for some of the earliest recorded anti-Jewish activity.[60] Furthermore, though the Jewries of medieval England disappeared when the Jews were expelled in 1290 and would have been very old memories indeed for a fifteenth-century writer, East Anglian attitudes toward Jews might well have persisted. There are several places in the *Book* where Kempe might have used stereotypical depictions of the Jews as enemies of Christ. In chapter 6, for example, Margery "sees" the sequence that includes Saint Anne's pregnancy, the holiness and simplicity of the child Mary, the birth of Saint John the Baptist, and the nativity of Christ. The first portion of this sequence is extrabiblical and can be found in works like Jacobus de Voragine's *Golden Legend,* the *Revelations of St. Elizabeth of Hungary,* and Nicholas Love's *Mirror of the Blessed Life of Jesus Christ.* The N-Town cycle, with its emphasis upon the Virgin devotes a good deal of space to dramatizing the contrast between the holiness and faith of Joachim and Anna,

60. Dobson, "The Jews of Medieval York and the Massacre of March 1190"; Lipman, *The Jews of Medieval Norwich.* In the Middle Ages, Jews were always thought the serfs of the Crown, which profited by them, exploited them, and (sometimes) protected them. As Jordan has demonstrated in *The French Monarchy and the Jews,* anti-Jewish activity cannot, therefore, be considered apart from royal policies and/or power.

Mary's parents, and the literal-minded and profit-oriented spirituality of their fellow Jews. Kempe is clearly more than content to embroider upon these scenes, for she describes Margery as becoming the handmaiden of Mary, keeping her until she is twelve years of age, "wyth good mete & drynke, wyth fayr whyte clothys & whyte kerchys" (18). She even goes so far as to have Margery precede Gabriel in announcing Mary's role as mother of God. But she does not mention the Jews or the Temple here or, later, in chapter 28, when Margery visits Jerusalem and the site of the Crucifixion. By placing her account of Margery's vision of the Passion, with its anti-Jewish comments, late in the first part of the *Book* (chapters 79–80), Kempe employs the Jews who "cruelly" torture and kill Christ as a means of indicting Margery's neighbors for their deliberate unwillingness to recognize the holy woman in their midst.

As Jeremy Cohen has pointed out, attitudes toward Jews changed during the course of the Middle Ages.[61] Saint Augustine and his followers tolerated the Jews, seeing them as ignorant of the nature of Jesus, and maintained that they should be left alone since their conversion would precede the Second Coming. But in the thirteenth century, the Jews began to be seen as deliberate unbelievers and, increasingly, as villainous. Medieval antagonism toward the Jews coincided with the increasingly antiheretical mission of the Church, a mission that dominated Crusader rhetoric, energized the early days of the mendicant orders, and helped to define the outlines of a Christian society. Thus Berthold von Regensburg in the early thirteenth century described Christian society as *not* containing Jews, heretics, or heathens, groups he insisted were without place.[62] The virulently anti-Jewish attitudes of the late Middle Ages, which were encapsulated in fraternal attacks upon them, need also to be seen in relation to political tugs-of-war and to the economic complexities and social changes of the same period.[63] In a Europe where feudal bonds were

---

61. See Cohen, *The Friars and the Jews: The Evolution of Medieval Anti-Judaism,* 233–54. See also Cohen, "The Jews as Killers of Christ in the Latin Tradition, from Augustine to the Friars"; Rembaum, "The Talmud and the Popes: Reflections on the Talmud Trials of the 1240's"; Synan, *The Popes and the Jews in the Middle Ages,* 88–89. In addition, Jordan's *The French Monarchy and the Jews* contains a wealth of information as well as an extensive bibliography.

62. Quoted in Cohen, *The Friars and the Jews,* 233–35.

63. On politics, see Jordan, *The French Monarchy and the Jews.* For comments about the language of nationhood, see Cohen, *The Friars and the Jews,* 248–54. Jordan, 214, quotes the sixteenth-century author, Yosef ha-Cohen as attributing the following statement to Philip the Fair, "Every Jew must leave my land, taking none of his possessions with him; or, let him choose a new God for himself, and we will become One People."

celebrated by means of Christian rituals and where labor—indeed, *civitas* itself—was defined according to the explicitly Christian ideology of the guild, the language of community was, more and more, used to mark the boundaries between what was excluded from it and what was not. Since the community was linked to the Church, or to the *corpus Christi,* the Jews were definitely not a part of it. Furthermore, the age's own discomfort with the moral ambiguities of mercantilism, with debt and credit, must have influenced its growing antipathy to a minority group in its midst whose very presence seemed to embody the realities of an economy based on gain even as its moneylenders and pawnbrokers bespoke the financial deficiencies of a Christian population.[64] It is, of course, always easier to isolate an already marginalized group and to use it to objectify fear of change, moral queasiness, and guilt. As William Jordon points out, though England could expel its Jews in 1290, English merchants were unable to undermine the positions of the alien Italian merchants who also functioned as moneylenders.[65]

Kempe's use of the stereotypical portrait of the Jews as killers of Christ must be understood in terms of what she could and could not have known about Jews. First, as an Englishwoman, she probably had no more first-hand knowledge of Jews than did the authors of the mystery plays. Since her intent is not to direct a reader's attention to any resident group within a contemporary population—something we might well encounter in Europe during the notoriously volatile season of Lent—Kempe's references can only be symbolic. Furthermore, her depiction of the Jews as fearful of Christ's power (189), but nonetheless as violent and disrespectful (190) and sadistically cruel (192), reflects the late medieval belief that the Jews deliberately willed their unbelief and hence engaged in consciously malicious acts against the holy.[66]

However, by locating the Passion sequence late in the *Book*—when, in fact, Kempe notes that this vision came to Margery *before* she went to

64. On the moral uneasiness of Christian society in the high Middle Ages, see Baldwin, *Masters, Princes, and Merchants;* Fleming, "Charity, Faith, and the Gentry of Kent 1422–1529"; Frugoni, *A Distant City: Images of Urban Experience in the Medieval World,* 92–93; Little, *Religious Poverty and the Profit Economy in Medieval Europe.* I do not mean to suggest that the Jews of medieval Europe were any better off than their neighbors. Despite a few quite well-off families, the Jews endured the privation of a world that increasingly delimited their ability to make a living.

65. Jordan, *The French Monarchy and the Jews,* 182.

66. See Cohen, "The Jews as Killers of Christ in the Latin Tradition." See Rubin, *Corpus Christi,* 122, 124, 130–31. Chaucer gives to the Prioress a classic tale reflecting such anti-Judaism.

Jerusalem (see 208)—Kempe gives herself time to establish a standard for willful disbelief and cruelty that has nothing to do with Jews but everything with contemporary Christians. As a number of critics have pointed out, Kempe's account of the Passion is one of the least effective—and most heavily indebted—sections of the *Book*.[67] The energy we sense in Kempe's accounts of Margery's own sufferings at the hands of her fellow Christians is nowhere present in her treatment of Christ's suffering at the hands of the Jews. Rather than chastise Kempe for bad writing in this section, perhaps we should recognize the scene for what it is, a comment upon a world that refuses to acknowledge what it knows to be the truth. Kempe depicts Margery as challenging her contemporaries in many of the ways in which Jesus challenged his fellow Jews. She breaks the rules of nature; she offends against social rituals; she refuses to observe degree; she ignores boundaries. She is, accordingly, scorned, "banned," and tormented. Her community decides that she can only be understood in the terms it uses for its persons without place: she must be a heretic. In depicting Margery's contemporaries as treating her like the Jews treated Christ, Kempe may also be echoing the late medieval interpretation of "judaizing," that is, regarding others not as brothers but as under a different set of rules that permitted forms of exploitation forbidden within the circle of brothers and friends.[68] If so, she accuses her fellow English of practices that willfully exclude holiness from society.

Her treatment of Margery is thus intended to suggest the ways in which her identification with Christ forces her to transgress those very boundaries by which society has excised some from its midst. Her actions pose a direct threat to a society that identifies its good with its goods. She not only gives away her own money, she gives away her guide's money; she is reduced to begging and to living among the poor. In so doing, she crosses the lines of social stratification, choosing to associate with those beneath her in degree. Kempe's brief account (see chapter 74) of Margery's dealings with the local lepers is likewise designed to emphasize her decision to cross what are normal boundaries of definition. By the first third of the fifteenth century, English lepers were almost as rare as English Jews, so Kempe's inclusion of this detail is almost certainly intended to do more than associate Margery with a persistent contemporary problem.[69]

---

67. See particularly Goodman, "The Piety of John Brunham's Daughter of Lynn," 349–50.
68. The wording here is Jordan's. See Jordan, *The French Monarchy and the Jews*, 45.
69. See Richards, *The Medieval Leper and His Northern Heir*, 11, 83.

Most obviously, Kempe aligns Margery with a venerable lineage of holy men and women who kissed the sores of lepers as a sign of their devotion to Christ's Passion. So, when Margery sees a leper, especially one with visible wounds, "sche cryid & so sche wept as ȝyf sche had sen owr Lord Ihesu Crist wyth hys wowndys bledyng" (176). Margery then asks permission of her confessor to kiss lepers but is told she may only kiss female lepers, "ȝyf sche wolde al-gatys kyssyn, sche xuld kyssyn women" (177). Lepers were not only contained in special places in communities, they were separated from the communities of the living by a special ceremony of the Church, which, in essence, celebrated the metaphoric death of one yet alive. Henceforth, the leper would live as the dead among the living, observing rules that delimited all sorts of normal communal relations with the rest of the population.[70] In order to kiss female lepers, then, Margery must go to a distinct part of town ("a place wher seke women dwellyd whech wer ryth ful of þe sekenes"), where Kempe describes her as finding and kissing two lepers. One of these women is clearly a victim of more than physical disease: she is sorely tempted by lascivious thoughts, thoughts that Margery herself helps her conquer. Kempe here plays upon the ancient (and false) connection between leprosy and lechery, but she does so in a way that echoes her description of Margery's own previous temptation to lechery, for the woman is "labowryd wyth many fowle & horibyl thowtys, many mo þan sche cowde tellyn" (177; cf. 15).

In the following chapter, Margery encounters another woman whose experience recalls her own earlier difficulties.[71] Like the young Margery, the woman has just had a child and has gone mad, attacking anyone who comes near her. Upon seeing Margery, the woman becomes civil, welcoming her and recognizing her holiness in the company of angels she sees about her. What is particularly interesting about this incident is the way in which Kempe suggests that the woman, like the lepers of the previous chapter, has been cast out from the community. Kempe says that the woman "roryd & cryid so boþe nyth & day . . . þat men wolde not suffyr hir to dwellyn a-mongys hem . . . Þan was sche had to þe forthest ende of þe town in-to a chambyr þat þe pepil xulde not heryn hir cryin. & þer was sche bowndyn handys and feet wyth chenys of yron þat sche xulde smytyn no-body" (178). Once or twice a day, Margery makes the journey to visit

70. See Collins, ed., *Manuale ad Vsum Percelebris Ecclesie Saribūriensis*, 182–85.

71. Gibson, *Theater of Devotion*, 64–65, has also made the point that with this event Margery comes "full circle."

the woman and prays for her recovery, which is embodied in the rite of "churching," that ceremony whereby newly delivered mothers were, after a specified period of time, brought once more into the community of Christ's body, "And þan was sche browt to chirche & purifijd as oþer women be" (178).[72] As the figure who can move between the world of the living dead and the world of the dead but living, Margery manifests a freedom that she owes to her imitation of Christ. What she has been freed from is the power of a hierarchical and profit-driven world to circumscribe her actions.

In her depiction of a society dominated by a mercantilist ethic Kempe employs strategies designed to shield her from the charge of being a dissenter. Like Chaucer, for example, she employs negative constructions in a pointed way. When Margery visits the Archbishop of Canterbury in order to plead for the right to choose her own confessor and to receive the Eucharist every Sunday, Kempe says that "he grawnt it her ful benyngly all hir desyr wyth-owtyn any syluer er gold, ne he wold latyn hys clerkys takyn anythyng for wrytyn ne for seelyng of þe lettyr" (36). The sentence operates on two levels. First, Kempe praises Thomas Arundel for granting Margery's request for relative spiritual autonomy. But she also provides a glimpse of a church whose bishops and their clerks do not do favors for nothing, of a church whose spirituality is too often rooted in the prospect of commercial gain.[73] By using one story to conceal another, Kempe reveals herself as adept at the art of veiled narrative. In chapter 24, she discusses the ways in which the priest who served as Margery's scribe comes to recognize his dependence upon her superior knowledge of events. Though ostensibly telling a story illustrating the priest's gullibility and Margery's canniness, Kempe actually offers a look at the pervasive worldliness of the contemporary Church. Thus, Margery's friend deliberates over the purchase of a portable breviary, saying to the man who urges him to buy it sight unseen: "why profyr ȝe me þis boke raþer þan oþer men or oþer prestys whan þer arn many mo thryftyare, richare prestys in þis cherch þan I am" (57–58).

---

72. For the ceremony, see Collins, *Manuale ad Vsum Sarisburiensis,* 43–44. For discussion, see Thomas, *Religion and the Decline of Magic,* 38–39, 59–61.

73. Compare Chaucer's praise for the Parson in the *General Prologue* and the way in which it also functions as an invective against the commercialism of the contemporary church. For remarks about Chaucer's use and inversion of conventional satiric criticism of the clergy and his corresponding ability to locate such figures as the Parson in particularity, see Mann, *Chaucer and Medieval Estates Satire,* 55–67. For a discussion of the Church and the "merchandizing" of benefits and favors, see Swanson, *Church and Society in Late Medieval England,* 65.

The prominent position of the phrase "other men" deflects attention from the following words, "or other priests." Kempe then amplifies her critique of the clergy by having the priest say in two different ways that there are many more priests who are more prosperous, or richer, than he. Our attention is, however, on the shell game being played out before our eyes, not on Kempe's well-aimed criticism of the more current subject of clerical possessions and wealth. Similarly, she focuses on Margery's ability to prophecy that a chapel patronized by "ryche men, worshepful marchawntys," who "haddyn gold a-now, whech may spede in euery nede" (59), will not be granted baptisms and purifications and not upon the more abstract, and potentially dangerous, issue of a church too often willing to sell its licenses. She nonetheless offers us a sharp look at a world whose tensions are in part a manifestation of the new mercantile wealth of the period, suggesting her scrutiny of the complicated spiritual and secular life of the late medieval townsperson.[74]

In contrast to her hints about the worldly comfort of the merchant class, Kempe provides some passing glimpses into the poverty of those who occupy a marginal social status. As David Aers has demonstrated, the subject of poverty was a charged one in the later Middle Ages. In sermons and treatises the obedient face of Labor threatened to displace the beloved Lady Poverty of Saint Francis and the apostles, as the goods of communal productivity began to outweigh the good of individual generosity.[75] In Rome, when Christ tells Margery to become poor for his sake, she gives away all her money and is forced to rely on charity. Kempe then provides a special perspective upon the city that was the center of Christendom, peopling it with poor men and women, with beggars, with those in need of a brotherly love that can be very hard to find (see 92ff.). Later, Kempe offers a more graphic description of medieval poverty when, on her final trip in Germany, Margery is forced to join a company of poor folk, who give her vermin in exchange for their fellowship. Kempe deftly sketches in the realities of life on the road:

74. For discussions of the new money to be found in the late medieval merchant class, see Coleman, *Medieval Readers and Writers, 1350–1400;* Du Boulay, *An Age of Ambition: English Society in the Late Middle Ages,* chapter 3; Platt, *The English Medieval Town;* Reynolds, *An Introduction to the History of English Medieval Towns;* Thrupp, *The Merchant Class of Medieval London, 1300–1500.*

75. See Aers, "*Piers Plowman* and Problems in the Perception of Poverty: A Culture in Transition." On medieval poverty, see Dyer, *Standards of Living in the Later Middle Ages,* chapter 9; Mollat, *The Poor in the Middle Ages.*

Whan þei wer wyth-owtyn þe townys, hir felaschep dedyn of her clothys, &, sittyng nakyd, pykyd hem. Nede compellyd hir to abydyn hem & prolongyn hir jurne & ben at meche mor cost þan sche xulde ellys a ben. Thys creatur was a-bauyd to putte of hir cloþis as hyr felawys dedyn, & þerfor sche thorw hir comownyng had part of her vermyn & was betyn & stongyn ful euyl boþe day & nyght tyl God sent hir oþer felaschep. (237)

By temporarily forcing Margery out of her own social group, Kempe is able to suggest other forms that community might take. Her diction betrays her irony: words like "felaschep" (used twice) and "comownyng" underline her recognition that we can be bound together by more than law. We can find ourselves forced, like our fellows, to sit naked on the ground, picking lice from our clothes while others ride by, well-fed and amply clothed.

That Kempe grounds her account of Margery's spiritual quest so thoroughly in the actualities of late medieval life suggests much about her sense of the *Book*'s scope. Although the very immediacy of her account can create the impression that we are reading a chronicle or a diary, Kempe's apparent artlessness is deceptive. In numerous ways the *Book* evinces the control of a keen literary intelligence. Kempe is not only careful to note the sources for Margery's spiritual understanding (see 152–53), but also to note specific chapters in such books as the life of Mary of Oignies or "Þe Prykke of Lofe."[76] She frequently signals her own sense of a relationship with a private reader of the *Book* by noting that a certain incident has been previously mentioned or that we have already read a reference to something now to be treated in detail. Furthermore, the very circumstances (fictional or accurate) of the *Book*'s composition seem designed to underline its craftsmanship. The *Book* was apparently written between 1436 and 1438, some twenty or more years after Margery's conversion (see 3, 6). In 1438 a Margery Kempe was admitted into the Guild of the Trinity, the most important of Lynn's civic organizations. The Guild of the Trinity regulated the whole volume of trade that poured through the town of Lynn from Gascony, the Rhineland, Zealand, the Hanse towns,

76. For discussions of the sources for the *Book*, see the notes of both Meech and Allen in *The Book of Margery Kempe*. For other comments, see Atkinson, *Mystic and Pilgrim*, chapter 5; Gibson, *Theater of Devotion*, chapter 3; Kieckhefer, *Unquiet Souls*, 182–90; Lochrie, *Margery Kempe and Translations of the Flesh*, 114–22.

and Dacia. As Alice Stopford Green points out, the Guild controlled everything: it owned the quay, regulated a boat's right of passage, and had the monopoly of various trades that were secured to its members, who were the bankers and capitalists of Lynn. Its authority extended even further, for it was the real governing force of the town.[77] If, as most medievalists agree, this is the Margery Kempe of the *Book,* we are forced to come to terms with an author, an accepted member of a clearly defined and exclusive social group, who creates a self whose social liminality is a necessary part of a literary fiction. It is equally likely that such an author might decide to create an image of community that at once serves as the background for Margery's spiritual quest and functions as a commentary on the tensions and inconsistencies of the late medieval community.

Kempe's ability to maintain authorial control over this world seems inextricably bound up with her strategy as a social critic. First, she creates in her *Book* a world as recognizable as any reported by any of the Pastons: Margery's experience occurs in actual towns—Leicester, Rome, York, Canterbury, Norwich, Lynn, Jerusalem—where she encounters persons we know to be real. She not only names herself, she also names her father and her husband. She appears in situations where we might expect her appearance to be a matter of legal or ecclesiastical record. On the other hand, Kempe manages to suspend the work in the shadowy realm between fact and fiction. Just as Chaucer could offer us real towns and towns now lost (once real?), names of evidently real people, and pilgrims so many medievalists have sought to link to fourteenth-century Londoners, creating a work at once true and profoundly untrue, so Kempe offers us a book whose foundations in the actual world seem at once firm and tenuous. For example, Kempe did not need to visit Jerusalem to write an account of Margery's experience there; she could easily have drawn upon written accounts of journeys to the Holy Land, which were designed to simulate the immediacy of

77. Green, *Town Life in the Fifteenth Century,* 404–7. See Black, *Guilds and Civil Society in European Political Thought* for a general discussion of the relationship between such corporate organizations and the theories of government. For relevant studies exploring English civic organizations and late medieval town life, see Goodman, "The Piety of John Brunham's Daughter of Lynn"; Gottfried, *Bury St. Edmunds and the Urban Crisis, 1290–1539;* Green, *Town Life in the Fifteenth Century,* especially chapters 14 and 15; Hillen, *History of the Borough of King's Lynn;* Hilton, "Towns in English Feudal Society," in *Class Conflict and the Crisis of Feudalism,* 174–86; Parker, *The Making of King's Lynn;* Platt, *The English Medieval Town;* Thrupp, *The Merchant Class of Medieval London,* especially chapter 1.

actual experience.[78] Of Santiago, she tells us almost nothing, but she describes in detail the meanness Margery encounters in Bristol before taking ship for Spain (see 105–10). Kempe's account of Rome is a story about the persons Margery encounters, not a tour of the city. The attention to detail, the place-names, what may be called the *impression* of accuracy, anchors the *Book* and particularizes it, helping to locate it in what Lee Patterson has called a "recognizable and yet alien world."[79] As a writer, Kempe, like Chaucer and Langland, is most interested in capturing the fundamental reality of her times, a reality that, for her, is best expressed in a disturbing image of community.

In depicting that community in terms of its stifling conformity, incipient violence, and persistent commercialism, Kempe offers a highly selective picture of the conditions of late medieval life. Her analysis of her own world is a shrewd one, for she concentrates her focus upon the symptoms of the economic and cultural changes of the late fourteenth and early fifteenth century, changes that inevitably influenced the relationship between the individual and his or her community. As an East Anglian, the daughter of a former mayor of Lynn, Kempe was well positioned to capture the perspective of the merchant, the townsperson, the newly prosperous citizen, whose piety, literacy, and civic concern were manifestations of social and economic privilege. Lynn remained prosperous during the first third of the fifteenth century, and its economic stability was sustained by its traders and merchants. Kempe's pictures of English towns reflect this shift toward a kind of merchant oligarchy; she rarely mentions the great magnates of the time but instead depicts a nation made up of tightly knit "burgher" communities whose orderly structure is somehow threatened by Margery's way of eating, dressing, and living. When the urban equivalent of the "hue and cry" is raised against Margery, the stranger in their midst, she is sent, first, to civil magistrates, then to ecclesiastical authorities. By blurring the distinctions between the ecclesiastical and mercantile worlds, Kempe depicts them as two competing inter-

78. See, for example, *Anonymous Pilgrims* I–VIII (eleventh and twelfth centuries), trans. Stewart; *Guide-book to Palestine* (*c. 1350*), trans. Bernard; *John Poloner's Description of the Holy Land* (*c. 1421*), trans. Stewart; Ludolph von Suchem, *Description of the Holy Land* (*1350*), trans. A. Stewart.

79. Though Patterson refers to the *Morte Arthure*, his remarks about historicity in romance are apposite to what I think Kempe's purpose in the *Book*. See Patterson, "The Historiography of Romance and the Alliterative *Morte Arthure*." See Patterson, *Negotiating the Past*, 197–232. See also his essay, "On the Margin: Postmodernism, Ironic History, and Medieval Studies."

est groups. Furthermore, although she includes a few references to the very real world of aristocrats and their networks of power, she presents England as composed of towns linked by roads. In repressing certain kinds of social realities, Kempe focuses her critique on what she sees as a central failing of her age, a commercialism that has lost sight of the values on which society was ostensibly based.

Kempe's dominant concerns in the *Book*—the threat of violence, the commercial basis of contemporary life, the constraints imposed by gender, and the strictures of conformity—reflect her keen appraisal of an age and milieu whose values were those of a merchant community in a period of change. How sharp her eye was is apparent from other sources, for she seems to capture a general feeling of national insecurity. A lack of confidence in Henry IV; complaints about the state of law and order in England during the later years of Henry IV and, again, in 1426, just after the accession of the child-king, Henry VI; the impact of Lollardy and the Lollard trials; and the shifting status of women all contributed to a world, by then more than slightly different from Chaucer's, in which men and women felt "a sharpening self-consciousness" about their status in the community.[80] Kempe writes to and for a society at once more fluid and more insecure than Chaucer's, a society whose codes and rituals have come to signify exclusivity, rather than community. Kempe's reasons for imaging that society the way she does are directly related to her analysis of its weakness and to her sense of the danger she might incur as a social critic.

By the time Kempe wrote, the experience of the Lollards had made the dangers of dissent real enough, so it is more than likely that she would wish to screen herself from the charge that she attacked the commercialism of either the church or the community. She employs screens in several ways. First, by keeping Margery squarely in the foreground of each scene in the *Book*, she focuses our attention upon Margery's spiritual growth

---

80. The phrase is Du Boulay's; see *An Age of Ambition*, 61. For the concern about law and order, see Fortescue, *The Governance of England*, ed. Plummer, introduction; Bellamy, *Crime and Public Order in the Later Middle Ages*, 3, 7, 12, 37. For studies suggesting the social impact of Lollardy, see Aers, "Rewriting the Middle Ages"; Aston, *England's Iconoclasts*, 154ff.; idem, *Lollards and Reformers*, chapter 1; idem, "Lollardy and Sedition, 1381–1431"; Hudson, *The Premature Reformation*; Reynolds, *An Introduction to the History of English Medieval Towns*, 169; Tanner, ed., *Heresy Trials in the Diocese of Norwich, 1428–31*. For studies concerning the changing status of women, see Bennett, *Women in the Medieval English Countryside*, 196ff.; Cross, " 'Great Reasoners in Scripture' "; Hilton, "Women Traders in Medieval England"; Howell, *Women, Production, and Patriarchy in Late Medieval Cities.*

and on her frequently outlandish behavior. Kempe here establishes and maintains a complicated relationship between her protagonist and her reader, for, as compelling as Margery's spiritual insights can be, we are nonetheless not eager to sever our own ties to our communities by risking the hostility that repays the nonconformist. Kempe thus jockeys her reader into a curious and uncomfortable empathy with the very society whose rituals Margery refuses to observe.[81] Furthermore, by keeping what is a primary concern in the background, Kempe implicitly disavows her role as social critic. Traditionally, holy men and women were seen as having a corrective or prophetic relation to their societies; by emphasizing Margery's relationship to Christ, however, Kempe suggests that the *Book* is less a critique than a sacred biography.

Our response to Margery is made even more problematic by Kempe's use of the third person, "this creatur," to refer to Margery. On only one occasion does she slip into the first person, and the effect is electrifying. Kempe describes Margery and John's visit to the Bishop of Lincoln, Philip Repingdon, employing her usual third-person pronouns in reference to Margery. After John tells the Bishop that he is ready to take a vow of married chastity, however, Kempe writes: "& þe Bysshop dede no mor to *us* at þat day, saue he mad *us* ryght good cher and seyd *we* were ryght wolcome" (emphasis added) (34). In the following sentence, Kempe resumes her more impersonal style. But her momentary slip into the first person points up the effect she achieves by using third-person pronouns and the phrase "this creatur" to refer to her protagonist. Where a reader is subtly urged to identify with a narrator who recounts his or her experience in the first person, a writer achieves a more distant, and inevitably more judgmental, effect by using a narrator who recounts the experience of another. By creating such a space between Margery and the reader, Kempe gives herself a certain latitude as a writer and a social critic. If her reader is sympathetic both to Margery and to her neighbors, how can we accuse Kempe of the sort of explicit critique of contemporary institutions that might well have been seen as dangerously heterodox?

Her cautious strategy seems well justified, as Kempe depicts a world where the conventional social model of orderly hierarchy seems hopelessly inapplicable.[82] Though Kempe's vision is not so bleak as Langland's, we do

---

81. This is a technique also used by Thomas of Cantimpré in his life of Christina Mirabilis.

82. For a searching look at this issue, see Hilton, "Ideology and Social Order in Late Medieval England," in *Class Conflict*, 246–52. For a provocative exploration of social metaphors

her a disservice to think that in chronicling her time she merely provides a background for a sacred biography; her account of Margery cannot be separated from her portrait of Margery's community. Held together by those rituals that signify shared practices, her community is revealed as indifferent, if not hostile, to spiritual development, particularly if spiritual growth results in nonconformity. Kempe thus depicts her protagonist as a destabilizing force in that community, whose unwillingness to observe social rituals places her in a dangerously liminal position. If Margery's story is an account of her flight away from such circumscription—from conventional patriarchal figures such as husbands, confessors, or civil-authority figures—it is also the story of a society whose order can only finally be described as an illusion, as the empty ritual we too often use to enforce a kind of peace. In depicting such a world, Kempe suggests the spiritual poverty that can be found amidst such evidence of material commerce. Though Margery returns, in the end, to Lynn, she does not return to her old position in the world she left. The romance we might wish to find in the *Book* is there only if we agree that the community was right in wishing a world where women knew their places and neither left their husbands, dressed strangely, nor abstained from meat and wine, and were filled with good cheer at dinner. The collection of Margery's intercessory prayers that end the *Book* suggest no such resolution, but further define the distance Kempe has created between Margery and her community by imaging her as the figure whose communal value ultimately lies in her *dis*sociation from society.

Kempe's handling of the relationship between Margery and her community is a tribute to her understanding and exploitation of the conventions of sacred biography. Initially, the *Book* presents itself as a certain type of reading experience. Each of the two prologues describes the *Book* as a "schort tretys." Although we may well quibble with the adjective, the noun defines the book we are about to read as treating of some particular subject. Hence, the authors of the *Lay Folks Mass Book* (c. 1375) and the *Cursor Mundi* (early 1300s), as well as Chaucer in the *Treatise of the Astrolabe,* all employ the term to define the limits of the works they introduce. The first of the *Book*'s prologues defines "treatise" in relation to

---

and the subject of social disunity, see James, "Ritual, Drama, and Social Body in the Late Medieval English Town."

the work's public, saying that it will give solace and comfort to the "synful wrecchys" who read it. The second prologue focuses attention upon the protagonist, whose life follows a classic pattern of conversion: "A schort tretys of a creature sett in grett pompe & pride of þe world" (5). The particular subject of the treatise can only be the holy woman, whose exemplary life will nourish a reader by providing a picture of the true plentitude to be found in God as manifested in and through the sacramental Church. However, the *Book* itself begins abruptly with marriage and childbirth, with hints of an inadequate priesthood and an unsympathetic community. Where the prologues appear to introduce a work where meaning can be deduced from polarities, where the focus will be concentrated upon a single figure whose simple sanctity elicits our ready response, and where social criticism will be subordinated to the business of imaging the holy, the *Book* plunges us into a realm of complexity and uncertainty.

However, by providing the text with an internal gloss, Kempe prevents her *Book* from suffering the fate of a work like Margaret Porete's *Mirror for Simple Souls,* where the emphasis upon the primacy of individual enlightenment is used to point up the hypocrisy and spiritual vacuity of the organized Church. Where Margaret Porete explicitly attacked the contemporary Church as "lesser" than the church of the spirit, as more allied to the world, Kempe avoids the dangers of overt social and ecclesiastical criticism that are latent in works devoted to the soul's ability to achieve spiritual knowledge on its own. Though Kempe would certainly not have known the textual history of the *Mirror for Simple Souls,* she was clearly alive to the dangers she might incur if she appeared to focus too sharply upon either the ecclesiastical or the civil communities. The scribe who narrates Kempe's short treatise continually insists on the orthodoxy, the veracity, and the relevance of the life he recounts, validating it as the late fourteenth-century translator of the *Mirror for Simple Souls* found it necessary to gloss his own translation and thus ensure its reception as an orthodox text.[83] Moreover, Kempe's scribal narrator insists on keeping Margery in the foreground. In so doing, he helps to deflect attention from the *Book's* troubling picture of contemporary society. That picture is nonetheless integral to a treatise that would be far shorter if its au-

---

83. See Colledge and Guarnieri, "The Glosses by 'M.N.' and Richard Methley to 'The Mirror of Simple Souls.'" For a Middle English text of the *Mirror,* see Doiron, "Margaret Porete: 'The Mirror of Simple Souls.'" For remarks on Porete's challenge to regal authority, see Lerner, *The Heresy of the Free Spirit in the Later Middle Ages,* 76–77.

thor's only purpose had been to write a simple life. The conventions of sacred biography that would have been available to Kempe certainly provide the opportunity to engage in social commentary, but the use Kempe makes of those opportunities evinces her awareness that, in order to speak, she must find a way of speaking not simply in but *through* the official modes or voices of her world.

3

The Image of Ecclesia

 *The Book of Margery Kempe* does more than use the conventions of sacred biography to address fundamental issues of medieval Christian society. By her decision to ground her narrative in the conventions of *female* sacred biography, Kempe inevitably chose to employ the language and the topoi of gender. I do not mean that Kempe "wrote like a woman," but rather that she fully exploited the rhetoric of gender, which itself served as a kind of code through which writers of either sex could raise and examine issues relating to authority.[1] They could do so because the medieval language of gender was grounded in a tacit recognition of certain polarities that also served as the basis for the perceived relationship between hierarchy and order. By alluding to such homologous categories as male / female, prince / state, Christ / Church, reason / flesh, or rider / horse, writers could refer to a single image or topic and, by a species of conceptual synecdoche, suggest the integral relation between that part and the whole of the natural order.[2] Thus such insignia as the

1. For expositions of theories of relating gender to the acts of reading and writing in the works of Chaucer, see Dinshaw, *Chaucer's Sexual Politics;* Hansen, *Chaucer and the Fictions of Gender.* For Dinshaw, male acts of reading are attempts to subdue or to interpret texts as means of containment. That which is subdued or contained is female, indeterminate and therefore threatening.
2. In "The Dominion of Gender: Women's Fortune's in the High Middle Ages," Susan Stuard notes that in the late twelfth and thirteenth centuries, theologians reconstructed their

Wife of Bath's spurs are intended to introduce the idea of female mastery (and hence of misrule) into our preliminary picture of the Wife, an idea borne out by the image she presents of herself in her prologue as challenging a status quo that she identifies as male. As the Wife suggests, if authority is male, then rebellion is frequently female. That there were various ways of exploiting such hegemonic conventions has been amply demonstrated in recent years. Carolyn Walker Bynum has offered a number of extensive analyses of devotional writers' use and reversal of gender categories to express their understanding of concepts like divine mercy and nurture, the humanity of Jesus, and the human apprehension of the holy. Peter Brown has demonstrated the ways in which the subject of physicality, inextricably tied to gender, served the thinkers of the late antique period as a means of exploring the tensions—the identity crises—of a period of rapid social change and metaphysical and cultural ferment. R. Howard Bloch and Natalie Zemon Davis have examined the relationship between the use of gender configurations in the medieval and early modern periods and expressions of public morality.[3]

Scholars of the late medieval period are increasingly becoming aware that the preoccupation with physicality and gender found in devotional prose and theological treatises also offered secular writers a language, a series of conventions, with which to describe concerns arising from shifts in power, status, and prosperity.[4] For example, the challenge to social hierarchies implicitly offered by femininity—perhaps most movingly voiced in the *Magnificat*—not only linked the topics of authority and power to the intrusion of the feminine into dramatic space but provided medieval dramatizations of Christ's Incarnation and Passion with an underlying theme of ironic reversal.[5] The language of gender was also used to describe what were conceived of as two separate discursive orders: one dominant, orthodox, linked to Latinity, allegorical interpretation, and objective inquiry; the other subordinate, vernacular, literal, experiential, and potentially hereti-

---

ideas of gender in ways that featured oppositions, not likenesses. She sees Thomas Aquinas as formally advancing a notion of polarities with which twelfth-century thinkers had experimented.

3. For references see the Works Cited section.

4. For example, see Bloch, *Medieval French Literature and Law,* 224, 258; idem, "Wasteland and Round Table: The Historical Significance of Myths of Dearth and Plenty in Old French Romance"; Köhler, "Les Troubadours et La Jalousie."

5. For a survey of recent work on such themes as they relate to medieval drama, see Emmerson, *Approaches to Teaching Medieval Drama,* in particular, Coletti, "A Feminist Approach to the Corpus Christi Cycles."

cal.[6] Such thematic or metaphoric extensions of a moral universe that the Wife of Bath hears elaborated in the "authoritative" language of Jankyn's book of wicked wives were formally expressed through a rhetoric in which garrulity established itself as a mode of speech that Lee Patterson has described as "feminine." Those vices associated with women, such as inveterate talking, were transformed into a rhetoric of subjectivity.[7] That Chaucer was keenly aware of the possibilities encoded in the feminine is manifest not only in the prologue to the Wife of Bath's Tale, in which the Wife presents her sermon as an instance of revolutionary rhetoric, but also in *The Legend of Good Women,* which poses as a sort of revisionary history, and in Chaucer's depiction of Criseyde's position in a Troy dominated by the "male" concerns of war and politics.[8] Through his women, Chaucer frequently raises and explores issues of authority that demanded the sort of screen afforded by a marginal figure whose subjectivity, garrulity, or physicality signified her fundamental powerlessness.[9]

In her recognition of her need for strategies of concealment or defense, Margery Kempe is a worthy heir to Chaucer. As I have argued, Kempe constructs for her protagonist, Margery, an image of a "holy woman" that serves as a screen for a penetrating analysis of contemporary English society. The subjective, in effect, blurs the subject; Kempe's primary focus upon Margery herself is designed to deflect the force of her portrayal of the communal values and practices of the late medieval town. Kempe employs gender stereotypes to explore the potentially more dangerous issue of spiritual authority, a subject so laden with associations of Lollardy that any exploration of it would have needed a screen as opaque as the one Kempe provides. Her employment of the topoi of gender to address this subject suggests how finely attuned she was to the terms of exchange employed by her world: through Margery and her at times comic confrontations with ecclesiastical authority, Kempe points up the ultimate futility of seeking to use rules and conventions to restrict and repress the force of an "eyewitness" response to the living gospel. The surface she creates is

6. See Copeland, "Why Women Can't Read: Medieval Hermeneutics, Statute Law, and the Lollard Heresy Trials." For associations between the feminine and the heretical, see Hanna, "The Difficulty of Ricardian Prose Translation: The Case of the Lollards," 328–29.

7. Patterson, *Chaucer and the Subject of History,* 282, 286–91.

8. See, for example, Aers, "Criseyde: Woman in Medieval Society"; Dinshaw, *Chaucer's Sexual Politics,* chapter 1; Patterson, *Chaucer and the Subject of History,* 237–43; idem, "Court Politics and the Invention of Literature: The Case of Sir John Clanvowe."

9. See Johnson, "Contexts for the *Melibee*"; idem, "Chaucer's Tale of the Second Nun and the Strategies of Dissent."

one that reflects conventions Chaucer likewise evokes and reshapes in the Wife of Bath's prologue and Tale, but for Kempe the surface merely establishes the language for what is a searching look at the foundations and thus the mission of Ecclesia in fifteenth-century England.

If subjective garrulity is a quality we should associate with female speech, Kempe's presentation of the *Book* as "recorded sound" locates the text within a rhetoric of femininity that gives primacy to experience and, like the Wife of Bath's prologue, manifestly draws its internal logic not from an externally imposed system of order but from the more associative realm of memory. Not only does she consistently direct our attention to the scribe who takes down Margery's dictation; she also frequently suggests that this method of composition has important implications for her underlying narrative method. In the proem, which serves to authorize the text before us, Kempe at once describes Margery as the tablet on which God writes and the *dictator* of her own sanctified experience. Margery thus "schewed" (3) others the grace the Holy Ghost "wrowt" in her soul, serving as the mediator between her own private spiritual experience and a public imaged as viewing those signs of God's labors she makes available to them. She is then urged by others to "makyn a booke of hyr felyngys & hir reuelacyons" (3). What is to be a record of subjective experience demands a special method of organization:

> Thys boke is not wretyn in ordyr, euery thyng aftyr oþer as it wer don, but lych as þe mater came to þe creatur in mend whan it schuld be wretyn, for it was so long er it was wretyn þat sche had for-getyn þe tyme & þe ordyr whan thyngys befellyn. And þerfor sche dede no þing wryten but þat sche knew rygth wel for very trewth. (5)

Kempe here outlines a rhetoric for the text of Margery's life. We are told that we are reading a book of memory, organized not by chronological principles but according to a purely subjective process of retrieval and interpretation.[10] Margery serves us as both our text and our exegete.

Kempe reiterates these same rhetorical principles at the end of the first book. After acknowledging that "reuelacyons" can turn out to be "deceytys & illusyons," Kempe verifies one of Margery's by saying: "Neuyr-þe-lesse

---

10. For an explanation of these terms, see Carruthers, *The Book of Memory*.

as to þis felyng of þis creatur, it was very trewth schewyd in experiens"
(220), once more linking what is subjective (feeling) to a truth that is
showed in, or verified by, experience. The authority to which Kempe appeals
is, like that affirmed by the Wife of Bath, experiential. Kempe goes on to
describe Margery's anguished education in the hermeneutics of feeling:

> Sum-tyme sche was in gret heuynes for hir felyngys, whan sche
> knew not how þei schulde ben vndirstondyn many days to-
> gedyr. . . . For sum-tyme þat sche vndirstod bodily it was to ben
> vndirstondyn gostly, & þe drede þat sche had of hir felyngys was
> þe grettest scorge þat sche had in erde & specialy whan sche had
> hir fyrst felyngys, & þat drede made hir ful meke for sche had no
> joye in þe felyng tyl sche knew be experiens wheþyr it was trewe er
> not. (220)

That Margery grows out of the need to verify truth with experience is
clear from the next sentence, where Kempe notes, "But euyr blissyd mote
God ben, for he mad hir al-wey more myty & mor strong in hys loue & in
hys drede & ȝaf hir encres of vertu wyth perseuerawns." The conjunction
with which Kempe begins this sentence, signals a resolution of the conflict recorded in the preceding sentences, a conflict resolved by Margery's
own spiritual growth. Such subjectivity, or self-mastery, is one thing for
the Wife of Bath to proclaim in a poem of the 1380s or 1390s. It is quite
another to suggest Margery's spiritual autonomy in a text apparently
composed in the England of Henry VI. It therefore makes sense that
Kempe would choose to leave implicit in the sentence its assertion of
Margery's increased trust in her own "feelings" and her decreasing reliance on external verification.

Throughout the *Book,* Kempe seeks to characterize the experience of
reading the text as a response to a written record of an oral recitation. In
numerous phrases like "as is wretyn be-forn" and "þe creatur of whom
þis book is wretyn," she reminds us that our experience of Margery's life
is mediated through a scribe. She suggests the relationship between the
text and the memory it betokens by reiterating that the narrative is not
to be treated as though it were linear, interrupting an account of a friar's
preaching against Margery to say, "For, þow þe mater be wretyn be-forn
þis, neuyr-þe-lesse it fel aftyr þis" (165). By reminding us that we read
an account of Margery's feelings taken down by a scribe, Kempe re-
inforces the fiction that we overhear a voice recalling what can only be

organized according to the idiosyncratic principles of spiritual growth. Though the *Book* is, in fact, far less confusing (and more chronological) than Kempe suggests it will be, her reminders are designed to help us understand the episodic, and hence, experiential and disruptive, character of the text before us.[11] By pointing to the voice behind the *Book,* Kempe locates the text, the written record, in the unstable world of feelings and experience, not in a linear realm of didactic truth. She transforms the garrulity that Margery's time "wyth hir writer" (216) represents into a text whose subjectivity is at once its explicitly proclaimed and its necessarily hidden message.

Kempe's explicit emphasis upon the *Book*'s subjectivity places Margery's growth in spiritual understanding in the narrative foreground. In so doing, she presents an image of Margery that is squarely based upon the conventions of female piety.[12] Kempe's mastery of her material and of the conventions of female sacred biography is apparent in the first chapter of the *Book,* where she describes a moment of spiritual awakening whose inherent conflict is expressed in language that stresses the fundamental relationship between gender and power. Margery's story begins, not with childhood, but with her marriage and with the birth of her first child, events which mark her *rite de passage* into an adult identity as wife and mother.[13] Kempe begins the narrative by distilling into a single lucid sentence information that situates Margery in a highly particular way: "Whan þis creatur was xx ȝer of age or sumdele mor, sche was maryed to a worschepful burgeys and was wyth chylde wyth-in schort tyme, as kynde wolde" (6). She thus locates her protagonist in the stratified realm of the late medieval town and outlines an identity that is predetermined by the interlaced claims of society and nature. With sure narrative economy, Kempe uses her quick sketch of the implicit constrictions of medieval womanhood as a means of highlighting the conventions of female sacred

11. See Middleton, "Narration and the Invention of Experience: Episodic Form in *Piers Plowman.*"

12. For discussions of these conventions, see Atkinson, *Mystic and Pilgrim,* chapter 6; Atkinson, Buchanan, and Miles, eds., *Immaculate and Powerful: The Female in Sacred Image and Social Reality;* Bugge, *Virginitas;* Bynum, "Women Mystics and Eucharistic Devotion in the Thirteenth Century"; idem, "Women's Stories, Women's Symbols"; idem, *Holy Feast and Holy Fast;* Castelli, "Virginity and Its Meaning for Women's Sexuality in Early Christianity." For a discussion of subjectivity as it relates to female devotional prose, see Georgianna, *The Solitary Self: Individuality in the Ancrene Wisse;* Petroff, *Medieval Women's Visionary Literature,* introduction.

13. See Hanawalt, *The Ties That Bound,* 197; Schultz, "Medieval Adolescence." For men, the passage into adulthood was embodied in the assumption of roles of power and authority.

biography. What "kynde wolde" brings less the joys of motherhood, than complications and illness, causing Margery to despair of her life. Her need to "schewe" a matter in her conscience that has been previously undisclosed, precipitates a crisis. When she summons her "gostly fadyr" to hear her confession, he was "a lytyl to hastye & gan scharply to vndyrnemyn hir er þan sche had fully seyd hir entent" (7), causing her to fall silent. Because she cannot speak, Margery goes out of her wits, slandering others and attempting to do physical harm to herself. Bound and now literally powerless, Margery is restored to herself by the appearance at her bedside of Christ, who appears as a fair and sumptuously dressed young man, offering her the filial relationship she does not achieve with her "gostly fadyr." When she comes to her senses, Margery demands those very tokens of female authority of which she had been relieved, her keys to the buttery "to takyn hir mete & drynke as sche had don be-forn" (8). Margery thus signals her reentry into her society by claiming the symbols of admission into the territory that her gender allows her.

In this opening chapter, Kempe establishes the terms and the method of the entire text: she draws upon a series of cultural and literary conventions that are designed to elicit a certain series of controlled responses in a reader. Moreover, she only partly conceals the outlines of a narrative that challenges the very concept of ecclesiastical authority. Her strategy—as well as her success—rests upon her understanding and exploitation of the subject of gender. For example, she describes Margery's crisis of identity as rooted in the mores and expectations of a patriarchal and oppressive society.[14] In achieving a spiritual identity, Margery must place herself in opposition to those orthodox ideas of family and authority sanctioned by the *civitas hominis*.[15] By describing a conflict that goes back at least as far as the account of the martyrdom of Saint Perpetua or the apocryphal early church biography of Thecla, Kempe insinuates Margery into the ranks of the "holy woman," whose renunciation of earthly social and sexual roles prepares her for spiritual intimacy with Christ.[16] Like such medieval figures as Dorothy of Montau, Catherine of Sienna, Christina Markyate,

14. Many have talked about the oppressive patriarchy of Margery's world. See Aers, "Rewriting the Middle Ages"; idem, *Community, Gender, and Individual Identity,* chapter 2; Atkinson, *Mystic and Pilgrim;* Delany, "Sexual Economics"; Feinberg, "Thematics of Value"; Lochrie, *Margery Kempe and Translations of the Flesh;* Partner, "Reading the Book of Margery Kempe."

15. The phrasing is Heffernan's; see *Sacred Biography,* 188.

16. On Perpetua, see Heffernan, *Sacred Biography,* 197; on Thecla and the role of women in the early church, see Brown, *The Body and Society,* chapters 7 and 13.

Mary of Oignies, and Bridget of Sweden, Margery looks beyond the earthly identity formalized by a series of social contracts and relationships. However, the very conventionality of this first chapter—its sharply defined lines and carefully conceived metaphors—conceals an antinomianism that stands at the core of Margery's conflict with authority.

It is in Kempe's account of Margery's first, and aborted confession, that we can detect her attempt to use a conventional criticism to mask ideas that are not only less conventional but potentially threatening to the church of her own day. Most obviously, Kempe describes Margery's "gostly fadyr" as lacking the skills or the compassion that are needed to elicit truthful speech from penitents frozen into silence by despair. However, where Chaucer, who likewise exploited the confessional relationship as an inherently sexual one in which power belonged to the male questioner and judge, focused on the abuses to the system of penance embodied in figures like the Friar and the Summoner, Kempe uses the scene to pose a question about the system itself. She describes Margery's priest as "a lytyl to hastye" (phrasing whose unrealized sexuality subtly undermines the power embodied by the confessor) and too judgmental. If authority is male, hasty, and harsh, rebellion must be female, slow, and hesitant. As Kempe slyly suggests, however, femininity is also capable of a silence that triumphs by default, for Margery never reveals this hidden sin to any earthly priest nor to any earthly reader.[17] If she is unburdened of it, as she supposedly is, she unburdens herself to Christ in private, where she receives an absolution equally private. Since her visions of and conversations with Christ occur only in her head, Kempe is, in fact, hinting at (or not describing) a confession that any Lollard would be pleased to affirm.[18] If Margery's buttery keys, symbols of her worldly identity, can only be restored to her through the intercession of her husband (8), she needs no earthly mediator to restore her to her sanity.

Kempe thus uses what is obvious and conventional as a screen for a more searching probe into subjects that, by the fifteenth century were not lightly

17. Kristeva discusses the feminine in terms of what is withheld or not said (*non-dit*); see "Stabat Mater."

18. In one Wycliffite sermon, in reference to Mary Magdalene washing Christ's feet with her tears (see Luke 7), the author affirms: "He[e]re may we see hou pryuey shrifte is autorised of oure Iesu . . . ʒif man haue ful sorowe for his synne, ʒif he speke not aftir o word but do wel and leeue to synne, God forʒueþ þis synne." He goes on to talk of the harm done by the present method of shrift. (See Hudson and Gradon, eds., *English Wycliffite Sermons*, 3:299. See also Cronin, ed., "The Twelve Conclusions of the Lollards," 301–2; *The Examination of Master William Thorpe*, in Pollard, ed., 155–60.

discussed. The subject of "priuie shrift" was one such subject that was firmly tagged as Lollard or heretical; probably no writer would wish to explore the idea of confession in an overt manner. However, criticism of poor confessors was indeed possible; witness the numerous invectives against confessional laxity.[19] This first chapter of the *Book* suggests Kempe's estimate of the dangers inherent in the subject of private confession as well as her manipulation of the traditions of clerical criticism. She thus counters any suspicion we might have of her Lollardy early in the chapter by noting that the devil tempted her to think she needed no confession but could do solitary penance "be hir-self a-loone" (7). She then goes on to dramatize the inadequacies of a confessor who does not understand the techniques of spiritual conversation. She balances this scene with Margery's "gostly fadyr," whom Margery summons (to her bedside?), with the scene in which Christ appears as fair young man and as father, calling Margery daughter and assuring her of his fidelity and love. The picture of Christ is likewise conventional, recalling the phrasing of *The Mirror of the Blessed Life of Jesus Christ,* Nicholas Love's important translation of the treatise by the pseudo-Bonaventure, which counsels the female worshiper to think of Christ as a "fair ʒonge man" when contemplating the Passion.[20] But Love's is a carefully scripted reading experience. He encourages his reader to create a picture of Christ as a beautiful young man as a preliminary to his description of the horrors of the Crucifixion; that picture which Love calls up in the reader is, in turn, intended to function as a stimulus to an affective understanding of the nature of Christ's sacrifice. Where Love seeks to control what the reader will do with her private picture of Jesus, Kempe is less clear about what Margery does with her own visionary experience, leaving the reader a good deal more latitude. The conversation she does record is conventional enough; it is the conversation she does not record that may or may not trouble us. Does Margery achieve a full confession to this second person to appear before her at her bedside? Unlike her garrulous sisters, Kempe preserves her silence; neither she nor Margery ever tells. Kempe's hint in this first chapter that authority might be located in the self is submerged in the details of a chapter that prepares us for a text we are encouraged to classify as female sacred biography. But art is designed to conceal, and what Kempe leaves implicit in her scene is the central truth

19. See, for example, Owst, *Literature and Pulpit in Medieval England,* 247, 373, 581–82.

20. Sargent, ed., *Nicholas Love's "Mirror of the Blessed Life of Jesus Christ,"* 161. For remarks on Kempe's indebtedness to Love, see Gibson, *Theater of Devotion,* 51.

that Margery stands on the threshold of an autonomy she herself does not yet understand and can only learn *by experience*.

What therefore can startle or repel a modern reader would have had an entirely different effect on a medieval reader who would have expected to find certain strains in a narrative such as the one the *Book* proclaims itself to be. Thus, the drama of Margery's distaste for and struggles with her own sexuality and her efforts to forge a nonsexual relationship with her husband encapsulate the holy woman's rejection of a self shaped by communal expectations.[21] Kempe positions Margery in bed when she has her earliest apprehensions of her new vocation. Not only does Christ first appear by her bedside, but she is finally won from her worldly attachments by the sound of heavenly melody that she hears "on a nygth, as þis creatur lay in hir bedde wyth hir husbond" (11). The sound of heavenly merriment causes her to find sexual intercourse "abhominabyl," and it is from this point that she seeks a new covenant of marriage (see 11–12). Thereafter, on two separate occasions, Kempe describes Margery's spiritual temptations or tensions in terms of her struggles against her own sexuality. The first occurs soon after her conversion, when a man tempts her to commit adultery. As Kempe describes the events (see chapter 4, 13–16), Margery consents, only to learn the man had been testing her. She is thrown into a state of despair, alleviated only by her first long "conversation" with Christ. Later, she rejects her visions of the damned, and God punishes her for twelve days with "fowle thowtys & fowle mendys of letchery & alle vnclennes as thow sche xulde a be comown to al maner of pepyl" (144–45). Where she once had glorious visions, now she sees only "mennys membrys" coming before her eyes. Only after she accepts the doctrine of God's justice, are the holy desires, speeches, and dalliances of Christ restored to her (146).

Kempe's emphasis on Margery's sexuality deliberately raises an issue central to the structure of female sacred biography, which identifies female virtue with virginity, or with the ability to refuse the blandishments of a world sullied by its own physicality.[22] English devotional works like the poems of the *Catherine*-group and *The Life of Christina of Markyate*, by using the issue of virginity as the central point of conflict in the lives of these

21. On Kempe's handling of Margery as a sexual being, see Partner, "Reading the Book of Margery Kempe."

22. See Brown, *The Body and Society*, 297–304; Castelli, "Virginity and Its Meaning for Women's Sexuality in Early Christianity"; Heffernan, *Sacred Biography*, 295–98.

strong and combative women, make it clear that virginity confers status and hence power.[23] Accounts of the childhood of female saints like Catherine of Siena focus upon the child's wish to remain a virgin and thereby to reject her worldly role as wife and mother.[24] In the case of holy women who are already married, biographers—no doubt influenced by such prototypes as the legend of Saint Cecilia—stress their abilities to create marriages whose bonds are not physical.[25] Elizabeth of Hungary, Mary of Oignies, Dorothy of Montau, and Bridget of Sweden were all married with identities based upon their positions in worldly communities; accounts of them emphasize their shifts in allegiance from one sort of power group to another. Thus, in his prologue to his *Life of Marie d'Oignies,* Jacques de Vitry opposes the strength of the women of the diocese of Liège to the weakness and venality of the men. Mary's relationship with her husband, John, reverses the conventional roles, for John agrees to being led by his wife into a chaste marriage under her direction. His willingness to relinquish the "right" his gender accords, or his voluntary assumption of feminine status, signals his spiritual readiness, his beatitude. Dorothy of Montau fared less well with her husband, and her marriage can be described as a penance she endured for her vocation. She is granted freedom from male persecution only on the death of her husband.[26]

Kempe's emphasis upon the spiritual marriage between Margery and God is designed to suggest Margery's kinship with other notable married holy women, whose authority derives from their private relationships to God. For example, in the first chapter of *The Revelations of Saint Birgitta,* Christ tells her,

> I haue chosse & take the to me to be my spowse for to shewe the my privey concelles, for so itt lykyth me. And also thow arte myne be all maner of ryght, when in the deth of thyne hossebond thowe yeuyste þi wylle jne to myn hondes, and also after hys deth whan thowe thoughteste and praydeste how þow myght be-com poor for me and for me for-sake all thynges.[27]

23. For searching explorations of the relationship between virginity and power, see the plays of Hrotswitha of Gandersheim.

24. See Petroff, *Medieval Women's Visionary Literature,* 238–39.

25. On the interrelated subjects of Saint Cecilia, married virginity, and spiritual fruitfulness, see Kolve, "Chaucer's Second Nun and the Iconography of Saint Cecilia."

26. For a discussion of Dorothy of Montau, see Kieckhefer, *Unquiet Souls,* 22ff.

27. Cumming, ed., *The Revelations of Saint Birgitta,* 1.

By using an affirmation of Bridget's spiritual marriage as the proem to revelations whose didacticism might otherwise seem presumptuous, the author locates the source of her power. Bridget, in effect, contracts a second marriage after the death of her earthly husband, choosing Christ as her new love and master. Her espousal gives her the freedom to speak to a Christendom split by faction and in need of the reform she implicitly offers. However, that freedom or power is possible only because she has dissolved her ties to the world.

Kempe is clearly aware that the very topic of marriage, in its cultural associations with the idea of authority, introduces the subject of conflict between the sexes, a subject that is ultimately about power. Late in her career, in a conversation on intercessory prayer, God reminds Margery of her gratitude for the freedom John Kempe has given her:

> Also þu askyst mercy for thyn husbonde, & þu thynkyst þat þu art meche beholdyn to me þat I haue ȝouyn þe swech a man þat wolde suffryn þe leuyn chast, he beyng on lyue & in good hele of body. . . . Dowtyr, ȝyf þu knew how many wifys þer arn in þis worlde þat wolde louyn me & seruyn me ryth wel & dewly, ȝyf þei myght be as frely fro her husbondys as þu art fro thyn, þu woldist seyn þat þu wer ryght meche beheldyn on-to me. & ȝet ar þei putt fro her wyl & suffyr ful gret peyne, & þerfor xal þei haue ryght gret reward in Heuyn, for I receyue euery good wyl as for dede. (212)

Kempe's strategy here is masterly. First, she sets these remarks within the context of an extended encomium by God for Margery's charity. Thus, for the entirety of chapter 86, God speaks to Margery; and we, through the mediation of the scribe ("on a tyme owre Lord spak to þe sayd creatur whan it plesyd hym" [209]), are privileged to overhear his words. Only after praising her for her powers of prayer, for seating the Trinity on three cushions in her soul, and for loving him so, does God discuss the subject of marriage. Like the Wife of Bath, God suggests that what women really want is mastery. Not only should Margery be grateful for a husband who has "suffered" her to live in chastity, but she should be aware of "how many wifys" there are who would like to be as "frely fro" their husbands as Margery is from hers. God then affirms his willingness to help wives evade male authority, saying that, though they are "putt fro her wyl," he will reward will for deed in heaven. By placing himself on the side of the feminine, God not only places himself on the side of a mutinously silent host, but affirms the primacy of what is private, subjective, and unauthorized. God goes on to praise Margery for her care for the sins of her confessor, establishing her as a figure whose intercessory power implicitly places her beyond the control of the clergy. He ends his encomium by touching on the nature of the spiritual marriage between them. Their private relationship is the source of her power; he thus praises her for welcoming both himself and the Blessed Virgin into her bed.[28]

Kempe here uses what is conventional—an intimate conversation between the holy woman and God—to frame remarks about spiritual autonomy that are expressed in terms of gender. Thus husbands—obvious figures of authority—restrict the devotional impulses of their wives, those without authority. But God, in whose mouth Kempe shrewdly places the entire sequence, not only looks kindly on female insubordination, but will reward inner rebellion with mercy in heaven. Similarly, he suggests Margery's superior powers of prayer, since she is able to ask mercy for her own "gostly fadyr." God, the true husband of the soul, therefore preempts all other figures of male authority, husbands and priests, who presume to circumscribe inner (or feminine) experience.

The eroticism of the *Book* is likewise a conventional element of devotional prose. From the elegant Latin of Saint Bernard's expositions of the Canticles, to the finely articulated expressions of Beguine spirituality, and the at times baroque descriptions of Richard Rolle, the literature of devotion describes mystic rapture or spiritual union in the language of physical love. It is clear from Kempe's references to Margery's fervent love for Christ and to the signs she receives of their intimacy—tears, sweet sounds and smells, strange visions, a burning sensation (see 88–89)—that Kempe is well aware of the literature of devotion, particularly of its English expression in the writings of Richard Rolle. As Karma Lochrie has pointed out, in a number of places Kempe's language suggests her familiarity with the *Incendium Amoris,* a text that Margery says was read to her (see 153–54), along with the works of other devotional writers, such as those by Walter Hilton and Saint Bridget.[29] In Rolle, in particular, Kempe would have found an emphasis upon physical sensation as a sign of mystic union.

28. That Kempe's language here disturbed a later reader is suggested by a marginal emendation. The reader, using red ink (as he does throughout the manuscript) has placed a caret before *bed* and written *gostly* in the outer margin.

29. Lochrie, *Margery Kempe and Translations of the Flesh,* 115–18. See also the notes by Allen in Meech, ed., *The Book of Margery Kempe.*

At least one of the *Book*'s early readers, who annotated the manuscript using red ink, signals a response to the text as belonging to the school of Richard Rolle.[30] This reader, like the anonymous M.N., who carefully annotated his English translation of Margaret of Porete's *Mirror of Simple Souls,* smoothing over parts that could be misinterpreted as heretical, offers a reading of Margery Kempe's *Book* that, in its obvious effort to characterize the *Book* generically, is designed to control any response to and, hence, understanding of the text.[31] It is clear from the way in which this reader emended the style, corrected the spelling, glossed the plot, and noted some of the errors of the original scribe, that he read the manuscript closely, paying special attention to the credibility and clarity of its argument. He also signaled the empathic and participatory nature of his approach by underlining words relating to affective spirituality and by writing "amen" or "thanks" at the end of chapters describing Margery's devotional life. In addition, the bulk of his marginal notations suggest his sense that the *Book* is generically affiliated with other significant affective texts. Phrases like "R. hampall" (39, 143, 154); "fervent loue" (40, 198); "ters with loue" (46); "ebrietas sancta" (98); "amor impaciens" (107, 149); "fire of loue" (111); "abundance of loue" (138); "langor amoris" or "langyng loue" (140, 176, 197); and "wel of ters" (141) provide evidence that he searched the text for tokens of Margery's state of grace.[32] He even wrote "tokyn of grace" in the margin near where the text refers to the "flawme of fyer" (219) Margery felt while she was writing the *Book.*

In addition to these notations, the reader included a number of marginal emblems that suggest his understanding of the possible uses of images as augmenting the experience of private reading.[33] The sacred monogram, IHC, occurs fairly often, frequently in rubric O's. Once, he drew a pillar (29); twice he drew a heart near a passage that is semierotic

30. Lochrie, *Margery Kempe and Translations of the Flesh* (119–22) also discusses these marginal comments. Meech's edition of the *Book* includes all such notations, along with a textual commentary. See also his comments on xxxii–xliii of the introduction. My own remarks are based upon my examination of the manuscript; see the introduction to *The Book of Margery Kempe,* ed. Staley.

31. For M.N., see Colledge and Guarnieri, "The Glosses by 'M.N.' and Richard Methley."

32. The page numbers refer to Meech's edition and not to the manuscript pages.

33. For remarks about the ways in which images might enhance the experience of reading, see Carruthers, *The Book of Memory,* 180; Woolf, *The English Religious Lyric in the Middle Ages,* particularly the second section dealing with fifteenth-century lyrics. On the experience of private reading, see Saenger, "Silent Reading: Its Impact on Late Medieval Script and Society."

(90, 211). He placed vertical wavy red lines near a section dealing with spiritual marriage (213) and drew a flame of love with the name R. hampall underneath it (88). To mark the Blood of Wilsnack, to which Margery journeys on her last trip to the Continent, he traced three hosts (232) and added the picture of a garment near a passage describing the Virgin's smock that was displayed at Aachen on Saint Margaret's Day (237). Finally, he marked a rhymed couplet inserted into the text, "Lord, for þi wowndys smerte drawe alle my lofe in-to thyn hert" (217).[34] The lines suggest his familiarity with the impulse to devotional poetry that is so pervasive a feature of late medieval lyricism.

If, as Lochrie has suggested, Kempe's references and allusions to Latin devotional works are designed to authorize the *Book* by reinforcing our sense of its Latinity, the notations in red ink suggest ways in which certain texts spoke to the needs and expectations of readers.[35] Such a reader, in responding to the text in so "scholarly" and affective a way, offers a sharply focused and thus controlled reading of the *Book* that throws into the foreground a particular image of its protagonist. Thus, Margery is presented as a mystic in the tradition of Richard Rolle, a presentation that governed Wynkyn de Worde's 1501 edition of extracts from the *Book,* entitled *A shorte treatyse of contemplacyon taught by our lorde Ihesu cryste, or taken out of the boke of Margerie kempe of Lynn.* The volume contains nothing of Margery's eventful career, nothing even remotely idiosyncratic, but in seven quarto pages offers us the prayers and sayings of what appears a conventional late medieval female contemplative. When Wynkyn de Worde's edition was reissued by Henry Pepwell in London in 1521, Margery Kempe had become "a deuoute ancres."[36] Shorn of her warts, no longer the uncomfortable, noisy, threatening woman who challenges male authority, Margery had been assimilated into traditions that a late medieval reader could understand without needing to explain away those sections of the *Book* that seem not to belong to the school of Rolle.

But it is only when we begin to scrutinize Kempe's handling of affec-

---

34. This couplet appears twice in the text. Both times, Kempe ascribes the couplet to God, who says it to Margery, reminding her of his care of her (see also 161). For other comments on the couplet, see *The Book of Margery Kempe,* ed. Meech, 326 n. 161/18.

35. Lochrie, *Margery Kempe and Translations of the Flesh,* 115ff.

36. See Meech, xlvi–xlviii. For De Worde's extracts, see appendix II in Meech. For a discussion of these extracts as constituting a "reading" of the *Book* done by a contemporary of Kempe's, see Holbrook, "Margery Kempe and Wynkyn de Worde." See also Lochrie, *Margery Kempe and Translations of the Flesh,* 220–22.

tive allusions and references that we begin to understand them as "orna-
ment" and not "substance." Here, the late medieval reader, who records
his response in so meticulous a way, serves as a useful guide to Kempe's
sense of one of her publics for the *Book*. What she builds into her narrative, the marginal notations signify, implicitly authenticating Margery's
experience as genuine. Those notations may stamp the *Book* with an "im-
primatur" for all subsequent browsers in the carefully tended library of
Mount Grace, which housed the manuscript of the *Book* for many years,
but they also excise most of the work itself. Like Wynkyn de Worde's
distillation of Kempe's flood of language into quartos, the wielder of the
red ink attempts to impose order (or genre) on a narrative that tests our
abilities to respond to what appears amorphous and, hence, threatens to
become chaotic. Thus, whereas in devotional treatises like *The Cloud of
Unknowing* or Rolle's *Incendium Amoris,* translated into English by Richard Misyn in 1435 as *The Fire of Love,* we find manuals of spiritual
instruction that are intended to guide the fledgling contemplative, Kempe
offers no sense that Margery's experience might be duplicated by another
devout woman or be seen as exemplary and therefore available. She neither counsels the reader in the techniques of devotional agility nor warns
the reader about the dangers of the contemplative way. Nor does Kempe
provide the detailed account of physical sensation or of spiritual insight
that we can find in other works of devotion. Where such descriptions are
integral to the *Incendium Amoris,* they are incidental to the *Book*. Instead,
Kempe uses language intended to arouse a response in a reader prepared
to associate a pious woman with a particular type of devotional experience. Rather than the first-person testimonies to mystic ecstacy found in
examples of Beguine spirituality or in the detailed account Rolle gives of
his apprehension of divine love, Kempe narrates the important events of
Margery's spiritual life through a scribe, punctuating that narration with
descriptions of Margery's intimate experience of God. Her decision to
employ third-person narration subtly alters the nature of our response to
Margery's experience by disallowing the carefully channeled subjectivism
that is aroused by purely visionary narrative. What might have been awe
becomes somewhat more and less—judgment, perhaps. All of these
"lapses," which I would describe as narrative techniques, at once suggest
and withhold meaning.

By including other details in the book of Margery's life that establish
Margery as a figure of active charity, Kempe also links the *Book* to the
traditions of female sacred biography. Some of these details, like Margery's

request to kiss lepers who live near her, are conventional. Saints such as Francis of Assisi, Catherine of Sienna and figures like Mary of Oignies expressed their humility and their devotion to the wounds of Christ by embracing diseased—and ostracized—members of the communal body. Margery's confessor expresses a due regard for decorum by giving her permission to kiss only female lepers: like that of Claire of Assisi, Margery's experience is explicitly circumscribed by society's sensitivity to gender categories. Kempe also presents Margery as comfortable among God's poor, particularly during her stay in Rome, where she gives away all her money at Jesus' admonition to become poor for his sake. She not only tends a poor old woman for six weeks, but finds herself the object of the charity of others, blessing them, in effect, through her own poverty.[37] Kempe also presents Margery as figuring in the ongoing spiritual life of her community, anchoring her firmly to the town of Lynn and to the locale of East Anglia. She is thus careful to include early in the *Book* an account of Margery's friendly relations with the local Dominican priory and her attachment to the church of Saint Margaret in Lynn.[38] She even gives Margery a "local" miracle by crediting her prayers with the sudden and uncalled-for snowstorm that saved the church from being destroyed by fire (see 162). She further anchors Margery in the community by describing her ability to foresee events relating to local religious figures and to heal a woman who had gone mad after the birth of her first child. Where Christ once appeared to a younger Margery, recalling her to herself, now Margery visits a woman "þat was alienyd of hir witte" (178). Through Margery's intercessory prayers, the "alien" is restored to the community by its ritual of purification after childbirth: "And þan was sche browt to chirche & purifijd as oþer women be." Kempe then verifies the significance of Margery's act through the scribe, who calls it a "ryth gret myrakyl" (178).

Kempe's handling of Margery as a saintly or intercessory figure is obviously intended to link Margery to female figures like Mary of Oignies or Christina Mirabilis, but it also suggests her grasp of the fundamental and oftentimes contradictory relationship between saint and community. The language with which God describes to Margery her vocation expresses the ambivalence society has toward the holy, "þow xalt ben etyn &

37. For discussions of evolving medieval attitudes toward poverty and the idea that the poverty of others conferred merit on the donor, see Little, *Religious Poverty and the Profit Economy in Medieval Europe;* Rosenthal, *The Purchase of Paradise.*

38. For an account of the religious foundations of Lynn and surrounding areas, see Taylor, *Index monasticus.*

knawyn of þe pepul of þe world as any raton knawyth þe stokfysch" (17). Where *knawyn* implies Margery's figurative dismemberment by the world, *etyn* connotes her nurture of the world. Similarly, Margery is at once rejected by her world and an active means of joining the fragmented sections of the social body. Those individuals who subsist on the margins of that body—lepers, the poor, the insane—are either temporarily or finally rejoined to it through Margery, who bridges the gaps between various social systems. Having received official permission to kiss female lepers, she goes to a place "wher seke women dwellyd whech wer ryth ful of þe sekenes" (177). There, Margery functions as an emissary of the societies of both heaven and earth, enjoining them to meekness and patience, bringing a sort of peace to that outcast community. We cast out as unclean what we cannot integrate into the systems of order we call our societies; by kissing the supposedly unkissable or by communicating with the insane, certain figures remind us that communities are organized around what may be relative ethical systems.[39] If Margery, a "ryth good woman" (178) can have a comprehensible conversation with a "madwoman," what are we if we cannot or will not? Or is our method of classification a reflection of an ill-developed ethical philosophy?

Kempe's handling of these scenes is not intended to shock her public, but to use the image of the holy woman she has detailed through Margery to adumbrate a redefinition of community. She thus attributes to Margery none of the odd behavior that characterizes figures like Christina Mirabilis; nor does she refer to Margery's crying in these scenes. Furthermore, Kempe is careful to be explicit about the social niceties of gender rules and to proclaim that, with the exception of her husband, Margery only ministers to other women. The potentially disruptive response aroused by an account of Margery kissing lepers of both sexes or holding conversations with the mad is disallowed by a brief description of a handful of female lepers and one woman whose experience is so like Margery's own that she seems to offer consolation to her former self.[40] Jonathan Hughes has suggested that,

---

39. This is a train of thought I owe to Mary Douglas and to Peter Brown. See Douglas, *Purity and Danger*; Brown, *Society and the Holy in Late Antiquity*.

40. For a discussion of the ways in which lepers and Jews were associated and, consequently, persecuted in medieval France, see Brown, "Philip V, Charles IV, and the Jews of France: The Alleged Expulsion of 1322," especially 301–2. Kempe's references to lepers may at once be conventional (recalling figures like Francis of Assisi) and intended to adumbrate a "society" whose very marginalization by the community indicates the threat it is perceived as posing to social order. See also the discussion in the preceding chapter.

through the initiative of Archbishop Thomas Arundel, the late medieval English church began to emphasize the value of the mixed life in an effort to meliorate the growing popularity of the works of Rolle and his followers. Writers, such as Nicholas Love, who sought to rechannel the contemplative urge back into the community inevitably reinforced the importance of the family and of the local community by implicitly defining an arena for charitable action.[41] In her handling of Margery, Kempe seems sensitive to the expectation that a holy woman might—or should—bridge both the contemplative and the active spheres. Such a model was, of course, provided by Jacques de Vitry in his *Life of Marie d'Oignies,* and, though Mary is imaged as a far less difficult and thus more serene and attractive personality than is Margery, Kempe underlines Margery's involvement with her fellows, despite their frequent hostility to her.

What is conventional about the *Book* points toward Kempe's grasp of the traditions in which she is working. As the work of scholars like Sanford Meech and Hope Emily Allen demonstrates, the *Book* seems to beg for annotation, and there are times when we find ourselves tempted to emulate our predecessor, the wielder of the red ink, and check off a sort of tally in the margins of the *Book.* If we were to do so, we would discover how much of the text does not quite conform to that pattern of devotional and hagiographic prose Kempe convinces us we are reading. For where Jacques de Vitry, another third-person witness to the life of a holy woman, carefully divides his account into parts, one for the outer woman and one for the inner, and those parts into chapter headings, creating a seamless account of sanctity manifested in the singularly focused life of Mary of Oignies, Kempe's *Book* has a far looser, perhaps an elusive, structure. Where significant portions of the lives of holy women are frequently devoted to accounts of their feats of fasting or self-mutilation—signs of their triumphant physicality—Kempe's handling of subjects like food focuses our attention upon the community's hostility to her eating practices, not upon Margery's victorious mastery of her flesh or her symbiotic imitation of Christ crucified. In fact, in the annals of the holy, Margery's is a rather tame story: she moderates her eating and drinking, wears white clothing, and weeps boisterously. She does not tie her body into knots, cut off pieces of her own flesh, drink pus, or develop the signs of the stigmata. She does wear a hairshirt for a while, but Kempe's assertion that her husband never knew of it though she conceived and bore children

41. Hughes, *Pastors and Visionaries,* 113–18; 198; 228–30, 299.

during the years she was wearing it may say more about male desire or late medieval sexual practices than it does about holiness (see 12). Nor does the *Book* end—as countless holy lives do—with an account of Margery's death. The "scribe," who says he felt impelled to add a second book after he finished copying the work of the first scribe, does not continue with his project and add a coda to the life he recounts. Neither does any other witness step forward to describe the death of this English holy woman. The *Book* "looks" or sounds traditional, but its shape finally suggests Kempe's ability to exploit a set of traditions or literary conventions as screens for a more unconventional narrative.

If the *Book* can sometimes seem punctilious about the details of late medieval female sanctity, it is because Kempe, like Chaucer, knew that writers must evolve ways of speaking that at once drew upon and transformed traditional images and modes. The overarching fiction of the *Book* as recorded sound and the references to Margery's religious impulses and experience are designed to serve as "generic stimuli" in a reader. However, as I have reiterated, the *Book* finally is not "about" that religious experience; instead, it uses Margery to examine what were some extremely provocative issues. One of these is the issue of spiritual authority. Rather than openly confront a subject that Wyclif and his followers had made all too provocative, Kempe focuses upon Margery and traces her spiritual growth, a growth that is inevitably away from the patriarchy of the established Church. Here, too, Kempe's handling of gender categories is integral to her purpose. She at once uses them to point up the inadequacies of the contemporary Church and to hint at a charity as radically simple as that imaged through the actions of the women in the Gospel, who, in their single devotion to Jesus, are privileged to be the first witnesses to the Resurrection.[42]

Central to her purpose is the image of female weakness and vulnerability Kempe projects through Margery. Kempe establishes the outlines of this image early in her account of Margery's career. At the same time that Margery begins to experience special marks of God's favor—holding pri-

---

42. One Wycliffite sermon says of John 20, "þis gospel telliþ hou Crist apperide to Mary Maudelen, for Crist wolde þat womman kynde hadde þis priuylegie bifore man þat he shewide hym aftir his deþ raþere to woman þan to man, for wymmen ben freele as water and taken sunnere prynte of bileue" (*English Wycliffite Sermons*, ed. Hudson and Gradon, 3:199). In reference to the last chapter of Mark, another says, "Furst Crist aperude to þese hoolye wymmen for to graunten a pryuylegie unto wommanys kynde" (*English Wycliffite Sermons*, 1:430).

vate conversations with Christ, serving as the handmaiden to the Blessed Virgin, miraculously surviving an apparently fatal accident, winning a vow of chastity from her husband, and telling a monk of his secret sins— she is described as extremely vulnerable to the opinions of representatives of the organized church. Kempe balances scenes that depict Margery's nascent spiritual power with those that dramatize her physical isolation and vulnerability in a world where actual power is described as male. Thus, directly after a chapter recounting Margery's reformation of a monk, who with her help had become "a wel gouernyd man" (27), Kempe includes a chapter describing a visit to Canterbury, opening with a scene where Margery is the only woman in a host of unsympathetic men:

> On a tyme, as þis creatur was at Cawntyrbery in þe Cherch a-mong þe monkys, sche was gretly despysed & repreuyd for cawse sche wept so fast bothyn of þe monkys & prestys & of seculer men ner al a day boþe a-for-noon & aftyr-noon, also jn so mech þat hyr husbond went a-way fro hir as he had not a knowyn hir & left hir a-loon a-mong hem . . . (27)

Not only is Canterbury described as "male" and hostile to Margery, but Kempe links the ecclesiastical to the secular power structure in the person of an old monk, "whech had ben tresowrer wyth þe Qwen whyl he was in seculer clothyng, a riche man & gretly dred of mech pepyl" (27). Though Margery does not hesitate to reprove him for his scorn of her, she is placed in jeopardy by the monks who follow her out of the monastery and accuse her of Lollardy. Like Lot in Sodom, who is similarly surrounded by a threatening crowd, Margery is finally rescued by "tweyn fayr ȝong men" who lead her to safety and take her back to her lodging, where her husband awaits.[43] Since "Sodom" was a common Wycliffite signifier for "simony," Kempe may here be inferring an even sharper critique of an English church that had coupled unnaturally with secular institutions.[44] If so, she would certainly want to conceal any such reference behind the sort of screen Margery herself, "tremelyng & whakyng ful sor in hir flesch," provides. (If the crowd threatens Margery with a heretic's fire, do we turn

---

43. For an account of that scene that stresses the physical beauty of the two angels, see *Purity*, ed. Menner, lines 788–95.

44. For contemporary references to simony as the sin of Sodom, see Hudson, *The Premature Reformation*, 217; *The Lanterne of Light*, ed. Swenburn (1917), 12.

and accuse Margery's maker of views Margery forcefully denies?) Kempe then concludes a chapter that dramatizes the worldliness of the institutional Church with Christ's private assurance of his extraordinary love for Margery, whom he describes as a "peler of Holy Cherch" (29).[45]

Similarly, in Leicester, where she is arrested and accused of Lollardy, Kempe juxtaposes Margery's female vulnerability and weakness with the powers of the mayor and the steward who are, naturally, male. Her sex makes her even more vulnerable to their proceedings against her. Her jailor, who seems sensitive to the dangers of prisons, is loath to imprison her with men and places her under house arrest in the care of his wife. The Steward of Leicester (whom the jailor's wife seems not to trust; she thus keeps Margery from a private audience with him) later entraps her and threatens her sexually (see 113). Although Margery must depend upon the craftiness of women and the intercession of men to ensure her physical safety, there is no doubt as to her spiritual power. Publically examined for her faith (see chapter 48), she triumphs over her ineffectual accusers by asserting her orthodox views of the eucharist.

Kempe once again focuses upon the issue of gender in her account of Margery's experience in Beverly, where she is arrested by the yeomen of the Duke of Bedford. On her way to Beverly, under guard, she is accosted by "men of þe cuntre," who say to her, "Damsel, forsake þis lyfe þat þu hast, & go spynne & carde as oþer women don, & suffyr not so meche schame & so meche wo. We wolde not suffir so meche for no good in erthe" (129). Kempe here not only suggests that Margery's life is particularly threatening to a male power structure, but also that the men of Beverly find her willingness to suffer even more troublesome. Margery's willing assumption of suffering, her imitation of Christ, wins her one of the Duke's men as a convert and turns a forced march into a preaching tour. When they arrive in Beverly, she is indeed imprisoned, but in a private home, where her room has a window. She uses the window as a pulpit, "þan stode sche lokyng owt at a wyndown, tellyng many good talys to hem þat wolde heryn hir, in so meche þat women wept sor & seyde wyth gret heuynes of her hertys, 'Alas, woman, why xalt þu be brent?' " (130–31). Since the jailor has the key to Margery's chamber, the "good wyfe" of the house cannot give Margery a drink when she is thirsty. But a way is found around this obstacle:

45. In the far margin, there is a pillar drawn in red, a sort of silent guarantee of Margery's orthodoxy.

And þan þe women tokyn a leddyr & set up to þe wyndown & ȝouyn hir a pynte of wyn in a potte & toke her a pece, besechyng hir to settyn a-wey þe potte preuyly & þe pece þat whan þe good man come he myth not aspye it. (131)

Kempe here exploits gender stereotypes in ways that point to her interest in gender as a sign of communal power. As the chapter begins with a picture of female vulnerability in the face of male privilege, it ends with a scene of female triumph as potentially riotous as any presented by the Miller or the Wife of Bath or the Merchant, all of whom stress the fundamental chicanery and intractability of the weaker sex. Not only do the men of Beverly wish not to suffer (something every medieval woman must have known was inscribed in her bones as a daughter of Eve), but, for all their locks and keys, they are outsmarted by their wives. The women of Beverly who gather beneath Margery's window to hear the "good tales" she tells them have access to ladders, pots, and cups and sense enough to know how to hide the evidence. In the end, the Archbishop of York intervenes to free Margery, but the details of chapter 53 nonetheless stand as testimony to the good wives of Beverly, who rally around Margery as she talks to them from her prison. Like a latter-day Saint Paul, Margery witnesses to Christ, bringing word of a new order to those fixed in an older, patriarchal world.

It is therefore not surprising that Kempe should describe Margery as frequently in conflict with the expectations of her spiritual fathers. The tension inherent in the *Book*'s opening chapter, along with its hint of male, or priestly, inadequacy, is repeated throughout Margery's life. In fact, her life describes an effort to forge a spiritual autonomy that would have been seen as directly threatening to the organized Church, and thus, as heretical. Such an effort is perhaps best, and most covertly, presented as rooted in a conflict between an obstreperous woman and her male confessors and spiritual guides. Kempe's presentation of this conflict is designed to underline Margery's orthodoxy while, at the same time, suggesting the incapacities of the contemporary Church. If Margery's physical vulnerability blunts the challenge she presents to authority, the very tears that signal the "femaleness" of her devotion also remind us of the spiritual dryness of a church unwilling to confront such emotional, or subjective, piety. Put another way, can the church cope with or minister to spiritual needs and impulses we can metaphorically describe as female? That Chaucer felt the force of such an inherent conflict is clear from his positioning of the Wife of Bath's Tale. By grouping it with those of the Friar and the Summoner, he adumbrates a conflict between "wives" and friars that the Wife herself recognizes in her tale, where she says that friars have supplanted elves in present-day England, going on to pun on these *lymytours* and their *lymytaciouns* and to suggest that women are no safer walking out today than they once were, since the friar has become the modern incubus.[46] This same conflict, of course, provides the Wife with the subject for her sermon / prologue in which she seeks to confront a world of male authorities, deity itself, as well as exegetes and husbands.

Like Chaucer, Kempe is at once concerned with the obvious lapses and with the more fundamental issue of spiritual authority. Where Chaucer describes a friar who is all too familiar with the taverns and the wives of every town, Kempe has Margery take as a companion on the last part of her final journey a poor friar through whom Kempe suggests some of the potential limitations of his order:

> þe frer, beyng euyl for thryst, seyd to þe creatur, "I knowe þes cuntreys wel a-now, for I haue oftyn-tymys gon þus to-Romeward, & I wote wel þer is a place of recreacyon a lityl hens. Late us gon þedyr & drynkyn." Sche was wel plesyd & folwyd hym. Whan þei cam þer, þe good wife of þe hows. . . . (239)

Though Kempe does not satirize the Friar, her description of him has a certain affinity for Chaucer's description of Friar Hubbard in the General Prologue. There, Chaucer notes that the Friar is "famulier" with "worthy women of the toun," "knew the tavernes wel in every toun," and prefers "selleres of vitaille" to lepers.[47] While Kempe nowhere satirizes the fraternal orders so sharply as Chaucer, there are enough details about Margery's difficulties with various members of the fraternal orders scattered throughout the *Book* to provide the outlines of a less-than-flattering portrait of the heirs to Dominic and Francis.[48] The point for Kempe, as for Chaucer, is the town, that very community seen as the target for the evangelism of those orders, a significant component of which was the women of the

---

46. *The Canterbury Tales* III (D) 865–81.
47. *The Canterbury Tales,* I (A) 217, 240, 248.
48. For a study of anticlericalism during the later Middle Ages, see Scase, *Piers Plowman and the New Anticlericalism.*

town.[49] As Kempe implies, when preachers banish female piety from their sermons, the Church has not only denied a part of its ministry by ruling out what is subjective and erratic but risked shutting its doors against the Holy Spirit, whose force is manifested in Margery.

If Chaucer pointedly suggests the sexual indiscretions of ecclesiastical figures like the Friar and the Monk, Kempe also hints at the untrustworthy character of certain churchmen. Thus, on her difficult journey to Aachen, Margery and her unsympathetic companion meet with a monk, "a ful rekles man & euyl gouernyd, & in hys cumpany weryn ȝong men, chapmen" (235). They travel with the monk and his company, coming "forby an hows of Frer Menowyrs hauyng mech thrist." When they bid Margery to come in with them for wine, she replies, "Serys, ȝe xal haue me excusyd, for yf it were an hows of nunnys I wolde al redy gon, but for-as-meche þei arn men I xal not gon be ȝowr leue" (235). Since Kempe makes no apology for Margery spending time alone with those male members of the clergy who read to her and write for her, her sudden concern for social decorum seems intended to point up an incipient recklessness within the Church's institutions. Her subtle emphasis upon gender at once underlines Margery's vulnerability and the Church's accountability.

Kempe also presents many ecclesiastical figures as lacking the devotion that ought to undergird authority. She characterizes the households (*meny*) of Thomas Arundel, archbishop of Canterbury, and of Thomas Peverel, bishop of Worcester, as scornful to Margery, the lone woman in a group of men. Kempe's description of these households as made up of men who swear great oaths, live ill-disciplined lives, and wear fashionable clothing points up the affinities between ecclesiastical and aristocratic households (see 36, 109). She also describes some churchmen as frankly hostile to Margery. One, an English priest she encounters in Rome, turns against her because "sche wold not obeyn hym." As Kempe notes, "sche wist wel it was a-geyn þe helth of hir sowle for to obeyn hym as he wolde þat sche xulde a don" (84). Others turn against her for her clothing or her tears, and a noted Franciscan preacher refuses to allow her to hear his sermons because her tears of devotion are disruptive (see 84, 120, 123, 148–54). Such figures suggest the outlines of a contemporary Church

49. The antifraternalism of the Lollards is well known, but one Wycliffite sermon explicitly castigates friars for the false counsel they give to women. See *English Wycliffite Sermons,* ed. Hudson and Gradon, 2:298.

within which social codes have come to dominate spiritual concerns. Thus, Margery's affective piety and her idiosyncratic life-style offend churchmen in the same ways as they offend mayors and stewards. Her increasing ability to resist control over her person threatens the very concept of an order conceived of as hierarchical.

Both parts of the *Book* therefore trace a movement away from the patriarchal control of confessors, or "gostly faders" by focusing on the ineffectual nature of male authority. In her handling of such an explosive topic, Kempe displays a keen sense of strategy. Thus, early in the first part of the *Book,* she describes Margery's successful efforts to win the approval of key members of the early fifteenth-century English church, Philip Repingdon, bishop of Lincoln, and Thomas Arundel, archbishop of Canterbury. She then goes on to recount Margery's acceptance by local, East Anglian figures, the anchorite attached to the Dominican priory at Lynn, and three representatives of Norwich devotional circles: Richard Caistyr, vicar of St. Stephen's; William Southfield, the Carmelite; and Dame Julian, the anchoress. Having established Margery's orthodoxy by naming her spiritual supporters, Kempe begins to recount Margery's conflicts with other figures of ecclesiastical authority. These conflicts center on the authority Margery should be granted to interpret her private conversations with Christ and to translate what is private and subjective into a public self. She thus complains to the anchorite at Lynn, who is her primary confessor:

> Good ser, what xal I do? He þat is my confessowr in ʒowr absens is rygth scharp vn-to me. He wyl not levyn my felyngys; he settyth nowt by hem; he heldyth hem but tryfelys & japys. & þat is a gret peyn vn-to me, for I lofe hym wele & I wold fawyn folwyn hys cownsel. (44)

Kempe's language here establishes the problem as a conflict between that which is feminine and subjective (feelings) and that which is male and objective. Margery's feelings come between her and this other confessor, thus between Margery and her ability to follow his advice. Since he will not believe in her, she cannot obey him. Kempe signals Margery's good intentions ("I lofe hym wel"), but, in linking female obedience to male tolerance and tractability, she hints that what is harshly logical is fundamentally ineffectual. She has, of course, raised a provocative issue: should a person reserve the right to judge confessors on purely subjective grounds or, more explicitly, should spiritual obedience be based on personal approbation?[50] Kempe contains the effect of such a question by having Margery's confessor tell her that unsympathetic priests can be seen as scourges sent by God to refine her belief: "þe mor scharp þat he is to ȝow, [þe mor] clerly schinyth ȝowr sowle in þe sygth of God, & God hath ordeyned me to be ȝowr norych & ȝowr comfort. Beth ȝe lowe & meke & thanke God boþe of on & of oþer" (44–45). Though Kempe here describes the confessor as recommending meekness and obedience, she depicts Margery's steadily decreasing reliance on the advice of such spiritual fathers. Those men who are supposed to serve Margery as "nurse and comfort" fail to offer her a relationship as satisfying as that she achieves through contemplation.

Moreover, Margery's search for confessors becomes a search for those who are willing to grant her spiritual autonomy and authority. Her need for priests is the more acute since she had won from Archbishop Arundel both the right to choose her own confessors and the right to receive communion every Sunday. Margery's wish to receive the sacrament frequently links her to other holy women, who likewise focused their devotions upon the body of Christ present in the sacrament of the altar, but it also underlines her reliance upon a church whose priests may impede her spiritual needs.[51] Thus, in choosing a confessor, Margery must convince him of her holiness. Kempe consistently uses the verb "show" to describe Margery's conversations with potential confessors: Margery shows herself, which is to say, her life, to a priest, who must choose to believe or disbelieve the text she presents for his verification. Her choice of him, then, depends upon his favorable reading.

Through scenes that purport to depict Margery's obedient bearing to representatives of the church, Kempe describes a complicated social and spiritual dynamic. First, such scenes occur between two individuals, each of whom can "read" the other. The confessional that physically separates penitent from priest did not exist in the Middle Ages, and the act of penance was inherently both more personal and more communal than it

50. The question, or my phrasing of it, is rooted in Wyclif's theory of dominion, his semi-Donatist assertion that the spiritually unworthy do not possess true spiritual authority. If such a question was dangerous to raise in the late fourteenth century, it was even more so in the early fifteenth century.

51. For a discussion of the relationship between gender and eucharistic devotion, see Bynum, "Women Mystics and Eucharistic Devotion"; on the broader issue of frequency of communion, see Rubin, *Corpus Christi*, 147–54.

became.[52] For example, Kempe describes Margery as observing Richard Caistyr (whom God has already recommended to her) walking up and down with another priest before she approaches him for an audience. He then sits down in the church with Margery, where she "shows" him "all þe wordys whech God had reuelyd to hyr in hyr sowl[e]" and "al hyr maner of levyng fro hyr chyldhod as ny as it wolde come to hir mende" (38). Offering her memory of her life as her confession (and notice it is not the same "memory" that is inscribed in the *Book,* which begins with adulthood, not childhood) and going on to tell him of her "feelings," Margery convinces Caistyr of the quality of her faith. He becomes her supporter and, afterwards, her confessor whenever she comes to Norwich. Kempe's account is less an account of a confession than of a relationship. By emphasizing the inherently communal nature of confession, Kempe implicitly points up its reciprocity: if Margery is to present herself as a text for verification, she demands an exegete capable of making an accurate interpretation. As Kempe repeatedly implies, only the virtuous can read.[53] Margery's search for confessors is therefore a hunt for those members of the clergy whose blameless lives give them the ability to see Christ in her. If her obedience is a testimony to priestly virtue, priestly virtue is a condition of her obedience.

Kempe's account of Margery's experience in Rome suggests her appraisal of a Church that cannot recognize an embodiment of its own ideals. Margery is cast out of the congregation of the Hospital of Saint Thomas of Canterbury in Rome by the slander of an English priest "þat was holdyn an holy man in þe Hospital & also in oþer placys of Rome" (80). As Kempe implies, what passes for holy in Rome has less to do with spiritual insight than with worldly pomp. Though his malice deprives her of both a confessor and the eucharist, Kempe provides for Margery a new and compensatory series of relationships that are based upon spiritual understanding. Her account of the first of these relationships is especially curious. Upon being informed of her plight, the priest of a nearby congregation invites Margery to confess to him though he says he does not understand English. Kempe does not say whether or not Margery accepts the invitation; instead, she describes another sort of confession:

---

52. Bossy, "The Social History of Confession"; Hughes, *Pastors and Visionaries,* 121.

53. This is an opinion she shares with the author of the general prologue to the *Wycliffite Bible.* For a discussion of this issue, see pages 134–35. For further discussion of the episode involving Richard Caistyr, see the Conclusion.

Than owyr Lord sent Seynt Iohn þe Evangelyst to heryn hir confessyon, & sche seyd 'Benedicite.' & he seyd 'Dominus' verily in hir
sowle þat sche saw hym & herd hym in hire gostly vndirstondyng
as sche xuld a do an-oþer preste be hir bodily wittys. Than sche
teld hym alle hir synnes & al hir heuynes wyth many swemful
teerys, & he herd hir ful mekely & benyngly. & sythyn he enioyned
hir penawns þat sche xuld do for hir trespas & asoyled hir of hir
synnes wyth swet wordys & meke wordys, hyly strengthyng hir to
trostyn in þe mercy of owyr Lord Ihesu Crist, & bad hir þat sche
xulde receyuen þe Sacrament of þe Awter in þe name of Ihesu. &
sithyn he passyd awey fro hir. (81)

Though the preceding description of the non-English-speaking priest
implies that Margery is confessing to another human being, what Kempe,
in fact, describes here is "priuy shrifte." Margery confesses to herself, or to
her private vision of Saint John, is absolved by that same vision, and
directed to the sacrament. Kempe's wording insists on the reality of what
is a new, spiritual relationship. Margery sees and hears Saint John in her
spiritual understanding as she would actually see and hear *another priest*.
Kempe's nomination of Saint John as Margery's confessor may owe a debt
to the *Revelations of St. Elizabeth of Hungary* where the Virgin presents the
Evangelist to Elizabeth as a witness to the private charter between them.
Signifying his obedience to the Virgin's spiritual authority as well as his
own episcopal and literary authority, Saint John then writes the charter.
The scene, however, is devoid of any social commentary or even of any
social context. Kempe's use of Saint John links Margery to Elizabeth of
Hungary, but it also suggests her ability to exploit incidents she found in
the literature of the holy that served her complicated and intentionally
ambiguous purposes.[54]

That Kempe is interested in the nature of the confessional relationship
is clear from another incident that occurs during Margery's stay in Rome.
Seeing a priest celebrate at the church of Saint John Lateran, she believes
him to be a good and devout man. She wishes to speak with him, but he is
German, and they cannot understand one another. However, they pray
for thirteen days, and they are granted a sort of Pentecostal gift: they can
understand one another though neither can actually speak the other's

54. Bokenham, like Kempe an East Anglian, includes Saint Elizabeth in his *Legendys of Hooly
Wummen;* see lines 9607–24 for her devotion to Saint John.

language. Bound by their love of Christ, they contract a new society. He forsakes his office to support her, taking her for his mother and his sister, and enduring a good deal of ill-will for Margery's sake. In exchange, Margery grants him her obedience, at his behest changing back into black clothing and serving an old woman for six weeks (see 82–86, 97). Where Margery directly challenges another English priest, who turns against her because she will not obey him, she meekly obeys the German priest because he is good (see 84–85). The relationship between penitent and confessor that Kempe describes is not described in the patriarchal language that defines a hierarchal unit. Instead, Margery is mother and sister to her priest; she is daughter only to Christ.

The subtle way in which Kempe substitutes God for male figures of spiritual authority reveals her awareness that, in describing Margery's life as a type of sexual revolution, she also provides a sharp look at the fundamental weaknesses of the ecclesiastical hierarchy. When Margery first feels the "fire of love" burning in her, God informs her that her private apprehension of him is more important than rituals signifying her conformity to accepted spiritual norms, such as fasting, wearing a hairshirt, saying many paternosters, or telling beads. By assuring her that "thynkyng, wepyng, & hy contemplacyon is þe best lyfe in erthe" (89) and by promising her that she will have more "merit" in heaven from "o ȝer of thynkyng in þi mende þan for an hundryd ȝer of preyng wyth þi mowth" (90), God (or Kempe) gives Margery the freedom of her feelings. God, both here and elsewhere, sounds suspiciously Wycliffite; compare the sentiments of the author of the important sermon "Of Mynstris in þe Chirche," which proclaims:

> For Crist nedude not hise apostlis to risen euermore at mydnyȝt, ne to faste as men don now, ne to be cloþud as þes newe ordris; but al þis is broȝt in by þe feend and fredom of Cristus ordre is left. For Crist wolde þat suche cerymonyes weron takon of hym by mennys frc wille aftur þat þei weron disposude to t[a]ke hem oþur more or lasse. But kepyng of Godus lawe, Crist wolde þat were grownd in his ordre. And Crist wolde teche as nede were chaunghyng of oure cerymonyes; for as God tolde Adam and Ioseph by luytul and luytul what þei schulden do, so Crist wolde telle men of his ordre how þei schulden worche and seruon hym.[55]

55. *English Wycliffite Sermons,* ed. Hudson and Gradon, 3:362.

Just as the author of this sermon presents Christ as founding an order owing allegiance to no earthly figure, Kempe substitutes God for more conventional figures of spiritual authority. When one anchor bids Margery "be gouernyd" by him, she evades him, saying "sche xulde wete first ȝyf it wer þe wil of God er not" (103). Later, she sends the anchor word that God does not wish her to be so "governed." When Margery is despised by all for her weeping, God himself places the unsympathetic priest under heavenly interdict, "Dowtyr, ȝyf he be a preyste þat despisith the, knowyng wel wher-for þu wepist & cryist, he is a-cursyd" (155). When one such priest is won over to her, Kempe notes, "þus God sent hir good maystyrschep of þis worthy doctowr" (166). By using a term—*maysterschep*—that connotes sexual hierarchy (a term also beloved of the Wife of Bath), to describe the priest's change of heart, Kempe makes it clear that what is at issue here is the very nature of, or foundation of, spiritual authority. She therefore describes God as complicit in Margery's efforts to compensate for ecclesiastical strictures against her. He tells her "þer is no clerk in al þis world þat can, dowtyr, leryn þe bettyr þan I can do" (158). When the church limits her access to knowledge by forbidding Master Aleyn ("by vertu of obedience") to instruct her or to speak with her, God tells her that he is more worthy to her soul than the anchor and, since she now lacks spiritual conversation, he will speak more often with her (168–69). By offering her spiritual love and companionship, God provides Margery with a way around the strictly hierarchical relationship offered by the Church.

What Margery moves toward is a reliance on Christ that finally obviates the need for obedience to any representative of the earthly priesthood. This is nowhere more apparent than in the second part of the *Book*. Structurally, the second part seems designed to mirror the first: both parts open with scribal testimonials, recount conflicts rooted in gender roles and conventions, and finally outline the process by which Margery achieves a spiritual enfranchisement that liberates her from the constrictions society imposes on women. Thus, the first part of the *Book* ends with a picture of Margery as a fully empowered visionary and writer, a person whose power comes solely from her relationship to Christ. The image offers a sharp contrast to the initial portrait of Margery as a weak, maddened wife, dependent upon an inadequate priest as mediator between herself and God. Kempe begins the second part by pulling us back into the realm of the family and the community, describing Margery's concern for her son's lax living. Through her prayers, he is converted to a more regular life, marries a German woman, and settles down on the Continent. Later, when visiting England in the company of his wife, the son dies and a month later Margery's husband dies. A year and a half later, the son's wife wishes to return to her native Germany, and Margery begins to sense that she should accompany her. What might take another writer many pages to narrate, Kempe accomplishes in one and a half brief chapters. The point of these events is obviously not their effect on Margery, since Kempe never mentions grief and never describes any process of mourning. Kempe, for example, spends far more time describing Margery's fears for her son's spiritual condition than she does describing his death. Instead, the deaths of both son and husband provide the occasion for another type of story, whereby Margery as a sort of holy *pícaro* achieves a final and breathtaking dissociation from her community that places her beyond the reach of male authority.

Kempe begins her account of this last pilgrimage in Margery's church, specifically with a conflict between Christ and Margery's confessor. When Margery wonders whether she should take leave of her confessor and accompany her daughter-in-law home to Germany, Christ answers, "Dowtyr, I wote wel, yf I bode þe gon, þu woldist gon al redy. Þerfor I wyl þat þu speke no word to hym of þis mater" (225–26). Though Margery takes this to mean she will not have to contemplate another sea voyage at her age, she does ask for and receive permission from her confessor to take her daughter to Ipswich. When they are in route to Ipswich, Margery feels commanded to take her daughter all the way home to Germany. What Kempe then goes on to describe is the conflict Margery feels between Christ's command and her confessor's paternal care, "Lord, þu wost wel I haue no leue of my gostly fadyr, & I am bowndyn to obediens. Þerfor I may not do thus wyth-owtyn hys wil & hys consentyng" (227). Christ answers these objections by asserting the primacy of Margery's private feelings, "I bydde þe gon in my name, Ihesu, for I am a-bouyn thy gostly fadyr & I xal excusyn þe & ledyn þe & bryngyn þe a-gcyn in saftc" (227). That Kempe was aware of the force of these words is clear from the next incident, in which Margery recounts her feelings to a Franciscan she meets in Norwich. This "doctowr of diuinyte" has heard of her holy living and is well disposed to her; he counsels her to obey the voice of God, saying that he believes it is the Holy Spirit working in her. By having this man verify Margery's feelings as the stirrings of the Holy Spirit, Kempe maintains the fiction that Margery is an obedient daughter of Holy Church. But the incident nonetheless points up the difficulties of obeying someone if you do not believe he is right, and Kempe presents Margery as docile only when a priest's reading of a situation agrees with her own. With Christ and a doctor of divinity supporting the trip and only her confessor opposing it, Margery takes ship.

If Margery's final pilgrimage begins with hints of her disengagement from ecclesiastical authority, her return is even more potentially explosive. Kempe first describes Margery as enjoying a triumph in London. Not only does Margery face down her detractors; she also speaks out boldly against the worldly life-styles of Londoners. Since her devotions make her an unwelcome communicant in the churches of London, she becomes a peripatetic worshiper and a figure of special holiness to the common people:

> . . . sche suffyrd ful mech slawndyr & repref, specyaly of þe curatys & preistys of þe chirchis in London. Þei wold not suffyr hir to abydyn in her chirchys, & þerfor sche went fro on chirch to an-oþer þat sche xulde not ben tediows on-to hem. Mech of þe comown pepil magnifijd God in hir, hauyng good trost þat it was þe goodnes of God whech wrowt þat hy grace in hir sowle. (245)

Kempe follows up her account of Margery as a quasi-populist preacher, a potentially radical identity, by describing her as proceeding next to the Carthusian abbey of Shene, which had been founded by Henry V in 1415.[56] Not only was Shene a royal foundation; along with its sis-terhouse, the Bridgettine abbey of Syon, Shene was a center for mystical piety during the later Middle Ages and was responsible for the descemina-tion of devotional texts like those Kempe evokes throughout her own *Book*. By locating Margery at Shene during Lammastide (see 245–46), Kempe appears to realign her with the Church and consequently with the spirit of obedience. First, as Kempe twice repeats, Margery goes to Shene to purchase her pardon on the day that was the "principal day of pardon." On Lammas Day, August 1, which was also one of the quarter days for rent-paying, loaves made from the new wheat were consecrated in English churches as signs of the congregation's thankfulness for harvest. On that

---

56. For a detailed account of the history of this abbey, see F. R. Johnson, "Syon Abbey," in Cockburn et al., *A History of the County of Middlesex*, 182–91; Meech, *The Book of Margery Kempe*, 348–49.

day, which commemorated the settling of secular and spiritual debts, Margery goes as a devout daughter of the Church to purchase her own pardon. Kempe, however, neglects to detail this particular act of exchange, instead describing two events that focus our attention upon Margery's own assumption of authority: Margery's spiritual direction of a young man who observes her devotions in the church at Shene, and her successful negotiation of the final obstacle standing in her way back to Lynn. While she is in church to "purchase" this pardon, she sees the hermit who had led her and her daughter-in-law out of Lynn to Ipswich. She approaches him about leading her home and learns that her confessor has "forsaken" her because she went to Germany without telling him of her plans. Margery, the renegade penitent, nonetheless manages not only to persuade the hermit to accompany her back to Lynn but also to make peace again with her confessor. The end of the *Book* is worthy of Chaucer:

> Whan sche was come hom to Lynne, sche obeyd hir to hir confessowr. He ȝaf hir ful scharp wordys, for sche was hys obediencer & had tekyn vp-on hir swech a jurne wyth-owtyn hys wetyng. Þerfor he was meuyd þe mor a-geyn hir, but owr Lord halpe hir so þat sche had as good loue of hym & of oþer frendys aftyr as sche had be-forn, worschepyd be God. Amen. (247)

What Kempe describes is a female victory. Though she twice refers to obedience, even calling Margery her confessor's *obediencer,* denoting someone who has vowed obedience to a rule, such as a novice, the nature of that obedience is ambiguous.[57] Now that Margery has returned from her journey, every step of which she determined herself, and from a life as a sort of holy vagabond, preacher, and mystic, she obeys her confessor. Furthermore, as the passage suggests, her confessor is most annoyed because she went without his permission; in other words, because Margery contravened the terms of a relationship based upon hierarchy. Margery, like many an Eve before her, endures his wrath and soothes his ruffled pride. As Chaucer's Merchant gives May Persephone's help when old Januarie confronts her with marital infidelity, so Kempe gives Margery, who has broken her vows, the Lord's help, "so þat sche had as good loue of hym & oþer frendys as sche had be-forn." The "amen," repeated in red at the end of the chapter, helps to muffle the resonating irony of a

---

57. According to the *Middle English Dictionary, Obediencer* is a late medieval word.

scene that only appears to validate the authority vested in priests by women who feel compelled to go well beyond the boundaries those men have established for them.

The intercessory prayers with which the *Book* ends likewise image Margery as an obedient daughter of Holy Church, but they also suggest that her special relationship with Christ somehow allows her to transcend gender categories. Thus, along with sentences attesting to her charity and piety, there are those that hint at a new understanding of the nature of spiritual authority. Requests like "Lord, make my gostly fadirs for to dredyn þe in me" (249) or "for alle þo þat feithyn & trustyn er xul feithyn & trustyn in my prayerys in-to þe worldys ende, sweche grace as þei desiryn" (253–54) hint that Margery's power extends well beyond that of the churchmen who presume to direct her. What Kempe achieves through the conventional language of intercessory prayer is that same delicately poised ambiguity that characterizes her entire text. For Margery is at once a textbook exemplar of late medieval female piety and a reminder of the essential unruliness of the subjective, the feminine, and its fundamental urge to master those authorities who seek to contain what is, finally, uncontainable.

The comic irony inherent in the reversal of gender roles is, of course, designed to point up the folly of seeking to control the "feminine" with instruments inadequate to the task. If Jankyn will not, then his "book of wicked wives" cannot make order out of hierarchy, particularly when that hierarchy rests on foundations as shaky as the marriage of Jankyn and Alisoun. Through Margery and her comic insurrection, Kempe provides an image of the Church that underscores its inadequacies. Her point, however, is hardly satiric: through Margery she projects a community where harmony is a manifestation of true spiritual authority. Such authority rests on a literal and personal interpretation of the Gospel story, which Kempe presents to us through Margery whose visions and conversations with God mediate the central doctrines and events of Christianity.

What can be described as Kempe's "Passion sequence" (187–99) owes, as Gibson has pointed out, a genuine debt to Love's *Mirror of the Blessed Life of Jesus Christ*.[58] Both sequences heighten the pathos of the Gospel accounts of the Passion by dramatizing scenes of primarily human interest. Thus, the intricate courtroom scenes on which the medieval dramatists expended so much care are not included. Instead of depicting the

---

58. Gibson, *Theater of Devotion*, 49.

ironies of law and empire that undergird such public scenes in the mystery plays, both Kempe and the *Mirror* describe extratextual scenes like Jesus' parting from his mother, Mary's terrible grief, the exhaustion and bewilderment of Holy Saturday, and Jesus' appearance to his mother very early on Easter morning. By concluding Margery's experience of the Passion with her apprehension of the Purification, Kempe suggests her awareness that, in privileging the affective piety of Mary and the early followers of Christ in her treatment of the Passion, she foregrounds the feminine. The feast of the Purification, or Candlemas, is, of course, a woman's feast, for it celebrates Mary's offering in the Temple as her thanksgiving for the safe delivery of a male child (see Luke 2:22–35).[59] Rather than the pair of doves required by the law and that Luke recounts Mary and Joseph as offering, Kempe describes Mary as offering only her son, thereby suggesting Mary's awareness that the baby in her arms needs no symbolic pair of doves; he himself will satisfy the law of sacrifice. Kempe then describes Margery as responding to a moment of female ritual: "Sche thowt in hir sowle þat sche saw owr Lady ben purifijd & had hy contemplacyon in þe beheldyng of *þe women* wheche comyn to offeryn wyth *þe women* þat weryn purifijd" (198; emphasis added). Margery weeps because the Passion sequence she has just seen is the denouement of that joyful presentation. Like Mary, she understands the significance of the one act in the light of the other.[60]

However, though Kempe appears at times simply to imitate the affective emphasis of works like the *Mirror,* she, like Julian of Norwich before her, subtly alters a reader's response to these scenes by locating authority in the female beholder.[61] The reader of the *Mirror* is directed by an authoritative male voice to imagine or "behold" these scenes, and is implicitly urged to use the Virgin as her point of reference. In empathizing and identifying with Mary, she participates in the Passion. In contrast to such a prescriptive narrative technique, Julian of Norwich presents herself as

59. In a paper delivered at the 1992 meeting of the Medieval Academy of America, Gail McMurray Gibson elaborated upon the communal ritual of Candlemas. For a "fictional" account of Mary's Purification that became canonical, see *The Golden Legend.*

60. The N-Town Purification pageant depicts Mary as first laying her son on the altar as a sign of her recognition of his role in human salvation history. It is a more literal-minded figure, the Chaplain, who reminds her that she still must make an offering, the pair of doves required by the Law. For a cogent discussion of the ways in which depictions of the experience of the Virgin are designed to link maternal joy with sorrow, see Gibson, *Theater of Devotion,* 155–66.

61. For work on the "gender-implications" of the gaze, see Stanbury, "Feminist Film Theory: Seeing Chrétien's *Enide*"; idem, "The Virgin's Gaze."

the visionary, telling the reader what she saw—how, for example, Christ's body appeared dried out after much time on the Cross in the "dry sharp wynd, wonder colde," of the day of the Crucifixion.[62] Julian thereby focuses our attention on the sight itself, on the pictures she passes on to us, that then demand the sort of highly intellectual analysis she provides for each of her visions. Thus, the picture she evokes of Christ's dried-up flesh is used as a means of understanding his words from the Cross, "I thirst," which as she comes to understand signify both a physical and a spiritual thirst. Julian offers the reader not only the images and scenes she has been privileged to behold, but also the picture of a mind thinking and guiding our understanding of those visions upon which she has spent so many years' efforts. In her presentation of the same scene of sacrifice, Kempe betrays her awareness that she who directs the reader's line of sight governs the reader's response to the act of viewing. The "scribe" describes for us what Margery "sees," using Margery herself as a key participant in the drama of the Passion. Instead of Mary, Margery becomes our focal point. Mary is Margery's point of reference; she empathizes with the Virgin's grief and love in the way the *Mirror* directs its female reader to respond to the pictures the narrator composes for her. But for the reader, the viewer, Margery is the active participant, our spiritual directress. Kempe uses the voice of the scribe in a particularly sophisticated way in such scenes: it appears to function as the narrator of the *Mirror* functions. In fact, however, that voice focuses the reader on Margery herself, whose authority is verified by the reality of vision.

Kempe also suggests the nature of Margery's authority by dramatizing her literal application of the Gospel to her own life. She seeks to imitate Christ's poverty, meekness, self-sacrifice, and charity. Moreover, when the Archbishop of York tries to order her not to "teach" or "challenge" (reprove) people in his diocese, she firmly replies,

> And also þe Gospel makyth mencyon þat, whan þe woman had herd owr Lord prechyd, sche cam be-forn hym wyth a lowde voys & seyd, "Blyssed be þe wombe þat þe bar & þe tetys þat ʒaf þe sowkyn." Þan owr Lord seyd a-ʒen to hir, "Forsoþe so ar þei blissed þat heryn þe word of God and kepyn it." "And þerfor, sir, me thynkyth þat þe Gospel ʒeuyth me leue to spekyn of God." (126)

---

62. See Colledge and Walsh, eds., *The Showings,* the Long Text, chapter 8, 357–59. The quoted passage is on 358.

Though Margery goes on to defend herself against the charge that she preaches, her use of the Gospel as precedent for her actions underlines her increasing reliance on her own, in opposition to ecclesiastical, authority. In fact, her "translation" of the passage (Luke 11:27–28) suggests her presumption of authority, for she does not translate word for word, but "sense for sense." First, she heightens the effect of verse 27 ("sum womman of the cumpany reysinge hir vois") by saying the woman who had heard Jesus preach spoke with a *loud* voice. Second, she recounts Jesus as agreeing with, rather than differing from, the woman's words. Where Luke reads, "*Rathere* blessid ben thei, that heeren Goddis word, and kepen it," Margery uses *forsope so,* which implies agreement and not distinction.[63] Since Margery, like the Wife of Bath, seems to have no qualms about validating her own actions by quoting and (mis)translating Scripture, it seems fitting that one good wife should reply to one of Margery's prognostications by saying, "Now Gospel mote it ben in ʒowr mowth" (202).[64] Kempe's characterization of Margery as basing her actions upon a literalist reading of the Gospel would also have had Wycliffite associations for any astute fifteenth-century reader. She thus follows up Margery's audacious use of Scripture with the tale of the bear and the pear tree, a fable that it is unlikely any Lollard preacher would have used. Rather than tell tales, the Lollards, who described themselves as "Bible men," focused on Scripture; mendicants and other popular preachers were more likely to weave stories into their sermons. By inserting the fable into the scene with the Archbishop of York, Kempe contains the effect that Margery's words might well produce by focusing our attention on her faintly scatological tale about the bear whose defilement of a fair pear tree is intended to suggest the need for clerical purity. That the fable, as I have suggested, may have more than a surface relevance adds one more layer of irony to an already dense episode. Kempe could wish for no finer advocate for Margery than Henry Bowet, archbishop of York, whose

---

63. I quote from the *Wycliffite Bible,* ed. Forshall and Madden. Carruthers (*The Book of Memory,* 61) has suggested that such "mistranslations" reflect the medieval way of memorizing sense for sense and that what appear to us as lapses may, instead, suggest the techniques of "memoria ad res." If this is the case in the above passage, it highlights Kempe's internalization of the text as well as the close connection between translation and interpretation. For a discussion of this issue, see pages 133–35; Copeland, *Rhetoric, Hermeneutics, and Translation in the Middle Ages,* 91–95.

64. The prologue to the Wycliffite glossed gospel known as "Short Mark" (London B.L. Additional MS. 41175) defines "gospel" as "good telling." For a discussion of these manuscripts, see Hargreaves, "Popularizing Biblical Scholarship."

zeal against the Lollards was well known; she therefore notes his liking of the tale as well as his judicious support for such a Bible-quoting woman. Kempe's strategy here follows a familiar pattern; she at once suggests Margery's own assumption of authority and her assimilation into the patriarchal hierarchy of the contemporary Church. Archbishop Bowet serves Kempe as an official stamp of approval for a protagonist whose words and actions actually indicate her break with all earthly fathers.

It is clear moreover that Margery's "Gospel" is not the Church's, that what Margery is, the Church is not. Margery, with her private visions of the life of Christ (which serve as a type of unauthorized translation), with her certainty that the Gospel provides a precedent for her own provocative life, and with her growing espousal of a literalist interpretation of that Gospel, presents a challenge to a Church whose authority rested on privilege, hierarchy, and the tradition of biblical exegesis and allegory that had defined patristic culture for a thousand years. Kempe characterizes the nature of that challenge by dramatizing the negative effect Margery's strictly regulated behavior has on contemporary churchmen. In particular, Margery's espousal of a doctrine of apostolic poverty would have been seen as a direct threat to a Church that, since the days of Richard II, had sought to defend its secular wealth and privilege from those who wished to see the Church divest itself of temporal goods that compromised its ability to function as a spiritual power.[65] The subject of poverty was also linked to the ongoing controversy about (and within) the mendicant orders, which had long since abandoned a literalist interpretation of Christ's injunction to genuine poverty.[66] It is therefore appropriate that Christ's command to become poor for his sake comes to Margery in Rome, the center of Christian power. Margery, now poor, must, like the original followers of Francis, depend upon the charity of others for her food, clothing, and shelter. As she discovers, not every churchman meets her poverty with goodwill. In losing the safety net her money gives her, Margery loses the nominal respect she is granted by virtue of her social status.

In exchange, however, Margery gains a new community, organized according to a system of relations defined in familial language. Kempe not

65. For a study of apostolic poverty as it relates to English ecclesiastical and political trends, see Aston, "Caim's Castles"; Hudson, *The Premature Reformation*, 114–15, 338–40. See also "The Clergy May Not Hold Property" in Matthews, ed., *The English Works of Wyclif*; "Of Mynystris in þe Chirche," in *English Wycliffite Sermons*, ed. Hudson and Gradon, 2:329–65.
66. See Leff, *Heresy in the Later Middle Ages*, chapter 7; Little, *Religious Poverty*, 177–78.

only suggests the ineffectuality and the harshness of a male priesthood and, in Margery's visions, the male violence visited upon the body of Christ; she also presents Margery as a figure who nurtures her converts in ways the male-dominated church does not. She therefore describes Margery's male converts as her sons, even when many of these supporters are priests and supposedly have care for her soul. An English priest she meets in Rome who offers to relieve her physical want displays filial piety toward Margery, "mekely he cleped hir modyr, preying hir for charite to receyuen hym as hir sone" (96). When Margery suddenly decides to accompany her daughter-in-law to Germany and is therefore without provisions, the master of her ship provides for her needs and "was as tendyr to hir as sche had ben hys modyr" (231). The young man she encounters in the church at Shene asks her to counsel him in the Christ-like life, saying, "Schewith modirly & goodly ʒowr conceit vn-to me" (246).[67]

Kempe also offers a rather startling picture of the way in which that new community is constituted in a series of phrases intended to preface another incident. Kempe writes, "On þe Fryday aftyr, as þis creatur went to sportyn hir in þe felde & men of hir owyn nacyon wyth hir, þe whech sche informyd in þe lawys of God as wel as sche cowde—& scharply sche spak a-gayns hem for þei sworyn gret othys & brokyn þe comawndment of owr Lord God" (101). Kempe here images Margery as a Lollard preacher, poor for Christ's sake, speaking in the open air against swearing and the taking of oaths, as well as against breaking the laws of God. Thus one Wycliffite sermon notes that it is better to hear God's word and pray than to be encumbered by a wealthy and corrupt Church, going on "and þis is comunly beture doon in þe eyr vndur heuene; but often tyme, in reyny weder, chirchis don good on holy day."[68] As it turns out, rainy weather chases Margery and her group home to shelter, but Kempe nonetheless provides a glimpse of a fellowship that has formed around Margery, a community that is not circumscribed by parochial boundaries. The authority Margery claims for herself and is granted by her listeners derives from her private relationship with God. But the very terms of that private relationship inevitably point up the inadequacies of a Church whose buildings, ecclesiastical households, worldly power and wealth, and frequently

---

67. We can find a similar emphasis upon a differently configured "kinship" group in Wycliffite treatises, such as the sermon on Matthew 12 ("here is my mother and my brother") collected in *English Wycliffite Sermons*, ed. Hudson and Gradon, 2:280–81.

68. Ibid., 2:101. Oath-taking was, of course, inimical to the Lollards; see pages 147–50.

self-interested interpretation of Christ's literal commands suggest the need for a new understanding of the nature of spiritual authority.

By using Margery as such a radical figure for charity and devotion, Kempe suggests the ways in which the Church might function as a transcendent (or transnational) community. Despite the fact that she speaks only English, Margery is able to communicate very well with a wide variety of people. Whereas her fellow English scorn her for her tears, the Saracens Margery encounters in the Holy Land make much of Margery and lead her where she wants to go (75). In Rome, a Dame Margaret Florentyn communicates with Margery by "syngnys er tokenys & in fewe comown wordys" (93). She is invited into a poor woman's house where the sight of a little boy reminds Margery of the love Mary had for her son. Although Kempe records no actual conversation on this visit, Margery nonetheless leaves with Jesus' words in her ear, "Thys place is holy" (94). This gift of tongues is likewise verified in her relations with those foreign priests and confessors she meets in Rome, whose virtue, meekness, and holiness render them capable of communicating with Margery. Finally, Margery herself serves as a figure for translation; she translates into contemporary terms the Christ-like life, just as her private visions translate "her gospel" for the reader. Furthermore, in her handling of the Passion, where the women of Jerusalem step forward to offer Mary their sympathy and to acknowledge that "owr pepil han don hym so meche despite" (195), Kempe implicitly draws a distinction between the "cruel Iewys" (192) who crucify Christ and the women who align themselves with those who follow him, mourn him, and take care of him. Similarly, it is frequently women who come to Margery's aid, offering her food (79), wine in a stone cup (94), compassion for her spiritual sorrow (99), aid in prison (130), or safety when she is on the road. By linking gender to such works of mercy, Kempe adumbrates the character of a new Church that ministers to those in need. Just as Margery is drawn to devotion of the Christ child when she sees the women of Rome carrying male children, so many of the women in the *Book* remind us of the ways in which the Church might minister to a world increasingly ruled by economic relationships.

As the bride of Christ, Margery emerges as a figure for a new *ecclesia,* where love, vision, and purity of life are the criteria for authority. The multiplicity of roles that Kempe describes Christ as assigning to the pri-

vate relations between himself and Margery early in her spiritual career,
she elaborates on throughout the *Book:*

> Þerfor I preue þat þow art a very dowtyr to me & a modyr also, a
> syster, a wyfe, and a spowse, wytnessyng þe Gospel wher owyr
> Lord seyth to hys dyscyples, "He þat doth þe wyl of my Fadyr in
> Heuyn he is bothyn modyr, broþyr, & syster vn-to me." Whan
> þow stodyst to plese me, þan art þu a very dowtyr; whan þu
> wepyst & mornyst for my peyn & for my Passyon, þan art þow a
> very modyr to haue compassyon of hyr chyld; whan þow wepyst
> for oþer mennys synnes and for aduersytes, þan art þow a very
> syster; and, whan thow sorwyst for þow art so long fro þe blysse of
> Heuyn, þan art þu a very spowse & a wyfe, for it longyth to þe
> wyfe to be wyth hir husbond & no very joy to han tyl sche come to
> hys presens. (31)

Kempe here glosses Christ's words about spiritual kinship (mother,
brother, and sister) solely in terms of female roles—daughter, sister,
mother, and wife—each of which she describes as directed by a special
type of love. She goes even farther than some Lollard preachers, who
made a point of underlining the centrality of women to the Gospel community. As one sermon notes in reference to this same scriptural passage,
"And þus tellep Crist a sutylte þat is of gostly breþren in God: for be it
man, or be it womman, þat seruep God trewly, he is on þes þre maners
knyt to Crist in sybrede," going on to explain that we are Christ's brothers
by soul, sisters by flesh, and mothers by both. The explanation ends with,
"And þis is betture cosynage and more sotyl þan is of kynde."[69]

By describing Margery as substituting a network of spiritual kinship for
a natural or fundamentally literal network, Kempe emphasizes the genuine freedom to be found in a fellowship of "gostly breþren." Where the
kinship of "kynde" restricts Margery to roles and activities sanctioned by
social hierarchies and expectations, her new and divinely ordained spiritual identity releases her into a new realm of meaning where those roles
used to define the limits of womankind become signifiers of a different
order. Thus the "mulier fortis" of Proverbs 31, whom the Wycliffite
translator(s) renders as "strong woman," was conventionally identified

---

69. Ibid., 2:280–81. Atkinson (*Mystic and Pilgrim,* 133–34) also remarks on Kempe's wording, noting Saint Anselm's use of bisexual and multifunctional language.

with the Church.[70] Her activities are those writ large of womankind: she is a figure of fruitfulness and nurture, upholding her husband's honor, providing food, clothing, and livelihood for her family, and charity for the poor, blessed, in turn, by her many children. As Theresa Coletti has suggested, the *mulier fortis* may well underlie Chaucer's portrait of the Wife of Bath, whose real and metaphoric barrenness, rampant sexuality, and selfish mercantilism set her in opposition to the common good.[71] When translated, however, out of the realm of the actual, those very activities that delimit woman's sphere of activities in earthly relationships can be used to define the mission and thus the authority of the Church by reference to the feminine. The Wycliffite glosses upon the passage in Proverbs are especially illuminating:

> Cristen doctours expownen comynly this lettre, til to the ende, of hooly chirche, which bi figuratif speche is seid a strong womman; hir hosebonde is Crist, hir sones and dou3tris ben Cristen men and wymmen; and this is the literal vndurstonding, as thei seyen; and this exposicioun is resonable and set opinly in the comyn glos. But Rabi Salomon seith, that bi a strong womman is vndurstondun hooli Scripture; the hosebonde of this womman, is a studiouse techere in hooly Scripture, bothe men and wymmen; for in Jeroms tyme summe wymmen weren ful studiouse in hooly Scripture.[72]

The first part of this gloss echoes the conventional explanation for the passage that can be found in the *Glossa Ordinaria*.[73] The second part, which compares the woman to the sacred text, whose "housband" is its student and exegete subtly points up the Wycliffite challenge to conventional authority by stressing that this student may be either a man or a woman. For readers of Chaucer and Kempe, the passage resonates with additional ironies. Chaucer's Wife—the antitype of the *mulier fortis*—who defines herself as the physical text well and carnally "glossed" by Jankyn

---

70. The *mulier fortis* deserves a special note, for she has been translated in ways that adumbrate a history of the feminine. Thus, while the heirs to Wyclif, with a certain stake in privileging the feminine, offer her as a "strong" woman, the Renaissance translators who prepared the Geneva Bible present her as a "virtuous" woman, focusing our attention upon her womanly activities and underlining her obedience rather than her strength or her force as an allegorical figure. The translators of the Douai Old Testament equivocate and use "valiant."

71. Coletti, "Biblical Wisdom: Chaucer's *Shipman's Tale* and the *Mulier Fortis*," 180–81.

72. Forshall and Madden, *The Wycliffite Bible*, v. Proverbs 31, p. 51.

73. See *PL* 113:1114–16.

the clerk, or student, who is her fifth husband, situates herself in opposition to authorities like Saint Jerome, whom she sees as merely constricting the feminine. Kempe, perhaps echoing Chaucer and / or the gloss on Proverbs, likewise defines Margery as the text displayed for confessors and fellow townspeople, ultimately for the reader of her *Book*.[74] Kempe presents Margery as her own best exegete, even slyly using Saint Jerome, whose reputation for antifeminism was notorious in the Middle Ages, to authorize Margery's assumption of spiritual authority (see 99).

Throughout the *Book*, Kempe further extends the meaning and the range of female roles and thereby defines Ecclesia's role in contemporary life. Whereas Margery is constricted by her physical role as wife and mother, Kempe's emphasis upon her espousal to Christ and "mothering" of others is meant to underline Margery's translation into the freedom of the metaphoric. Her freedom of movement, her powers of communication and intercession, and her refusal to accept the limits of a hierarchical and conformist society proclaim the message of a radical gospel, a message the women who followed and ministered to Christ indeed bore to their skeptical and temporarily immobile brothers, who took the witness of women as madness (see Mark 16, Luke 24, John 20). As one Wycliffite exegete noted of John's account of the Resurrection, "While men gon awey, stronger loue haþ set þe womman in þe same place." He goes on to use a female figure, Mary Magdalene, as an example of the true preacher, "so must they that han office of preching, that if any sign of heuene is schewed to þem, bisily þey telle it to her neiȝboris."[75] Through the transforming power of the Resurrection, female garrulity, or gossip, has become "busy telling," or the Gospel itself. Like other contemporary gospellers, Kempe develops a revolutionary rhetoric, imaging through Margery what she could, perhaps, only image through a woman. The challenge to existing hierarchies she dramatizes in Margery's life is based on cultural assumptions about gender categories, but gender is, finally, the means of expressing what are radical ideas about spiritual dominion.

74. For the fullest exposition of textual metaphors in relation to the *Book,* see Lochrie, *Margery Kempe and Translations of the Flesh,* especially chapter 3.
75. This passage is taken from the Wycliffite glossed gospel, known as "Short John," MS. Bodley 243.

4

The English Nation

 In the preceding chapter I have intentionally drawn upon terms usually used in discussions of the beliefs and stances of Wyclif and his followers. I would not describe Kempe as articulating through Margery a program as detailed as we can find in explicitly Wycliffite texts of the period. Nor would I simply call her a Lollard. Nonetheless she uses Margery in a way that evinces her sensitivity to the whole range of issues that had accrued around the Lollard heresy and that suggests her sympathies for what might loosely be called Lollard views.[1] Since, by the fifteenth century, "heresy" and "treason" were inextricably linked, to be a Lollard was to be a traitor: both official and semiofficial documents proclaim the belief that Lollardy led to civil unrest.[2] Kempe was clearly aware of the con-

1. For accounts of these, see Compston, "The Thirty-Seven Conclusions of the Lollards"; Cronin, "The Twelve Conclusions of the Lollards"; Hudson, *The Premature Reformation,* especially 389. On the subject of the "submerged presence of Lollardy in the English consciousness," see Dickens, *Lollards and Protestants in the Diocese of York, 1509–1558.* For remarks about the relevance of Lollardy to literature, see Hudson, *The Premature Reformation,* chapter 9, "The Context of Vernacular Wycliffism"; Jeffrey, "Chaucer and Wyclif: Biblical Hermeneutic and Literary Theory in the XIVth Century."

2. See especially the *Rotuli Parliamentarum,* vols. 3–4; the *Statutes of the Realm,* vol. 2. See also Aston, "Lollardy and Sedition, 1381–1431"; Catto, "Religious Change under Henry V," in Harriss, ed., *Henry V: The Practice of Kingship;* and Haines, *Ecclesia Anglicana.* The request, in the first year of the reign of Henry IV that the new "secte" of people who dress in white clothing as a sign of great sanctity and who threaten to subvert the realm, be proscribed, voices an attitude that is repeated throughout the period (*Rot. Parl.,* 3:428).

temporary association between heterodoxy and sedition. In her accounts of the potential dangers Margery faces as a suspected Lollard, Kempe underlines the actual legal relationship between ecclesiastical and civil crime, subtly pointing up the ways in which the lines had been blurred between the institutions and laws of church and state. Kempe's descriptions of Margery's successful rebuttals of charges of religious heresy brought against her in civil proceedings by her fellow citizens therefore preserve Kempe herself from charges of either religious or civil dissent.

Such scenes may be designed to militate against any sense that Kempe sought to subvert English civil order, but they also suggest how analytical an eye Kempe cast upon order as a reflection of the national character. Her interest in England Kempe shares with her contemporaries. From the mid-fourteenth-century compiler of the Gough map, to the chronicle writers who created a learned Latin analysis of English events, to the continuators of the vernacular *Brut*, and to Sir John Fortescue who, in the mid-fifteenth century, sought to define England by analyzing the nature of its government, the men and women of the later Middle Ages proclaim their interest in establishing or in understanding their national identity.[3] The care Kempe takes to create in Margery a character who exists within a specific geographic and historic context signals her awareness that though kingdoms may reckon their strengths by evaluating their institutions, their geographic boundaries, or their records of significant events, national identities are reckoned in less concrete ways. The fiction any nation promulgates about itself is a self-conscious act of creation that emerges from actual conditions but does not necessarily reflect them. The Lancastrian kings, in particular, understood the need to create a national myth whose claims to primordial unity would belie their own violent seizure of regal power, and none understood the art of mythmaking as well as Henry V, during whose reign the bulk of Kempe's narrative is set.

In her own fiction, Kempe is scrupulous about her presentation of both time and place, situating Margery in particular towns at particular times, and describing her confrontations with actual representatives of civil or ecclesiastical power.[4] In so doing, Kempe provides a glimpse of England

3. For a consideration of the ways in which Chaucer was assimilated to a growing sense of a "national literature" by his fifteenth-century editors, see Lerer, "Textual Criticism and Literary Theory."

4. The very fact that Meech could abstract a list of dates from the *Book* suggests its author's interest in localizing the narrative; see Meech, ed., *The Book of Margery Kempe*, xlviii–li.

during a particularly difficult period for those with Lollard views. The map of England that is submerged in the narrative of Margery's life is one where the names of major towns in central England like Leicester, Bristol, or London anchor the narrative in the relatively familiar world of English commercial activity. However, since it was also in these towns (and along the roads to these towns) that Lollardy flourished, Kempe's references serve as reminders of more than material profit and mercantile unity.[5] Though Kempe is nowhere explicitly critical, she nonetheless dramatizes the ambiguities of some of the conflicts of Henry V's England, a reign that most official documents tended to describe as a triumph of right over wrong. Like many a travel writer before and after her, Kempe plays upon the isolation of the traveler as a means of exploiting the mode's potential for social satire. Most of Margery's most threatening experiences occur within her own country, where she can seem as alien a figure—if not more so—as she is in Jerusalem or Rome. Kempe uses such experiences as a means of exploring the underlying "reality" of that national community that was officially described as unified by language, religion, and mission. Kempe's picture of nationhood, which is as tenuously grounded in actuality as Henry's, displays her adroit manipulation of the terms in which that official portrait of England was cast. Like the Lancastrian mythmakers, Kempe focuses upon the issues of language, authority, and community as signifiers of nationhood. If the *Book* is not a diary or a chronicle or a history, it is—like any of these—an attempt to understand a time by telling one piece of its story.

In the fifteenth century the subject of a national language became fundamental to England's sense of its own identity and unity at the same time that the subject of the vernacular was linked to impulses that might subvert that unified identity. There is certainly a good deal of evidence for linguistic nationalism throughout the late fourteenth century; writers explored the sanctions for and possibilities of English as a medium for the writing of literature, of science, of theology, and of devotion. Nor did English suddenly come into its own with Henry IV's accession to the throne at the end of the century. Though English increasingly appeared in letters and official documents as the national tongue, the Parliament Rolls continued to be kept in French, and Latin retained its prominence as the

5. Aston, *Lollards and Reformers,* 19; Hudson, ed., *Selections from English Wycliffite Writings,* 8.

language of the learned.[6] In 1362 Parliament had enacted a statute saying that all court proceedings must be conducted in English and, from its inception in 1394, the court of chancery had conducted most of its proceedings in English.[7] After the death of Henry V, we begin to encounter more entries in English in the Parliament Rolls. The signet letters of Henry himself suggest his sensitivity to the need for a standard for English, and in the year of his death in 1422 the members of the London Brewer's Guild elaborately justified their decision to keep their records in English:

> whereas our mother-tongue, to wit the English tongue, hath in modern days begun to be honorably enlarged and adorned, for that our most excellent lord, King Henry V, hath in his letters missive and divers affairs touching his own person, more willingly chosen to declare the secrets of his will, and for the better understanding of his people, hath with a diligent mind procured the common idiom (setting aside others) to be commended by the exercise of writing: and there are many of our craft of Brewers who have the knowledge of writing and reading in the said English idiom, but in others, to wit, the Latin and French, before these times used, they do not in any wise understand. For which causes with many others, it being considered how that the greater part of the Lords and trusty Commons have begun to make their matters to be noted down in our mother tongue, so we also in our craft, following in some manner their steps have decreed to commit to memory the needful things that concern us.[8]

The document links nationalism to the primacy of a written English. Thus the twice-uttered "mother-tongue"—according to the *MED,* a late fourteenth-century phrase and one that surely reflects a self-conscious nationalism—along with the encomium to Henry V as a sort of father of

6. For a more detailed account of the growing importance of English, see Fisher, Richardson, and Fisher, *An Anthology of Chancery English,* introduction, xv; Fisher, "Chancery and the Emergence of Standard Written English in the Fifteenth Century."

7. See *Statutes of the Realm,* vol. 1, 36 Edward III, pp. 375–76; Fisher, Richardson, and Fisher, *An Anthology of Chancery English,* xv. In 1362, Parliament was concerned about the ability of the ordinary citizen to understand court proceedings, to obey the law, and to defend himself and his property in a language other than "the Tongue of the Country" (*la lange du paiis*). Thus, though cases were to be pleaded in English, they were to be enrolled in Latin.

8. Quoted in Fisher, Richardson, and Fisher, *An Anthology of Chancery English,* xvi.

English, underscores the ways in which townsmen saw themselves as joined by a common series of concerns that are best expressed in a common language. When that tongue is embodied in a written form, it can be incorporated into a book, a "memory" of "the needful things that concern us." The Brewers also signal their awareness that the very definition of literacy has expanded to include vernacular literacy, consigning Latin and French (the currencies of privilege) to earlier times.

Despite the sanction for an official English that was frequently linked to the figure of Henry V, during his reign the link between the vernacular and heresy became most pronounced. By 1382, when Archbishop Courtney had mandated against the unlicensed explication of the Scriptures, either in the vulgar tongue or in Latin, the Church began to identify Wyclif and his followers with the provocative issue of language. As Anne Hudson notes, however, it was only in the last years of his life that Wyclif began to focus on the importance of the vernacular. Equally slowly did church authorities come to understand just how troublesome the issue of the vernacular might prove, since the use of it raised the possibility of general discussion of hitherto elitist subjects.[9] With the accession of Henry IV to the throne in 1400—and consequently of Thomas Arundel to the see of Canterbury—official promulgations against irregular preaching or interpretation of the Scriptures or translation of the Bible became more frequent, culminating in 1407 with the *Constitutions* of Archbishop Arundel, which specifically banned translation of the Scriptures into English, disputes about the nature of the sacrament, and possession of works by John Wyclif.[10]

The *Constitutions* made explicit the assumption that the subject of translation was pertinent to that of sedition. Since his own claim to the throne of England had been made before Parliament in 1399 in English (*in lingua materna*), there is a certain irony to Henry IV's attitude toward

9. Hudson, "Lollardy: The English Heresy?" On the problems the Lollards deliberately posed through the issue of translation, see also Hanna, "The Difficulty of Ricardian Prose Translation: The Case of the Lollards"; Hudson, "Wyclif and the English Language"; Peter McNiven, *Heresy and Politics in the Reign of Henry V,* 116. For other discussions of the vernacular as linked to reformist views, see Beckwith, "Problems of Authority in Late Medieval English Mysticism: Language, Agency, and Authority in *The Book of Margery Kempe*," 183–84; Johnson, "*The Shepheardes Calender*": An Introduction, chapter 1; Knapp, *Chaucer and the Social Contest,* 73–75.

10. For the official records of the English Church during the period, see Wilkins, ed., *Concilia Magnae Britanniae et Hiberniae,* vol. 3. For the above, see 123, 157–65, 166–72, 208, 210, 252–54, 254–63, 314–19.

those other "reformers," who argued for the need for a faith manifested in a national tongue. Thus Henry had implicitly imaged himself as one who restored England to its original foundations:

> In the name of Fadir, Son, and Holy Gost, I Henry of Lancastr' chalenge this Rewme of Yngland, and the Corone with all the membres and the appurtenances, als I that am disendit be right lyne of the Blode comyng fro the gude lorde Kyng Henry therde, and thorghe that ryght that God of his grace hath sent me, with helpe of my Kyn and of my Frendes to recover it: the which Rewme was in poynt to be undone for defaut of Governance and undoyng of the gode Lawes.[11]

Henry of Lancaster thus defined himself as a Christian king, who saved the realm from the "defaut of Governance and undoyng of the gode Lawes" into which Richard had impelled it. Henry's use of "defaut" seems a deliberately and delicately poised adjudication: he might here mean to indicate Richard's insufficiency or, more seriously, the damage he had done to government, or, possibly, the crimes Richard had committed in the name of order. The charge was later repeated by Sir William Thirnyng, the chief Justice of the Common Pleas, who announced to Richard (again, in English) the sentences of his deposition. Thirnyng remarked to Richard that the "articles of Defautes in zour Governance" led parliament to decide that Richard was not "worthy" or "sufficeant" or "able" to govern.[12] Henry, implicitly, is neither insufficient, nor unworthy, nor incapable of ruling a realm whose laws, the manifestation of its order, Richard's "defautes" had threatened to undo. If Henry wished his claim to the throne and Richard's crimes to be noted in English, as well as in the French and Latin of parliamentary records, he did not wish his subjects to ponder the articles of their faith in a language all might understand. Or perhaps he knew that revolutions—or reformations—are also rhetorical acts.

The subject of the translation of the Scriptures into English was key for Lollard sympathizers and preachers. Such figures as John Trevisa made

11. *Rotuli Parliamentorum*, III, 1 Hen. IV, nu. 53, pp. 422–23. I have altered abbreviations. McNiven (*Heresy and Politics in the Reign of Henry V,* 69) also talks about this speech, but from a different angle.
12. *Rot. Parl.*, III, nu. 59, p. 424.

eloquent arguments for the need for English translations of important works. For example, in the "Dialogue between a Lord and a Clerk upon Translation," which appears in his translation of Ranulf Higden's *Poly-chronicon,* Trevisa allows the Lord to become the major spokesman for the need for translation. Trevisa, like later apologists, based his argument on historical precedent, drawing upon the examples of important figures from England's significant past, like King Alfred, who translated, or had translated, works of philosophy, theology, and law, as well as portions of the Scriptures, into the vernacular, and Caedmon, who was inspired by the Holy Ghost to make poetry in English. After Caedmon, Trevisa moves to Bede, using him as a sanction for the translation of the Bible:

> Also þe holy man Beda translatede Seint Iohn hys gospel out of Latyn ynto Englysch. Also þou wost where þe Apocalips ys ywryte in þe walles and roof of a chapel boþe in Latyn and yn Freynsch. Also þe gospel and prophecy and þe ry3t [fey] of holy churche mot be tau3t and ypreched to englyschmen þat conneþ no Latyn. þanne þe gospel and prophecy and þe ry3t fey of holy cherche mot be told ham an Englysch, and þat ys no3t ydo bote by Englysch translacion. Vor such Englysch prechyng ys verrey Englysch translacion, and such Englysch prechyng ys good and neodful; þanne Englysch translacion ys good and neodfol.[13]

Trevisa first establishes historical authority for translation in the three sentences that begin with the word "also." Where Bede made an English book out of a Latin one, an unknown craftsman used the Church itself as his medium, translating the Book of Apocalypse into the very fabric of his building. Moving from something that is at once text and icon (or example) to the living word manifested in preaching, Trevisa draws the conclusions from these precedents in the final sentence, where the word "then" underlines the syllogistic nature of his proof. As he says, "telling" can only be accomplished through translation, for "such" English preaching constitutes an act of "very" translation, both of which are "good and needful" to

---

13. Ronald Waldron, "Trevisa's Original Prefaces on Translation: A Critical Edition," in *Medieval English Studies Presented to George Kane,* ed. Donald, Waldron, and Wittig, 292–93. For another edition, see John Trevisa, *Dialogue between a Lord and a Clerk upon Translation,* in Pollard, ed., *Fifteenth Century Prose and Verse,* 206–7. For discussions of Trevisa and of his patron, Lord Berkeley, see Hanna, "Sir Thomas Berkeley and His Patronage"; J. Taylor, *The "Universal Chronicle" of Ranulf Higden,* 134–37. Taylor also cites the above passage.

those who know no Latin. This argument, which would be repeated throughout the fifteenth and sixteenth centuries, established reform as a faithful rendering of venerable, and indeed nationalistic, tradition. The Lollards, like their sixteenth-century heirs, do not describe themselves as breaking with the past, but as reclaiming a past that has been obscured by the inequities of the present.[14]

Like Henry of Lancaster, whose claim in English to the English throne was based upon his assertion of his righteousness, his lineage, and his intention of restoring England to its primordial order, the heirs of Wyclif emphasized the anteriority of their status as faithful (and English) Christians. Their characteristic description of the mendicants as these "newe" orders was thus intended to recall the practices of the primitive Church and the consequent lapses or transgressions ("defaute" is commonly used) of the contemporary Church.[15] Most notably, they suggested that by declining to speak the language of the people, the Church failed to provide a foundation for faith. Possibly the most forceful apology for biblical translation is chapter xv of the general prologue to the Wycliffite Bible.[16] There, the translator not only identifies the labor as an act of "comune charite" but as an act designed "to saue alle men in oure rewme."[17] These prefatory remarks go beyond establishing the historic precedent for biblical translation and, as in Trevisa, link translation to interpretation as representing an extension of textual commentary.[18] The author therefore advocates translating "aftir the sentence" rather than "aftir the wordis," taking care to "make the sentence as trewe and open in English as it is in

14. On this subject, see Margaret Aston, *England's Iconoclasts;* Johnson, *"The Shepheardes Calender": An Introduction,* chapter 1.

15. My remarks here are drawn from the impression one gains on reading the three volumes entitled *English Wycliffite Sermons,* ed. Hudson and Gradon. The word "defaute" recurs throughout the collection, as does the constant repetition of phrases like "þes newe ordris." For a discussion of the ways in which the primitive Church was used in reference to reform, see Olsen, "The Idea of the *Ecclesia Primitiva* in the Writings of the Twelfth-Century Canonists." For Chaucer's use of the image of the primitive Church in the *Second Nun's Tale,* see Johnson, "Chaucer's Tale of the Second Nun and the Strategies of Dissent."

16. See Forshall and Madden, eds., *The Holy Bible,* 1:56–60. Hereafter, this will be cited as the Wycliffite Bible. Both the general prologue and other Lollard treatises commonly employ language that sounds semipopulist. Chapter xv is also reprinted in Hudson, ed., *Selections from English Wycliffite Writings,* 67–72. For Hudson's commentary on the chapter, see 173–77.

17. Wycliffite Bible, general prologue, 57.

18. The final phrase here is Copeland's. On the rhetorical convention of seeing translation as an act of interpretation, see Copeland, "Rhetoric and Vernacular Translation in the Middle Ages."

Latyn."[19] He ends the chapter by suggesting that good translation is a sign of both labor and grace: "Therefore a translatour hath greet nede to studie wel the sentence, both bifore and aftir, and loke that suche equiuok wordis acorde with the sentence, and he hath nede to lyue a clene lif, and be ful deuout in preirs, and haue not his wit ocupied about worldi thingis, that the Holi Spiryt, autour of wisdom, and kunnyng, and truthe, dresse him in his werk, and suffre him not for to erre."[20]

By associating good translation with good living, the author describes the translator as an emblem every bit as potent as the text that issues from his pen. Only if study is complemented by "clene lif" and devotion will the Holy Spirit find the translator an acceptable medium. The author then employs the New Testament metaphor of clothing to describe spiritual readiness and defines the fully prepared translator as "dressed" in God's own work, which is Scripture. Implicitly, the translator serves as a "text" inscribed by God, whose wisdom, knowledge, and truth are further manifested in a translation free from error. At once passive and active, the translator studies so that he himself may be infused with the wisdom necessary to do more than simply translate word for word. Like a true preacher, the translator, whom the author refers to as a "symple man," is the medium through which God's truth is made apparent to those otherwise prevented from apprehending the word of God.

Later Lollard arguments for biblical translation are more polemic than that found in the general prologue. Once Archbishop Arundel had linked biblical translation with heresy and treason, writers and preachers seemed to focus more on the erroneous assumptions of those who disallowed the translation of the Scriptures into English. For example, the early fifteenth-century tract, "On Translating the Bible into English," begins: "Aȝens hem þat seyn þat Holi Wryt / schulde not or may not be drawen into / Engliche, we maken þes resouns."[21] The author not only reminds the reader of examples from the past like Bede and King Alfred, but also recalls England's more recent history in the closing lines of the tract where he praises King Richard (and implicitly criticizes the present Lancastrian government) for his espousal of biblical translation, Queen Anne for owning a vernacular Bible, and then *Chancellor* Thomas Arundel for his

---

19. Wycliffite Bible, general prologue, 57. The latter expectation is repeated again on 58.
20. Wycliffite Bible, general prologue, 60. For a detailed discussion of Wyclif's views on "good" translation, see Jeffrey, "Chaucer and Wyclif."
21. Bühler, "A Lollard Tract: On Translating the Bible into English," ll. 1–3.

funeral sermon for Queen Anne in which he praised her for what *Arch-bishop* Arundel had ruled was illegal and dangerous: "not-wiþstanding þat sche was an / alien borne, sche hadde on Engliche al þe foure Gospeleris / wiþ þe doctoris vpon hem" (ll. 295–97). According to the author, Arun-del went on to recommend the value and integrity of a Wycliffite Bible, complete with glosses. Queen Anne is thus praised for an act of both devotion and patriotism: an alien, she nonetheless owned and read the Gospels in her adopted tongue. The treatise bears out Henry IV's fears that Lollard views might well lead to sedition; in criticizing Archbishop Arundel, the author inevitably objected to a national policy of suppres-sion and raised the dangerous specter of King Richard II, a ghost who was not laid to rest until Henry V transferred his remains to Westminster to lie beside Queen Anne.[22] Kempe's description of Margery as listening to the same texts ("þe Bybyl wyth doctowrys þer-up-on" [143]) is more cautious; she is careful to defend Margery's orthodoxy by reassuring her readers that Margery is illiterate and that a priest, a licensed member of the church, read such material to her.[23] As she implies, the truth Margery hears was filtered through and authorized by a church actively opposed to a translation that was judged an act of heretical interpretation.[24]

A similarly aggressive strategy can be found in other Lollard texts. A sermon from the Wycliffite sermon cycle that discusses the persecution Christ warned his disciples they would face establishes a link between the past and present by describing the anti-Lollard atmosphere of contempo-rary England. The author notes that one bishop of England is persecuting a priest for preaching Christ's gospel "wiþowte fables" and another for writing in English, concluding that "þe perelows tyme is comen þat Crist and Powle teldon byfore." He takes comfort, however, from the number of knights who yearn to read the gospel and "han wylle" to read in English "the gospel of Cristus ly3f."[25] The authors of the sermons look to the Bible for precedent, noting that Christ was able to read (see Luke 4).

22. For discussions of the "specter" of King Richard, see Aston, "Lollardy and Sedition, 1381–1431," 20, 34; Deanesly, *The Lollard Bible and Other Medieval Biblical Versions,* 282–83.

23. For a discussion of these texts, see Hargreaves, "Popularizing Biblical Scholarship: The Role of the Wycliffite *Glossed Gospels.*" Of the manuscripts Hargreaves refers to, I have used two that, combined, contain commentaries on all four Gospels: Oxford Bodleian MS. Bodley 243 (Luke and John) and London BL Additional MS. 41175 (Matthew and Mark).

24. The ways in which both the Wycliffite Bible and the Wycliffite gospel glosses are bol-stered by constant reference to exegetical authority suggests the writers' awareness of the relation-ship between the act of translating and that of glossing.

25. *English Wycliffite Sermons,* 2:64.

The author of the Wycliffite treatise, *Tractatus Regibus,* begins what is a book of political advice with remarks about the sorry state of English in England, "trowthe moveþ mony men to speke sentencis in yngelysche þat þai hav gedirid in latyne, and her fore bene men holden heretikis."[26] But it is the author of the radical Lollard text, the *Lanterne of Light,* who most explicitly draws a connection betwen literacy, translation, heresy, and treason. He says that these days the fiend (who is apparently alive and well in Lancastrian England) looks for

> ony peple þat wole rede priue or apert Goddis lawe in englische þat is oure modir tunge anoon he schal be sumned to come aforne hise iuggis to answere what is seide to him & bring his book wiþ him and eiþer he must forsake his book & reding of englische & algates he scal forswere to speke of holi writ. þei sein lyue as þi fadir dide & þat is ynow for þee. . . . For who dar now in þise daies talke of Crist or þe doom & certis þe bodi may not lyue wiþouten bodili food no more may þe celi soule wiþouten Goddis worde.[27]

As the author suggests, the person who separates himself or herself from others (including the illiteracy of his ancestors) and presumes to read the Bible in English shall be summoned to appear before judges. The book he must bring with him serves as a token of his act of separation, a book he must then forswear, along with his "modir tunge," and holy speech. Vernacular devotion is thus defined as heretical. The author goes on to say he lives in a time without true preachers and that any true one, like John the Baptist, will be persecuted "for a cursed Lollard."[28] John the Baptist was, of course, persecuted not by the ecclesiastical authorities but by (or through) Herod; as the author of the *Lanterne of Light* implies, the Church, like Herodias, works through the ruler to silence any criticism of its relationship to secular powers.

It is therefore no coincidence that English can seem a sign of radicalism when it appears in official records. For example, in the records of ecclesiastical legislation during the first half of the fifteenth century, the English statements of accused Lollards seem to proclaim their independence of

---

26. Genet, ed., *Four English Political Tracts of the Later Middle Ages,* 5.
27. Swenburn, ed., *The Lanterne of Light,* 100.
28. Swenburn, ed., *The Lanterne of Light,* 101.

contemporary convention. Inserted into the Latin records of Oldcastle's trial before Archbishop Arundel, for example, is his own statement of religious identity: "I Johan Oldcastell, knyght, lord of Cobham, wole, that all cristyn men wyte, and undirstond . . ." (Significantly, the *Fasciculi Zizaniorum* records a spurious *Latin* abjuration by Oldcastle, which focuses more on Oldcastle's submission to authority than on points of theology.)[29] In 1425, the official records contain (*in Anglico scriptam*) the recantations of the Lollard priest Robert Hoke of the diocese of Lincoln, made before the cross at Saint Paul's, and that of William Russell. Both men confessed to entertaining Lollard beliefs. In addition, Hoke confessed to owning a number of contraband books and Russell to teaching and preaching false doctrines. In 1428, the records contain further vernacular confessions, those of Thomas Gaventer and Richard Monk.[30] By recording such confessions in the native English of the speakers, the authorities signify not only the relatively low social status of the heretics, but the heretics' rhetorical dissociation from the official Church. They also signify their awareness that such a document recorded in English served to proclaim the fundamental weakness of a group that celebrated its identity as a movement away from the Latin of the compromised and materialistic Roman foundation. If we hear Hawissa Moone of Loddon in East Anglia forswear her heretical allegiances in the language we ourselves speak, are we not reminded of the power of an ecclesiastical authority that can bring to heel those who turn out to be no martyrs to the cause of heterodoxy?[31]

For this reason, figures like William Thorpe and John Oldcastle, who maintained their beliefs in the face of persecution were used to point up the dark irony of a Church turning upon members whose espousal of Christlike simplicity was their only crime. The sixteenth-century reformers, of course, saw the inherent value of the stories of Lollard persecutions, carefully transcribing manuscripts and collecting documents that provided their contemporaries with a link to the immediate past.[32] As Ritchie D.

29. Wilkins, ed., *Concilia Magnae Britanniae et Hiberniae,* 3:354–55; Shirley, ed., *Fasciculi Zizaniorum,* 414–16.

30. See Wilkins, ed., *Concilia Magnae Britanniae et Hiberniae,* 3:437, 438–59, 493–503. The most important collection of Lollard confessions is that edited by Tanner in *Heresy Trials in the Diocese of Norwich, 1428–31.*

31. For text and notes, see Hudson, *English Wycliffite Writings,* 34–37; 159–61.

32. On this important topic, see Aston, *England's Iconoclasts.* As Aston notes, both the *Lanterne of Light* and William Thorpe's account of his trial were in print by around 1530 (158).

Kendall notes, by seeking to uproot Lollards, the ecclesiastical authorities instead provided the reformers with their own "recurrent drama of redemptive sacrifice."[33] *The Examination of Master William Thorpe* served as a model text that presented the defendant as, like Susannah among the elders, innocent of and hard-pressed to defend himself against the crimes of which he is unjustly accused by lesser men.[34] The *Examination* is particularly important because it is a fiction, a re-creation of an actual event that is presented in dialogue form, hence, as drama.[35] Thorpe's preface to his *Examination* explicitly justifies his account (which he sees as a condemnation of the blindness and willfulness of his fellow Christians) on exemplary grounds. Not only does the account describe itself as creating a truthful written record of his trial before Arundel, but it serves as an example of "mine Apposing and mine Answering" that is available to all others who find themselves in dire straits.[36] What follows is a carefully and logically worked-out Lollard catechism, in which key topics like the sacrament, images, pilgrimages, tithing, oath-taking, and confession are raised by Archbishop Arundel and his clerk and discussed by Thorpe. Throughout, Thorpe presents himself as self-assured and rational and Arundel as increasingly irrational and bombastic. Where Thorpe's language is the dispassionate language of rhetorical persuasion, Arundel's tends to be colloquial, personal, and barely controlled. As Kendall suggests, the obvious model here is Christ's examination, where Christ's dignified silence throws into high relief the noise and frustration of Annas and Caiphas.[37] What Thorpe thus provides in his *Examination* is a text in the vernacular that illuminates the dramatic possibilities of the confrontation between Lollards and figures of civil and ecclesiastical authority. In so doing, he anchors the chief tenets of Lollard thought to a particular situation and set of personalities in a way that makes the abstract available and memorable.

33. Kendall, *The Drama of Dissent*, 57.

34. For a modernized text, see *The Examination of Master William Thorpe*. A small part of this examination is freshly edited by Anne Hudson in *English Wycliffite Writings*, 29–33. For Hudson's commentary on the text and its provenance, see 159–61. Thorpe's comparison of his own condition to that of Susannah comes early in the interview with Archbishop Arundel (113). As Hudson notes (*The Premature Reformation*, 153–54), in 1392, John Belgrave posted a pamphlet on the doors of Saint Martin's church in Leicester comparing the archdeacon's official who was due to hold court there the following day with the elders who condemned Susannah.

35. For a discussion of the text in relation to later reformist treatises, see Kendall, *The Drama of Dissent*, 59–67.

36. *The Examination of Master William Thorpe*, 102.

37. Kendall, *The Drama of Dissent*, 57, 59.

We find the same powerful use of English in the *credo* of John Oldcastle:

> I Johan Oldcastell, knyght, lord of Cobham, wole, that all cristyn men wyte, and undirstond, that I clepe allmyghty God in to wytness, that it hath ben, now ys, and ever wyth the help of God shall ben myn entent, and my wylle, to beleve feythfully and fully all the sacramentis, that evyr God ordeyned to be do in holy churche; and more over for to declare me in these foure peyntes: I beleve, that the most worschipfull sacrament of the auter is Cristes body in forme of bred, the same body that was born of the blyssyd virgyne, our lady seint Marye, don on the cross, deed and buryed, the thrydde day ros fro deth to lyf, the wych body is now glorified in hevene. Also as for the sacrament of penance, I beleve, that it is nedfull to every man, that shall be saved, to forsake synne, and do due penance for synne bifore doon, wyth trewe confession, very contrition and duhe satisfaction, as Goddes lawe lymiteth and techeth, and ellys may not be saved. Whych penaunce I desir all men to do. And of as ymages I undirstonde, that thei be not of bileve, but that they were ordeyned syth the bileve was zewe of Crist be sufferaunce of the churche, to be kalenders to lewed men, to represent and brynge to mynde the passion of our lord Jhesu Crist, and martirdom and good lyvyng of other seyntes, and that who so it be that doth the worschipe to dede ymages, that is duhe to God, or putteth seych hope or trust in help of them, as he shuld do to God, or hath affeccion in on more than in an other, he doth in that the grete synne of mawmentrie. Also I suppose this fully, that every man in this erthe is a pilgrime towarde blyss, or toward peyne, and that he that knoweth not, ne wole not knowe, ne kepe the holy comandementes of God in his lyvyng here, al be it, that he be goo on pylgrimage to all the world, and he dy so, he shall be dampned; and he that knowyth the holy comandementys of God, and kepeth hem hys end, he shall be saved, tho' he nevir in hys lyve go on pilgrymage, as men use now to Cantirbury, or to Rome, or to any othir place.[38]

---

38. In Wilkins, *Concilia Magnae*, 3:354–55. Almost directly after Oldcastle's statement of belief, a statement of official doctrine is included *in English*.

I have included Oldcastle's entire statement because it serves to epitomize the ways in which English could be used to present a public statement of belief that was at once an apology and a defense. The focus, here,
is on the self, its subjective recognition of guilt, use of *temporalia,* and
apprehension of the word of God. He goes through the same series of
topics as does Thorpe in his *Examination,* but Oldcastle presents them as
though he were reciting a creed, something that could be committed to
memory and used by anyone who might need the carefully worded sentences of Lord Cobham. Though neither Oldcastle nor Thorpe escaped
punishment, they nonetheless provided contemporaries with pictures, like
those of Susannah or Christ before their judges, that underscored the
ineffectual nature of worldly power and privilege and the ultimate freedom (and potentially subversive impulses) of the private self.

The heterodox were not, however, the only ones concerned with the
vernacular. A large body of vernacular devotional texts were sanctioned,
and in many cases commissioned, by key members of the Church. Works
like the relatively early *Lay Folks Mass Book,* which exists in a number of
manuscripts, attest to the need for a vernacular guide to the Mass. It is to
the Carthusians that we owe a number of works of devotion, such as *The
Chastising of God's Children,* as well as translations of the works of Rolle
and his school; and for the non-Latinate nuns of Syon, works like *The
Orcherd of Syon* and *The Mirror of Our Lady* provided the basis for devotional and liturgical instruction. The translators of such texts can, however, be differentiated from those with Wycliffite sympathies; they are
careful to justify their roles as translators in terms of their fundamental
orthodoxy and to specify the ways in which these texts should be used by
a private reader. The translator of *The Mirror of Our Lady* not only says
that the translation of the Office of the Virgin is intended for simple souls,
but inveighs against indiscriminate translation before going on to explain
each detail of the service and, inevitably, to seek to control the nun's
response at each point in it. Similarly, the very plan of Saint Catherine of
Siena's *Dialogue* suggests an orderly or prescribed reading experience: the
book is an "orchard" with "alleys" for refreshment, not a meadow
through which we wander at our wills.[39]

One of the great prose texts of the early fifteenth century is Nicholas
Love's *Mirror of the Blessed Life of Jesus Christ,* a translation of the Latin

---

39. See Blunt, ed., *The Mirror of Our Lady,* 3, 7; Hodgson and Leegey, eds., *The Orcherd of
Syon,* chapter 5.

Meditationes Vitae Christi, erroneously attributed to Bonaventure.[40] Conceived of as an answer to the Wycliffite Bible, the *Mirror* testifies to Archbishop Arundel's keen appraisal of his contemporaries' need for a vernacular Gospel. As Jonathan Hughes has argued, the circumstances surrounding the composition of the *Mirror,* which was begun in 1408, suggest that Arundel and his circle were consciously asserting control over the production and circulation of religious literature.[41] Love's work, like its Latin original, is designed as a guide to private meditation. In the final chapter of the *Meditationes* the author thus suggests that the reader, rather than be overwhelmed by the "weighty mass" of material in the entire volume, might divide the account of Christ's life according to the days of the week, reading only so much each day as can become the subject of private devotion. He notes that, by following such a weekly schedule of meditations, the reader will be able—like Saint Cecilia—to place Christ's life ("as she did the Gospel") "inseparably" in her heart.[42] The act of reading is conceived of as an aid both to meditation and memory, for the "text" of Christ's life is best inscribed upon, or preserved in, the heart. Love shifts this suggestion to his proem, using it as a means of prescribing the ways in which the *Mirror* is intended to be used by its readers:

> And for als mich as þis boke is dyuydet & departet in vij parties, after vij dayes of þe wike, euery day on partie or sume þerof to be hade in contemplacion of hem þat hauen þerto desire & deuocion. Þerefore at þe Moneday as þe first werke day of þe wike, bygynneþ þis gostly werke, tellyng first of þe deuoute instance & desire of þe holy angeles in heuen for mans restoryng, // and his sauacion, to stire man amongis oþer þat day specialy to wyrshipe hem, as holy chirch þe same day makeþ speciale mynde of hem. Also not

---

40. For analyses of Love's contribution to the history of English prose, see Salter, "Nicholas Love—A Fifteenth Century Translator"; idem, "Continuity and Change in Middle English Versions of *Meditationes Vitae Christi*"; idem, *Nicholas Love's "Myrrour of the Blessed Lyf of Jesu Crist."* Salter's monograph, in particular, considers the history of translations into English, as well as offering a careful stylistic analysis of Love's achievement.

41. For a discussion of the background for the *Mirror,* see Hughes, *Pastors and Visionaries,* 228–32. For a discussion of the English Church during the reign of Henry V, see Catto, "Religious Change under Henry V," in *Henry V: The Practice of Kingship,* ed. Harriss; Haines, *Ecclesia Anglicana;* Jacob, *Archbishop Henry Chichele;* Swanson, *Church and Society in Late Medieval England.*

42. See Ragusa and Green, eds. and trans., *Meditations on the Life of Christ,* 387–88. On the function of memory in relation to the act of reading, see Carruthers, *The Book of Memory,* 180, 255.

onelych þe matire of þis boke is pertynent & profitable to be hade in contemplacion þe forseide dayes, to hem þat wolen & mowen. bot also as it longeþ to þe tymes of þe ʒere, as in aduent to rede & deuoutly haue in mynde fro þe bigynnyng in to þe Natiuite of oure lorde Jesu & þere of after in þat holy feste of Cristenmesse, & so forþ of oþer matires as holy chirch makeþ mynde of hem in tyme of þe ʒere.[43]

By placing these remarks in the proem and by amplifying the suggestions he found in the final chapter of his original, Love establishes the relationship he maintains throughout the text between himself and his reader, who is probably, but not necessarily, female.[44] From the beginning of the *Mirror*, Love seems an omniscient and omnipotent guide, even less willing than the author of the *Meditationes* to sanction an entirely subjective use of the Gospel story. Where the pseudo-Bonaventure wrote in Latin to a female religious, offering a work that he clearly saw as both text and gloss (a text of Christ's life clarified by the words of authorities such as Saint Bernard), Love explicitly offers the *Mirror* for the edification of "symple creatures" whose ignorance of Latin necessitates images that arouse an understanding of the manhood of Christ: "ande þerfore to hem is pryncipally to be sette in mynde þe ymage of crystes Incarnacion passioun & Resurreccion so that a symple soule þat kan not þenke bot bodyes or bodily þinges mowe haue somwhat accordynge vnto is affecion where wiþ he may fede & stire his deuocion."[45] Love here directly confronts the Lollards, who saw the images of religious art as well as those produced by dramatic enactments of Gospel events or fanciful embroiderings on those events as extratextual and therefore potentially misleading, if not idolatrous. Love, like many an apologist before him, affirms the use of images as aids to devotion, since through the material world we can begin to estimate the nature of the spiritual.[46] In particular, for those "symple soules" who can only think in tactile or corporeal terms, images serve to "feed" and to "stir" devotion. If the followers of John Wyclif described the word of God in the vernacular as nurture enough for the simple souls who did not know

43. Sargent, ed., *Nicholas Love's "Mirror,"* 13.
44. See Sargent, ed., *Nicholas Love's "Mirror,"* 10.
45. Sargent, ed., *Nicholas Love's "Mirror,"* 10.
46. For the debate about images, see Aston, *England's Iconoclasts*, especially 124–54.

Latin, Love stresses their need for an English text that is "more pleyne in certeyne partyes" than the Gospels, "þe whiche as childryn hauen nede to be fedde with mylke of lyȝte doctryne & not with sadde mete of grete clargye & of [hye contemplacion]."[47]

Though Love is faithful to his original and does not exclude scenes like Christ's cleansing of the Temple, scenes that well might trigger Lollard remarks about the state of the contemporary Church, he nonetheless subtly guides the reader's response to certain events in an effort to convey the relationship between orthodoxy and order. For example, when discussing Christ's request that John baptize him, commonly glossed as an illustration of Christ's perfect humility, Love describes the "first degre" of humility in relation to contemporary social codes whereby "a man to be suget and lowed to his souereyne, & not preferred or hiede aboue him þat is euen with him in astate."[48] Love heightens our sense of the meaning of Christ's submission to John by offering two equivalents, *suget* and *lowed,* both of which reflect the strata of a social hierarchy, just as *preferred* and *hiede* suggest the dangers of social presumption. In his choice of the word *souereyne,* Love suggests the very basis for social organization and thus for the most basic and natural form of humility. Love does more than simply translate from Latin into English; he translates what is an abstract concept—humility—into language that speaks directly to the conventional stances of an age that conceived of chaos as something like social rebellion.

Love's treatment of the passage in Luke 4, where Jesus reads from the book of Isaiah in the synagogue, is carefully shaped to preclude the sort of emphasis upon literacy and the need for vernacular instruction in the Scriptures found in some Lollard discussions of Luke 4.[49] Where the author of the *Meditations* simply describes Jesus as humbly rising up to read in the synagogue, Love seeks to authorize Christ's assumption of the office of reader by stressing his priestly function. He says that "he rose vp fort rede in maner of a minstere or a clerke," and a few lines later repeats the simile by saying, "Now take hede of him how mekely at þe byginnyng

47. Sargent, ed., *Nicholas Love's "Mirror,"* 10. For remarks on Love's public, see Salter, "Nicholas Love—A Fifteenth Century Translator."
48. Sargent, ed., *Nicholas Love's "Mirror,"* 66. Compare, "The first is submission to a superior and not placing oneself before an equal"; *Meditations,* 107.
49. See Hudson and Gradon, eds., *English Wycliffite Sermons,* 3:26–27. In the Wycliffite glossed Gospel of Luke (MS. Bodley 243), the verses are described as emphasizing Christ's role as teacher and his perfect humility.

he takep vp on him þe office of a redere as it were a symple clerke."[50] By emphasizing Jesus' humility and his careful observance of decorum, Love subtly suggests that the office of reader does not belong to every man or woman, but to authorized servants of the Church.

In its picture of Jesus as a loving and obedient son, a nurturing leader, and a gentle and humble lord, the *Mirror* not only remains faithful to the devotional tone of the *Meditations;* it also conveys the social and familial values of the late Middle Ages.[51] Gospel events like the Marriage at Cana are described with an attention to detail that serves to translate the circumstances of Christ's first miracle into a language common to townspersons who understand the nuances of extended family relations and the distinctions of social degree. Like its source, the *Mirror* places Mary in the foreground, presenting her as the figure for whom Jesus has the most care, inserting her into scenes where we might not expect to find her, and transforming her into the matriarchal figure familiar to us from the *N-Town Cycle*. By emphasizing the feminine, however, the *Mirror* does not exploit the political or social implications of gender stereotypes and point up the revolutionary aspects of the gospel narrative. Instead, it offers a picture of Christ—and implicitly of the Church—as deriving authority from holiness, gentleness, and care for others. The work is sprinkled with similes that underline the "motherly" aspects of the divine. Love compares Christ's care for his disciples to a mother's care for her sons, since he rises up in the night "priuely and softly" to re-cover those who were "vnhilede," "for he loued hem ful tendurly knowyng what he wolde make of hem." Love also retains the scriptural analogy likening Christ and his disciples to a mother hen surrounded by her chicks.[52] The caregiver God is a fully social God, one who lives in a network of relationships and whose ministry is in some measure defined in relation to a fully social existence. The decision to translate the *Meditations* into English was an inspired one; in its emphasis upon everyday life, on the many details and images that compose a life, it locates the divine in a sphere we ourselves inhabit. By directing his translation at a reader whose involvement in the world does not preclude her hunger for a devotional life, Love testifies to

---

50. Sargent, ed., *Nicholas Love's "Mirror,"* 79.

51. For discussions of these, especially in relation to East Anglia, see Ashley and Sheingorn, *Interpreting Cultural Symbols: Saint Anne in Late Medieval Society;* Gibson, *The Theater of Devotion,* especially 29; idem, "Saint Anne and the Religion of Childbed: Some East Anglian Texts and Talismans," in Ashley and Sheingorn.

52. See Sargent, ed., *Nicholas Love's "Mirror,"* 80, 88.

the Church's wish to channel the devotional energy of its worshipers toward ends where subjective response did not become rebellion.

What emerges from even a brief survey of the subject of translation during the first decades of the fifteenth century is a dialogue about the uses of the vernacular. Translators were clearly aware that what was committed to the vernacular was potentially volatile, since it had escaped the implicit control effected by Latinity, the language of elite culture and instruction. Vernacular texts could be read by anyone who could read to anyone who would listen, inspiring a debate about the sort of texts that should be available in English. The history of works like *Piers Plowman* bears witness to the "usability" of vernacular works that might be variously categorized as spiritual autobiography, social criticism, or ecclesiastical satire: the number of manuscripts of all three versions of that poem suggests how many readers, well into the sixteenth century, found it meaningful to the various circumstances of their lives and times.[53] The fact that Love added an anti-Wycliffite treatise on the Eucharist as an epilogue to the *Mirror* reveals his (or Archbishop Arundel's) sense of the ways in which vernacular texts might, if "misinterpreted," work to unknown ends. Love's treatise on the sacrament attacks Wyclif for trusting to Aristotle and reason, rather than to the authorities of the Church—that is, to his own senses and not to his superiors, superiors like Hugh of Lincoln and Gregory the Great, or to his memories of miraculous stories that had accrued around the Host by the late Middle Ages: "he ʒaf more credence // to þe doctrine of Arestotele / þat stant onely in naturele reson of man. þan he dide to þe doctrine of holy chirch & þe trewe doctours þerof touching þis preciouse sacrament."[54] Love casts doubt on exactly the subjectivism he seeks both to stimulate and to ameliorate in his translation of the *Meditations* with its carefully scripted exercises for the private devotee.

Throughout the *Book,* Kempe reveals her sensitivity to the tone of the debate about literacy and the uses of the vernacular. Though she locates the *Book*'s action during a period of anti-Lollard activity, she maintains that the *Book* was written some twenty years or more after it was lived. Kempe thereby distances herself (and her reader) from Margery and from activities that are manifestly suspicious. Moreover, Kempe thoroughly

---

53. See Middleton, "The Audience and Public of *Piers Plowman,*" in *Middle English Alliterative Poetry and Its Literary Background,* ed. Lawton; King, *English Reformation Literature,* 319–47.
54. Sargent, ed., *Nicholas Love's "Mirror,"* 238.

muddies the issue of her own or Margery's literacy. The scribe, who plays a major role in the text, shields Kempe from authorities even as he authorizes the text she provides. That text is explicitly presented as Margery's life, memorialized, and then transcribed by one whose ability to read and write enables him to serve the will of God manifested through Margery, the holy woman. The *Book*'s fiction demands that its protagonist be illiterate, the embodiment of the living word whose memories of a lifelong relationship with Jesus are translated for us into our common tongue.

Since the scribe writes *about* Margery—as opposed to Kempe adopting the "I" of the autobiographer—he can present aspects of Margery's use of and attitude toward language that are suspicious, as well as defend her against charges of Lollardy. For example, the issue of swearing was a sticking point for those with Lollard sympathies: when Chaucer's Parson reproves Harry Bailey for swearing, the Host replies derisively, "I smelle a Lollere in the wynd" (II [B1] 1173). Margery's dislike of swearing, which Kempe mentions on at least three important occasions, is one mark of her isolation from the group. The first occasion suggests the possible dangers Margery's feelings might incur and confers official sanction for her disapproval of oaths. When at Lambeth, seeking an audience with the Archbishop of Canterbury, Margery warns the Archbishop's clerks that "þei schuld ben dampnyd but þei left her sweryng & oþer synnes þat þei vsyd" (36). With that, a woman steps forward and threatens her with a heretic's death by fire. Later, in a private audience with Archbishop Arundel himself, Kempe describes Margery as warning him about the behavior of his men, "My Lord, owyr alderes Lord al-myty God hath not ȝon ȝow ȝowyr benefys & gret goodys of þe world to may[n]ten wyth hys tretowrys & hem þat slen hym euery day be gret othys sweryng. ȝe schal answer for hem les þan ȝe correctyn hem or ellys put hem owt of ȝowr seruyse" (37). Kempe then describes Arundel as taking "benyngly" and "mekely" what is a critique of his spiritual stewardship for which he will be called to answer on Judgment Day. In her account of this sequence Kempe seems to raise the issue of swearing as a way of raising that of Lollardy. However, by doing so in her account of Margery's visit to the seat of the Archbishop of Canterbury and in a private conversation with the man who presided over the trials of William Sawtre, John Badby, and Sir John Oldcastle, Kempe "acquits" Margery of heresy.

Kempe's characterization of Archbishop Arundel as meekly suffering Margery's reproval is especially curious in light of William Thorpe's handling of the dialogue between himself and Arundel on the same subject.

Thorpe's alleged preaching against swearing is one of the points Arundel wishes clarified, and Thorpe's reply recasts the accusation into a conversation about the nature of and hence the use of material signs. Thorpe first says that one should swear (and only then taking God as a witness) only if "a man may not excuse him without oath to them that have power to compel him to swear."[55] Thorpe then goes on to explain why it is not "lawful" to swear upon a book because "every book is nothing else but diverse creatures, of which it is made of: therefore to swear upon a book is to swear by creatures! and this swearing is ever unleful." Backing himself up with authorities like Saint John Chrysostom and Saint Jerome, Thorpe affirms that the true Gospel is not the book, the tangible object, but the word of God engraved in the heart of the believer. Archbishop Arundel's reaction to Thorpe's dispassionate exposition upon swearing is far less meek than his reaction to Margery's attack on his pastoral care. To Thorpe he says finally, "Well, well, thou wilt judge thy sovereigns! By God! the King doeth not his duty, but he suffer thee to be condemned!"[56] What Arundel here responds to is Thorpe's temerity in reproving his superiors, an action that is cast as treasonous. A commentary about the nascent relationship between oath-taking and idolatry is consequently transformed into an act of political intransigency.

If Thorpe's purpose is to image himself as the imitator of Christ, who was also unjustly accused of fomenting revolution, Kempe's fiction is more ambiguous. Her picture of Archbishop Arundel is a positive one. He grants Margery a private interview in his garden, an interview that lasts until the stars appear in the sky, and gives her a letter granting her the right to choose her own confessor and to receive the sacrament every Sunday. He listens to an account ot Margery's life and approves Margery's manner of living. He then meekly accepts Margery's critique of his pastoral care. Later, on a visit to the diocese of York, Margery confronts Archbishop Henry Bowet, another ecclesiastic known for his anti-Lollard activities. Although Bowet can find nothing against her, he, like a modern-day Pilate, wishes her away from his jurisdiction. He asks her, "Ley þin hand on þe boke her be-forn me & swer þat þu xalt gon owt of my diocyse as sone as þu may" (125). Margery refuses to take a dishonest vow, saying, "Nay syr . . . ȝeue me leue to gon ageyn in-to ȝorke to

---

55. *Examination of Master William Thorpe,* in Pollard, 150. See also Compston, "The Thirty-Seven Conclusions of the Lollards," article 14.
56. *Examination of Master William Thorpe,* in Pollard, 155.

take my leue of my frendys."⁵⁷ Bowet then offers her another chance at oath-taking, "þow schalt sweryn þat þu [ne] xalt techyn ne chalengyn þe pepil in my diocyse." Margery refuses, "Nay, syr, I xal not sweryn . . . for I xal spekyn of God & vndirnemyn hem þat sweryn gret othys wher-so-euyr I go vn-to þe tyme þat þe Pope & Holy Chirche hath ordeynde þat no man schal be so hardy to spekyn of God, for God al-mythy forbedith not, ser, þat we xal speke of hym" (126).

Kempe's account, like Thorpe's, is cast in the form of a dialogue in which the accused seeks to evade the snares laid to catch the heretic. Thorpe describes himself as using the tactics of the university man—the logic, the semantic precision, the words of the fathers—to evade Arundel's net. Kempe's handling of similar incidents at once criticizes the contemporary church for its laxity ("vn-to þe tyme þat þe Pope & Holy Chirche hath ordeynde þat no man") and uses significant figures of the English episcopacy to verify Margery's mission. Furthermore, both here and elsewhere, she shows no interest in the sort of theological reasoning we see in Thorpe's *Examination* or in the works of John Wyclif. She is not interested in discussing the distinction between signs and things or in defining the limits of the material world. Instead, she wants to reform that world. Kempe describes Margery as capable of swearing on the Scriptures (see 115), but as unalterably opposed to the swearing she hears from those in the households of lords and bishops. Her strategy at once clears her protagonist of heresy and allows her to confront the issue of moral authority by dramatizing a fiction in which Margery's accusers are confounded by her holiness and her simplicity. Kempe herself is as free, and as shadowy, as Chaucer; for how can we accuse her of heterodoxy when (1) she is not her own writer; (2) the events she recounts absolve Margery of such charges; (3) her "text" records the approbation of men like Thomas Arundel, Henry Bowet, Philip Repingdon, or Richard Caistyr?⁵⁸

The third time the subject of swearing appears, Kempe links it to yet another provocative issue, unlicensed preaching. Henry Bowet, the Archbishop of York, unable to force her to swear not to preach in his diocese, is apparently unwilling to persecute her for insubordination or disobedience. A few chapters later (see 135–36), Kempe describes Margery as

57. Early in his dialogue, Thorpe describes Arundel as asking him to take an oath of obedience on the Bible. See *Examination of Master William Thorpe*, in Pollard, 112.

58. For a discussion of Chaucer's similarly strategic use of ambiguity as a means of dissent, see Johnson, "Chaucer's Tale of the Second Nun and the Strategies of Dissent."

doing what she said she could not swear not to do, preach against swear-ing.[59] When asked by "gret lordys men" whether they would be saved, she promises damnation to those who swear "swech horrybyl oþis," urging them to leave their sins and to be confessed. Her emphasis is upon inten-tion; she insists that the sinner be truly contrite, that he "wilfully" do penance, and that he not intend to return to his old ways. Though Mar-gery sends her converts to the Church for its sacrament of penance, she nonetheless preaches repentance to those around her. Apparently she must assume such a role because the Church will not fulfill its duties to the souls in its care.

Though Kempe does not explicitly say so, Margery uses language with a purity every bit as carefully conceived as Oldcastle's or Thorpe's or Henry IV's or Love's. When pressed, she admits only as much as she will, and the account she gives of her faith when she is on trial in Leicester is as precisely worded as any *credo*. This time (see 115–16), Margery swears on a book, clarifying her orthodox views on the sacra-ment and satisfying her accusers about the nature of her beliefs and the purity of her life. The very terms Margery uses to exonerate herself from the charges of heresy reveal Kempe's awareness of the Wycliffite argu-ment about the meaning of the sacrament: "I be-leue þat it is hys very flesche & hys blood & no material bred ne neuyr may be vnseyd be it onys seyd" (115). Where Sir John Oldcastle was careful to specify that "the most worschipfull sacrament of the auter is Cristes body in *forme* of bred," Margery is equally careful to affirm that no *material* bread re-mains after the priest ("be he neuyr so vicyows a man in hys leuyng") has blessed and transformed it. Her affirmation of her orthodoxy is curiously poised between submission and independence. Even as she takes the book and swears to her beliefs, she admits the possibility of "vicious living" in the priesthood, while a few moments later Margery uses her position as prisoner as an occasion to rebuke the Mayor of Leicester for his inadequacies, "ȝe arn not worthy to ben a meyr." Though her views are orthodox, the implications of her actions and beliefs are less so; she confronts the sacrosanct institutions of English order with their moral lapses, or, to draw upon contemporary usage, with their "defaults." Her persistent emphasis upon worthiness allies her

---

59. My wording is deliberate here. Kempe seems to be aware of the Lollard insistence that you should only take God as witness (1) when you are in dire straits and (2) when you can do so in truth.

with Wycliffite thinkers, who focused upon the need for moral purity and spiritual devotedness in figures of authority, arguing that authority was a sign of righteousness, not a benefit of office.[60] Though Kempe describes Margery as obedient to those in office, she nonetheless manifests a freedom from authority because she locates authority, not in the external world of mayorial office, but in the internal, subjective, world of devotion.

The freedom of which Margery avails herself is the freedom of language, English, her mother tongue. She continually denies that she can speak or understand any other language. When she is on trial in Leicester and is addressed in Latin, Margery says to her accuser, "Spekyth Englysch, 3f yow lyketh, for I vndyrstonde not what 3e sey. . . . askyth what qwestyon 3e wil in Englysch, & thorw þe grace of my Lord Ihesu Cryst I xal answeryn 3ow resonabely þerto" (113). Margery does more here than insist she does not understand Latin, the language of elite ecclesiastical culture. As her experience in Rome powerfully demonstrates, translation is intimately connected to moral authority. There, in the see of Christendom, Margery gathers around herself a number of non-English-speaking followers, a German priest and several Italian women, with whom she communicates by using a truly universal system of signs. Their common tongue is love of Christ, and, through Margery, Kempe presents an image of a Pentecostal church, whose members are bound together by devotion, not by the Latin of ecclesiastical power. In fact, wherever Margery goes, she is able to communicate with those who are receptive. There is consequently a good deal of irony underlying Kempe's descriptions of miscommunication, for it is predominately the English who refuse to understand Margery. As Kempe says of the German priest in Rome, "he cowde vndirstonde non oþer Englysch-man, so blyssed mote God ben þat mad an *alyon* to vndirstondyn hir whan hir owyn cuntre-men had forsakyn hir & wolde not heryn hir confessyon les þan sche wolde a left hir wepyng & spekyng of holynes" (emphasis added) (98). Kempe thus chastises the English nation in Rome, both resident priests and transient pilgrims, whose refusal to listen to Margery renders them more fundamentally alien than any actual foreigner.

---

60. For expressions of what are semi-Donatist views about the nature of authority, see Matthews, ed., *The English Works of Wyclif,* especially the sermons "Of Servants and Lords," "Of Dominion"; Hudson and Gradon, eds., *English Wycliffite Sermons,* vol. 2, "Of Mynystris in þe Chirche"; *Examination of Master William Thorpe,* in Pollard, especially 144–49. For discussions of these, see Aston, "Lollardy and Sedition; Hudson, *The Premature Reformation,* 314.

What Kempe offers in her account is a vernacular version of the Christ-like life, a life wherein Margery's own countrymen play the part of the persecuting Jews. Margery's judges are the figures of English civil and ecclesiastical authority, her tormenters, the townspeople of fifteenth-century England, whose communal codes Margery has threatened. Although the substance of Margery's "vision" of the passion of Christ is drawn from Love's *Mirror of the Blessed Life of Christ,* Kempe's account of Margery's life offers a translation of a more "radical" gospel than the one Love presents.[61] If Love "feminizes" the divine by emphasizing Jesus' care for his disciples, his tenderness toward his mother, and his compassion for humanity as manifested through his miracles, Kempe epitomizes the Gospel narrative in another way. She uses Margery to translate the apostolic poverty, humility, and single-minded devotion Jesus preaches into an English that still offends many readers. This is not to say that Kempe succeeds in ways Love does not, but that their ends are different. Love explicitly states that he seeks to stir devotion in a reader and that he desires to channel that devotion toward the sacraments of the church. From Love, who, as Elizabeth Salter has demonstrated, was an adept and self-conscious writer, we may learn much about the power and use of images and about their function in relation to the memory in the late Middle Ages. In the *Book* Kempe at once presents Love's public, the female reader whose devotion is certainly stirred by the sort of homely images Love prescribes, and the subject of a more subversive gospel, the Jesus who defined his distance from the constrictions of family life and the conventional ties of filial affection, from the power of either church or state, and from the codes of a tightly knit and inevitably constrictive community.

It is clear from the final movement of the first part of the *Book* that Kempe's use of Margery is designed as a corrective to her English contemporaries. Kempe's handling of chronology indicates what is a complicated perspective on Margery's communal function. Just before her account of the Passion, Kempe describes Christ as telling Margery, "I haue ordeynd þe to be a merowr a-mongys hem for to han grct sorwe þat þei xulde takyn exampil by þe for to haue sum litil sorwe in her hertys for her synnys þat þei myth þerthorw be sauyd, but þei louyn not to heryn of sorwe ne of contricyon" (186). If Margery is such a mirror, she can only reflect her exemplar, Christ. Moreover, she clearly is intended to reflect an image of Christ that, by prompting self-recognition, awakens a sense of spiritual

---

61. Love's own Passion sequence is described under Friday.

inadequacy and thus contrition in the viewer. Kempe next describes Margery as spectator, whose "sight" of the Passion and of scenes relating to the manhood of Christ is transcribed for us. After she has recounted these visions, however, Kempe notes that Margery had them early in her devotional life. Later, in her maturity, "owr Lord of hys hy mercy drow hir affeccyon in-to hys Godhed, & þat was mor feruent in lofe & desyr & mor sotyl in vndirstondyng þan was þe Manhod" (209). The previous scenes that focus upon the human nature of Christ—most of which are indebted to greater or lesser degrees to Love's *Mirror*—represent an early stage of Margery's spiritual development, but a stage that Kempe chooses to include in the final chapters of the first part.

Her reasons for doing so say much about her understanding of the translator's art. First, Kempe carefully locates these experiences of the manhood of Christ soon after Margery's "conversion," but before she and her husband take a vow of chastity or Margery goes to Jerusalem (208–9). Thus, near the end of the first part of her *Book* she describes the mental images that succeed her original vision of the "fair young man," who sits on her bed and awakens her to herself. The advice Nicholas Love gives in the opening paragraph of the Friday section of *The Mirror,* where he encourages the reader to imagine Christ as a fair young man before trying to "view" his Passion, Kempe has embedded in her own memorial account of her spiritual experience. By splitting the images and creating a kind of verbal dipytch, Kempe frames this first part of her *Book* with images whose source may be Love, but whose fundamental veracity rests in the memory and the use the memory makes of those signs.[62] If the first part of the *Book* is enclosed by reminders of the Passion, by her emphasis upon chronology, Kempe nonetheless insists that Margery's awareness of the Passion is the initial phase of a longer process. The growth of her understanding of the nature of God is manifested in the life she begins to lead, a life that her contemporaries find increasingly difficult to accomodate. That life is captured in the book that we read, the radical gospel of Margery Kempe, whose wanderings, uncomfortable sayings, and confrontations with authority "translate" Christ's life into the English of Lancastrian England, where Margery's welcome is all too like that Jesus received from his countrymen.

Kempe's exploitation of Love's advice is further complicated by an irony that goes to the heart of her purpose as a writer. Love seeks to

---

62. On this issue, see Carruthers, *The Book of Memory,* 213.

channel and contain devotion by prescribing the kinds of images that are most useful for meditation and by directing the meditative process toward the sacramental Church. Kempe employs many of the images Love provides, but she uses them in a more subjective manner. Margery may begin with scenes first depicted by the devotional manuals of others, but the last five chapters of this first part of the *Book* point up her ultimate freedom from the sort of control offered by either the Church or the community. The first three of these chapters are "set" in the Church and are thus contained by that physical structure. But the conversations with God recorded in these chapters (85–87) affirm Margery's singularity—her sanctification, her union with the Godhead, and the superior quality of her devotion. The last two chapters, in equating writing with meditation, effectively proclaim her independence from all outside control:

> Whan þis booke was first in wrytyng, þe sayd creatur was mor at hom in hir chambre wyth hir writer & seyd fewer bedys for sped of wrytyng þan sche had don ʒerys be-forn. &, whan sche cam to chirche & xulde heryn Messe, purposyng to seyn hir Mateyns & swech oþer deuocyons as sche had vsyd a-for-tyme, hir hert was drawyn a-wey fro þe seying & set mech on meditacyon. (216)

Kempe here defines Margery in terms that distance her from her community and her parish. She is a woman alone, more comfortable in her room with her male scribe—a woman unbound, even by the image she has created of herself as a holy woman. The time that formerly was spent in visible acts of devotion (beads and prayers in church) she now spends writing. God, however, quells Margery's guilt by authorizing her freedom:

> Drede þe not, dowtyr, for as many bedys as þu woldist seyin I accepte hem as þow þu seydist hem, & þi stody þat þu stodiist for to do writyn þe gracc þat I haue schewyd to þe plesith me ryght meche & he þat writith boþe. For, þow ʒe wer in þe chirche & wept bothyn to-gedyr as sore as euyr þu dedsit, ʒet xulde ʒe not plesyn me mor þan ʒe don wyth ʒowr writyng, for dowtyr, be þis boke many a man xal be turnyd to me & beleuyn þerin. (216)

God here is far more latitudinarian than any parish priest, then or now; he tells her what every writer wants to hear—that the beads she meant to say count as beads said, for time spent writing is time spent in public ministry. Kempe then goes on to outline Margery's inner development, a process that culminates in her ability to trust her own "feelings" and to need no external proof that God speaks through her. By growing toward an utter trust in the primacy of subjectivism, Margery inevitably grows away from the control offered by Love in his *Mirror*, a text that Kempe implies is a type of primer for the spiritual beginner. The *Book* Kempe writes mirrors the life, or the more mature experience of God, of her protagonist, who, in turn, mirrors that life inscribed in the Gospel. If the true translator must be "dressed" by God, as the author of the general prologue to the Wycliffite Bible affirms, then Margery's gospel is pronounced free from errors.

That gospel is not only presented in the English language but expressly directed to Lancastrian England, a nation adumbrated through the names of the towns and the people who compose it. Though Kempe indicates that the *Book* was written around 1336 or 1337, she locates the main events of Margery's life in the reign of Henry V.[63] Whatever the truth behind Kempe's fiction, her careful identification of both time and place demands our attention, since she thereby situates the *Book* in a period of self-conscious nationalism, the creation of Henry himself, whose care for his kingdom was manifested in a vision of social and religious unity. [64] Henry V's understanding of the ways in which a national image might be composed was inextricably bound to his composition of his own image as sovereign. Where the reign of his father was fraught with the threat of rebellion and shadowed by the Lancastrian seizure of the throne, Henry V sought to create and maintain an image of national harmony and stability. He did so in a variety of ways. Since Henry spent much of his reign out of the country making war against the French, he needed to project a royal

---

63. For dating, see Meech, ed., *The Book of Margery Kempe,* introduction, li.

64. I cannot do justice here to the figure of Henry V. For background, see Harriss, *Henry V: The Practice of Kingship,* particularly the essays by Catto and Powell; Haines, " 'Wilde Wittes and Wilfulnes': John Swetstock's Attack on those 'Poyswunmongeres,' the Lollards"; idem, "Church, Society and Politics in the Early Fifteenth Century as Viewed from an English Pulpit"; idem, " 'Our Master Mariner, Our Sovereign Lord': a Contemporary View of Henry V." For contemporary treatments, see Brie, ed., *The Brut or The Chronicles of England;* John Capgrave, *Abbreuiacion of Cronicles;* Hingeston, ed., *Johannis Capgrave Liber de Illustribus Henricis;* Cole, ed., *Memorials of Henry the Fifth;* Galbraith, ed., *The St. Albans Chronicle, 1406–1420;* Kingsford, ed., *The First English Life of King Henry the Fifth;* Taylor and Roskell, eds. and trans., *Gesta Henrici Quinti: The Deeds of Henry the Fifth;* Thompson, ed. and trans., *Chronicon Adae de Usk, 1377–1421.*

image whose power would promote the sort of empathy and awe that undergird national pride and successful tax levies. As R. N. Swanson has pointed out, Henry used the pulpits of England as major agents in royal propaganda, especially about the state of military affairs.[65] The crown distributed throughout the dioceses what were official newsletters that were intended to be incorporated into church notices. Operating as a kind of powerful affinity group in local affairs, the church disseminated an image of Henry as a "celestial warrior," "the column which supports the temple," or "the master mariner."[66] Similarly, the contemporary *Gesta Henrici Quinti*, written in 1415–17 to justify the King's second French expedition, presents Henry as a pious and able prince, justly ruling over a new Israel. Where the sermons and addresses that opened Parliament during the reigns of Henry IV and Henry VI frequently emphasized the King's need for good counsel, during the reign of Henry V speakers focused on Henry himself as a figure of good government, divine labor, courage, and providential force.

The greatest threat to the body politic was perceived to be heresy, or Lollardy. The author of the *Gesta* thus compares Oldcastle and his fellows to Cain, fleeing to "antris et diverticulis" or "antris et latibulis," or as taking refuge in those parts of the communal body that are separate from the whole.[67] If Oldcastle poses a threat to unity, England may preserve its prosperity by purging ("extirpare") itself of heresies, along with other acts of sedition and unrighteousness and make acknowledgment, *"more fully than before"* through public expressions of communal piety and nationalism.[68] As Taylor and Roskell note, on 8 May 1417, the Archbishop of Canterbury, Henry Chichele, issued a mandate (prompted by the King) urging both the clergy and the laity to greater participation in processions, litanies, and prayers for victory.[69] This move to conformity as a

---

65. Swanson, *Church and Society in Late Medieval England,* 118, 122. See also Jones, "The English Church and Royal Propaganda during the Hundred Years' War"; McKenna, "Popular Canonization as Political Propaganda: The Case of Archbishop Scrope."

66. Haines, "Church, Society and Politics in the Early Fifteenth Century." See also Catto, "Religious Change under Henry V," in Harriss, *Henry V: The Practice of Kingship,* 107.

67. Taylor and Roskell, eds. and trans., *Gesta,* 6–7. Taylor and Roskell translate both phrases as "holes and corners." While I do not wish to quibble with their translation, I nonetheless feel that the language is intended to suggest the very divisiveness that Henry wished to extirpate from his realm.

68. Emphasis added. See Taylor and Roskell, eds. and trans., *Gesta,* 99.

69. Taylor and Roskell, eds. and trans., *Gesta,* introduction, xxiv. For the account, see *Gesta,* 150–55. See also Jacob, *Essays in the Conciliar Epoch,* 59n., who reports that in May 1417,

means of promoting unity also underlay the preferment, again, prompted by the Crown, of the Sarum usage throughout England's churches and the gradual predominance of a single rite.[70] With its services for the blessing of the palms on Palm Sunday, for Maundy Thursday, or for the Easter Vigil, intermingled with those for marriage, for pilgrims, for new knights, for ships, for seeds and harvests, and for the dead, the Sarum Manual proclaims the unity of the body of Christ by presenting the human year as inextricably linked to the holy year. As the Manual subtly suggests, the human year is most fully understood in relation to the fellowship of the whole, whose boundaries it defines. The Manual contains rituals of reentry ("De purificatione mulierum") and rituals of excision ("Modus separandi leprosos"), ceremonies that indicated the ways in which uniform faith was perceived to be a key aspect of community.

The Crown's wish to enforce a uniform national usage was one local manifestation of an impulse that also drew England to play a prominent part in the Council of Constance, which, from 1414 to 1418, functioned as the diplomatic and religious center of a Christendom in which papal disunity was increasingly difficult to explain or to tolerate.[71] At the Council, the English delegates persistently insisted on the language of nationhood, defining the nation, rather than the diocese or the province, as a voting unit. As E. F. Jacob notes, this insistence "reflected more than the *ecclesia Anglicana*. It also represented the *regnum Angliae* . . . a unit of *imperium*, reflecting the sovereignty of its master."[72] While the English espousal of nationhood was no doubt aimed at blocking efforts by French delegates to dominate the Council, it nonetheless testified to Henry's wish to present an image of England as a single and uniform nation ruled over by a pious and forceful prince. Henry's agenda for national unity was reflected in his vision of ecclesiastical unity, including far more than the

---

Chichele sent out a mandate for prayers on Henry V's behalf since some "tepiditate causante" were ceasing to pray for the king. See also McHardy, "Liturgy and Propaganda in the Diocese of Lincoln During the Hundred Years War."

70. See Collins, ed., *Manuale ad Vsum Percelebris Ecclesie Sarisburiensis;* Frere, ed., *The Use of Sarum.* For discussion of this issue see Jacob, *Archbishop Henry Chichele,* 67; Jacob, *Essays in the Conciliar Epoch,* 80; Frere, ed., *The Use of Sarum,* 2:xxx–xxxi; Catto, "Religious Change under Henry V," in Harriss, *Henry V: The Practice of Kingship,* 108.

71. Jacob, *Essays in the Conciliar Epoch,* 48. See Johnson, "Chaucer's Tale of the Second Nun," for discussion and further documentation concerning Chaucer's reaction to schism.

72. Jacob, *Essays in the Conciliar Epoch,* 53. See also Mundy and Woody, eds., Loomis, trans., *The Council of Constance: The Unification of the Church.*

effort to return the papacy to a single figure: Henry sought to reestablish the purity of the faith, to champion orthodoxy, in England and in Europe.[73] Within the confines of the English Church, he encouraged a strong, well-educated, and energetic prelacy, appointing Henry Chichele to the see of Canterbury upon the death of Thomas Arundel in 1414. Archbishop Chichele, in turn, spent a long and productive career encouraging a high standard of education in and system of rewards for those whom he placed in important ecclesiastical positions.[74]

Despite the urgings toward unity that can be detected in the move to a uniform ecclesiastical usage and in explicit statements of national unity that we find in the opening addresses to Parliament as well as in sermons or other semiofficial texts of the period, Kempe offers a more problematic national image. For example, if, as Meech suggests, Margery left for the Holy Lands sometime around November, 1413, she would have traveled through Constance about six weeks to two months later.[75] A year later delegates from all over Europe would be gathering there for a major ecclesiastical effort in the direction of unity, but for Kempe Constance serves as a token of disunity.[76] It is on the way to Constance that Margery's fellow pilgrims reject her, cutting her gown short and forcing her to sit at the end of the table. They thus define community in terms of conformity to worldly codes and manners. At Constance, Margery finds an ally in a papal legate, who enjoins her company to accept her. His efforts to reconcile her fellow pilgrims to her fails, however, and Margery finds another guide for the journey from Constance to Bologna (see 61–65). Though Kempe does not place Margery in Constance during the years of the Council, her description of Margery's difficulties with her countrymen while in the neighborhood of Constance, along with her constant reference to the name of the city in this portion of the *Book,* point toward her awareness that conformity and unity are two separate, and perhaps mutually exclusive, qualities. More specifically, by locating a quarrel about the nature of community in and around Constance, Kempe implies that the English, by excising the holy from the realm of the ordinary, are themselves divided in ways that subvert any official move toward unity.

73. Jacob, *Essays in the Conciliar Epoch,* 52. On the subject of reform at the Council of Constance, see also Moody, "The Conciliar Movement," in Mundy and Woody, eds., *The Council of Constance,* 28.

74. See Jacob, *Archbishop Henry Chichele,* especially 72; Swanson, *Church and Society.*

75. See Meech, ed., *The Book of Margery Kempe,* 284 n. 60/18–19.

76. See Jacob, *Essays in the Conciliar Epoch,* 44.

Kempe was not alone in creating a carefully shaded portrait of Henry's England. As Lee Patterson demonstrates, John Lydgate's appraisal of Henry V, in raising the specter of Theban history, was designed as covert criticism of his regal authority or, at the very least, as cautionary praise.[77] Thomas Walsingham, author of the *St. Albans Chronicle,* does not criticize Henry, but neither does he provide an "official" picture of Henry as restorer of Israel and its glories. Like Adam of Usk, he offers a more balanced account of the reign, an account that includes noticeable threats to the health of the body politic—bad weather and poverty, for example, as well as the dangers posed by civil dissent and heresy. Even more explicitly, Adam of Usk's *Chronicon* presents a contemporary image of Lancastrian rule that points up its fundamental disunity. Unlike the official pictures of Lancastrian rule, especially of Henry V, which highlighted royal piety, valor and strength, and popular gratitude and adulation, Adam of Usk never fails to mention the tensions of either the reigns of Henry IV or Henry V. He includes Philip Repingdon's letter of warning to Henry IV, in which Repingdon urged the king to search his own heart before thinking to heal the sufferings of the people or to establish peace in the land. In sketching in the outlines of contemporary Europe, Adam of Usk presents a picture of Rome (where he lived for several years) as a crime-ridden and brutal city. For the reign of Henry V, Adam of Usk's praise is equally shaded: despite his explicit praise for his sovereign, he also meticulously points out Henry's frequent tax levies, those natural catastrophes that occured during his reign, and the king's military losses. The last few pages of his account seem almost intentionally chaotic: in quick succession he mentions taxation; Henry's return to France; English losses at the seige of Falaise; the capture and death of Sir John Oldcastle; the end of a papal schism that had, at times, given Christendom four popes at once; the siege of Rouen; the King's further war and victories in France (including his marriage to Katharine); the Duke of Clarence's upset by the Dauphin at the battle of Baugé and the terrible English losses. He then describes Henry as seeking to take revenge for this loss by raising another tax, "tearing to pieces" ("dilaniando") all with money, rich and poor, through the entire realm. He ends the *Chronicon* on a less than laudatory note, by talking about the "murmuring" of the people against Henry and their hatred of "excessum," warning Henry against joining the

---

77. Patterson, "Making Identities in Fifteenth Century England: John Lydgate and Henry V."

ranks of Julius, Assur, Alexander, Hector, Cyrus, Darius, or Maccabeus, who suffered God's wrath.[78]

Where more official accounts of the reigns of Henry IV and Henry V describe heresy as dividing the body politic, and where Adam of Usk describes a body politic fragmented by war, taxation, and economic dissent, Kempe's account of England is at once disarming and alarmingly specific. Her attention to chronologcial detailing situates the *Book* in both an apolitical and a political context. Her frequent references to the length of time between her religious experiences and the written record of those experiences seem to evoke a set of conventions relevant to the transcription of spiritual experiences, such as Julian of Norwich's similarly exact clarifications of chronology in the *Showings*. Kempe repeatedly reminds us that twenty years "and more" elapsed before she could bring herself to write down what she had seen and heard or specifies that a particular experience, such as her private vision of the Passion, occured early in her spiritual life, despite the fact that she places it near the end of the first section of the *Book*.

Kempe also provides the *Book* with references linking it to events that are external to the narrative itself. She includes specifically topical references that allow us to "date" the events she recounts.[79] For example, early in Margery's career, she has interviews with both Philip Repingdon (33), the Bishop of Lincoln, and Thomas Arundel, the Archbishop of Canterbury (35). By naming both figures, she provides a chronological frame of reference for the action, since Philip Repingdon assumed his see in 1405 and resigned it in 1419, and Thomas Arundel died in 1414. Similarly, her references to the Bishop of Worcester (109) and to the Archbishop of York (122) make it possible to identify Thomas Peverel and Henry Bowet. The references do more than locate the *Book* in time; they also locate it in a time of religious dissent, not in the era of uniformity so carefully promulgated by the official "portrait-painters" of Henry's reign. Three of these men, all of them illustrious prelates, were zealous in prosecuting Lollards, describing a sort of chain of ecclesiastical command in the

---

78. Thompson, ed. and trans., *Chronicon,* 65–69, 231–36; 120–33, 298–320; 131–33; 316–20. In a paper on Adam of Usk and the deposition of Richard II, presented at the 1991 International Congress on Medieval Studies, Chris Given-Wilson argued that Adam covertly presented a less-than-flattering picture of Henry IV.

79. For the details of dating, I, like every reader of Kempe's *Book,* am indebted to the work of Meech and Allen, recorded in the notes to their edition. Since these notes are keyed to pagination, I shall cite only the pages on which incidents occur.

history of the Lollard trials that the sixteenth-century reformers would, in turn, use to trace a venerable genealogy of martyrdom. John Badby, the Worcestershire artisan whose burning at Smithfield on 5 March 1410 became a landmark in the history of English heterodoxy, was first examined by Thomas Peverel, then handed on to Henry Bowet, who "recommended" him to the Archbishop of Canterbury, Thomas Arundel. The fourth, Philip Repingdon, had fallen into the Wycliffite camp in his youth, recanted and risen in the Church hierarchy, but resigned his see before he died. His will was as suspiciously bare of excess as any Lollard will, leaving the impression, at least, of a certain sympathy for Wycliffite simplicity.[80] While the references may, as Meech and Allen suggest, be intended to guarantee Margery's orthodoxy, they seem, instead, to recall England's history of dissent, a history of the divisions between the prelates of the English church and some of the English.

Even the towns whose "peace" Kempe describes Margery as troubling were those known for their concentrations of heretics. As Aston points out, Lollards, like earlier heretics and like the friars themselves, flourished along the main roads and found supporters among the tradespeople of large towns.[81] What Kempe thereby notes, with her accounts of Margery's experiences in Bristol, Leicester, York, or London, is the presence of division, of dissent. Kempe's account of English towns does not disagree with other contemporary chronicles of daily life, which suggest a similarly anxious awareness that the fabric of everyday life was not the whole cloth official pronouncements sought to weave. With her accounts of threatened earthquakes, unseasonal snowstorms, awesome thunderstorms, poverty, strife, and civic lawlessness, Kempe captures a sense we can find in many different types of texts that the times were difficult. If the Lollards sometimes intimated that such events signified that the Last Days were at hand, those of more orthodox leanings suggested that the Lollards themselves were the sign of an endemic distemper in the body

---

80. For Repingdon's life, see the *Dictionary of National Biography*; Aston, " 'Caim's Castles': Poverty, Politics, and Disendowment," 66; Crompton, "Leicestershire Lollards," 15. On Lollard wills and the contemporary trend towards a Lollard-like simplicity in death, see McFarlane, *Lancastrian Kings and Lollard Knights*, 210; Post, "The Obsequies of John of Gaunt"; Tuck, "Carthusian Monks and Lollard Knights: Religious Attitudes at the Court of Richard II"; Walker, *The Lancastrian Affinity*, 100–101; Vale, *Piety, Charity, and Literacy Among the Yorkshire Gentry, 1370–1480*.

81. See Aston, "Lollardy and Sedition," 15. For an account of the road system in late medieval England, hence of mobility, see Stenton, "The Road System of Medieval England."

politic.[82] Bishop Alnwick of Norwich's commission for the detection of offenders in 1428 at Bury St. Edmunds described those whom he wished to indict as

> heretics and their believers . . . as well as anyone celebrating private conventicles or making conventicles away from the common gathering of the faithful, and on festival days withdrawing themselves from churches or the general converse of men, or holding exceptional views on the faith or sacred matters, and possessing or learning from books in our vulgar English tongue, and those who are suspected, known, or reported of the above or anyone of them.[83]

The description, though ostensibly concerning the Lollard heresy, is less a description of Lollardy than a definition of community, since Alnwick identifies community with uniformity. Any movement away from the "common gathering" is a divisive separation from common views. Furthermore, Alnwick reveals his belief that the community is already fragmented, that the very act of finding and indicting "heretics and their believers" constitutes an indictment of the England of 1428. Though paeans to Henry V as the great champion of the English church and nation abounded in the 1420s, when his son was still a child, the continuing need to hunt out and indict those who had separated themselves from the English body of Christ is a constant reminder that the unity preached from the nation's pulpits seemed an elusive goal to those in power.[84] Just as her references to the significant prelates and religious figures of the time—Archbishop Arundel, Henry Bowet, Philip Repingdon, or Richard Caister—remind us of heterodoxy even as they signify the power and mission of the English church, so Kempe's "map" of England suggests a country fragmented by a variety of impulses. In fact, her depiction of England seems designed to place in sharp relief the

82. See, for example, the accounts of the reigns of Henry V and Henry VI in Gairdner, ed., *Historical Collections of a Citizen of London in the Fifteenth Century;* Riley, ed., *Memorials of London and London Life;* Wilkins, ed., *Concilia Magnae Britanniae et Hiberniae,* vol. 3. For an account of a fifteenth-century sermon collection (c. 1421–22) stressing the disjointed nature of the times, see Haines, "Wilde Wittes and Wilfulnes." For Lollard sermons on the same topic, see Hudson and Gradon, eds., *English Wycliffite Sermons,* vol. 2, sermons 15 and 17, and the important "Of Mynystris in þe Chirche."

83. From BL Additional MS. 14848, f. 109v, quoted in Swanson, *Ecclesia Anglicana,* 335.

84. For a powerful sense of the official awareness of the threat dissent posed to the common good, see Tanner, ed., *Heresy Trials.*

perilous nature of the times and the need for a new understanding of the nature of civil dominion.

Kempe's subtle pointing at certain key moments in the *Book* of figures linked to Lancastrian authority suggests less their strengths than their inherent limitations. Of Kempe's four references to the Crown, only two of them are explicit. The first reference evokes the King without naming him, naming instead the Duke of Bedford, brother to the King and lieutenant of the kingdom during Henry's frequent absences abroad. It is the Duke of Bedford's yeomen who arrest Margery and take her to Beverly. They speak in his name, "owr Lord . . . þe Duke of Bedforth hath sent for þe. And þu art holdyn þe grettest loller in al þis cuntre er a-bowte London eythyr" (129). These yeomen later accuse Margery of being "Combomis dowtyr . . . sent to beryn lettrys abowtyn þe cuntre" (132). As Meech notes, "Combomis" is probably a corruption of "Cobham's," meaning the famous Lollard Sir John Oldcastle, who was first arrested in 1413, then escaped and was at large until 1417, when he was arrested and executed. Kempe therefore seems to be dating the incident sometime before Oldcastle was finally captured. Her reference not only places the incident on a chronological grid; it also inserts Margery into Henry's own ecclesiastical or national agenda. During Henry's absence, it was his brother who stood for the order of Henry's reign. In his *Liber de Illustribus Henricis,* for the year 1417, Capgrave describes the Duke of Bedford as quelling the twin foes of revolt and heresy. Triumphing over the Scots on the one hand and overseeing the final trial of Sir John Oldcastle, the Duke of Bedford embodied the militance and the piety of the king. Just as *Prince* Henry had stepped in to halt temporarily the burning of John Badby in 1410 in order to seek Badby's repentance, so the Duke of Bedford first urged Oldcastle to penance, and then proceeded with the drawing, hanging, and burning of heretical flesh, dividing and destroying a body that itself had sought to tear apart the body politic which he presided over in his brother's name.[85]

Kempe's second reference to the crown is equally oblique. When Margery is brought before Henry Bowet, Archbishop of York, in the chapterhouse of Beverly, she is accused by a Dominican friar in the Archbishop's service of counseling Lady Greystokke, the daughter of Lady Westmorland, to leave her husband (133). The accusation can be

85. See Hingeston, ed., *Johannis Capgrave Liber de Illustribus Henricis,* 122. For Henry's response to Badby, see Jacob, *The Fifteenth Century,* 95.

read in two ways. First, the friar accuses Margery of threatening the institution of marriage, an accusation that echoes the fear expressed by the men of Beverly that Margery has come to lead their wives away with her (129). But the reference does more than simply suggest that Margery's presence is a destabilizing force in the community, since Lady Westmorland was Joan of Beaufort, daughter of John of Gaunt and Kathryn Swynford, and thus half-sister to Henry IV. Her elder daughter, Elizabeth, was married to John de Greystoke.[86] The denouement of this scene, in which Margery triumphs over the friar's malice and the archbishop's quandry ("I wote not what I xal don wyth þe" [134]) and leaves Beverly, protected by the Archbishop's letter and seal, which certainly owes its force to our appreciation of the comedy of gender, nonetheless leaves hanging in the air, the whisper of the king's name, his presence, summoned and never truly dismissed.

Kempe's most eloquent reference to Henry V is to his death. When a new prior is sent to the Carmelite priory in Lynn, Margery rejoices that he is a holy and learned man. But, he is shortly appointed to go "ouyr þe see to þe Kyng in-to Frawnce and oþer clerkys also of þe worthyest in Ynglond" (171). Despite the official summons, Margery "feels" that the prior will not leave Lynn. The prior is less optimistic about his fate: "Neuyrþe-lesse he wend hym-self to a gon & was al purueyd þerfor & wyth gret heuynes had takyn leue of hys frendys, supposyng neuyr to a comyn ageyn, for he was a ful weyk man & a febyl of complexion. & in þe mene-tyme þe Kyng deyid, & þe Priowr bood at hom" (171–72). By subordinating Henry and an ongoing war that was consistently described as crucial to the *nation*'s sense of its identity to the health and well-being of one prior from the town of Lynn, Kempe suggests the paradoxical state of affairs in England. Like Adam of Usk and Thomas Walsingham, both of whom imply that Henry's war was costing his people dearly, Kempe provides a hint of the costs of a different type of taxation.[87] The very weight of the chapter, which emphasizes the worthiness of the prior and

---

86. See Meech, ed., *The Book of Margery Kempe,* 317 n.133/23.

87. For Adam of Usk, see above. Walsingham's closing notes for the events of A.D. 1420 strike an odd note; he writes: "Transiit annus iste cum frugum fertilitate copia, fructum tamen penuria et pecuniari egestate per maxima. Nam rex noster in ultramarinis agens cum suis excercitibus taliter pelagus post se confluere iusserat quod vix in communi plebe nummismata tanta remanserant, unde competentem annonam poterant providere." See Galbraith, ed., *The St. Albans Chronicle, 1406–1420,* 126. For taxation, see also the Rolls of Parliament for the reign of Henry V.

his spiritual value to the community but is silent about the worthiness of Henry V, works to heighten our sense that English values are somehow askew. The terse "in þe mene-tyme þe Kyng deyid" serves as a preamble to the happy resolution of the difficulty among the Christians at Lynn; since the king no longer requires his presence, the prior "bood at home." Both here and in her earlier description of Margery's trouble in Bristol with finding passage to Santiago ("þer wer non Englisch schepys þat myth seylen þedyr, for þei wer arestyd & takyn up for þe kyng" [107]), Kempe implies that Henry, like other figures of civil authority, represents obstacles to Margery's vocation, that he is the agent of a type of motion that opposes spiritual progress.

It is in the closing chapters of the *Book,* which describe Margery's return from her final journey, that Kempe seems deliberately to oppose Margery's humility and poverty to triumph and magnificence. To some extent, Margery's progress is utterly conventional: like any traveler returning from France to England, she goes from Calais, to Dover, to Canterbury, to London. However, Kempe marks each stage of Margery's journey by linking events to exact place-names as carefully as the authors of the *Gesta Henrici Quinti* and *The Brut* specify Henry's route from France to London after the battle of Agincourt.[88] There was more than one contemporary account of Henry's progress, and each communicates the ways in which processional movement transforms neutral space into a theatrical *locus:* the city, in effect, becomes a site for the performance of social drama. Thus, though Margery returns as we would expect, Kempe does more than narrate her movement through space. In the details that elaborate that movement, Kempe suggests a way of understanding this return as a type of progress. The point of convergence between Margery's return and the progress of Henry V is the way in which both are designed to stage a drama of community and to do so by exploiting the relationship between the principal actor (Henry or Margery) and the citizens who hail that figure. The single figure is thus both the focus for the drama (and in that sense its audience) and its main player; the citizens are coalesced into a

---

88. See Brie, ed., *The Brut,* 380–81; Taylor and Roskell, eds. and trans., *Gesta,* 100–113. For the London festivities, see also Thompson, ed. and trans., *Chronicon,* 128–29, 311–13; Gairdner, *Historical Collections of a Citizen of London in the Fifteenth Century,* 112; Withington, *English Pageantry,* vol. 1, chapter 3. For verses on the pageant ascribed to John Lydgate, see *Gesta,* appendix IV, 191–92. The language I employ in my account of the pageant is drawn from the *Gesta.* Patterson also discusses this pageant in"Making Identities in Fifteenth Century England: John Lydgate and Henry V."

single body that also becomes player and audience.[89] Each step of Henry's deliberate progress to London suggests his remarkable grasp of the dynamics of civic ritual. Upon landing in Dover with his host of French captives, he rested a day before proceeding to Canterbury, where he stayed for two days. He then went to his manor of Eltham until Saturday, November 23, when he "honored" London by his bodily presence ("proponens sequenti die Sabbati urbem suam Londonie sua corporali presencia honorare").

The pageant with which Londoners greeted Henry's return on that Saturday can be read as a celebration of Henry as the representative of sacramental kingship and of London as a symbol for the mystically unified community. The pageants that greeted Henry in his progress through London toward Westminster were designed to unite the symbols of national myth and sacred, or salvific, history. He was met at Blackheath by the mayor, twenty-four aldermen, and "twenty thousand citizens dressed in red gowns riding horses," who accompanied the king to the entrance of London Bridge where he was saluted by giants. The giants at once recall similar civic pageantry for Richard II and the legendary history of Britain itself as inhabited by giants who were subdued by the heroes of national myth. Henry was then welcomed by Saint George and by a boys' choir singing "Benedictus qui venit in nomine Domini," language that conventionally welcomes Christ into the Mass. When Henry reached the conduit in Cornhill, he was greeted by the arms of Saint George, Saint Edward, and Saint Edmund and by the prophets, who released a flock of birds as he passed them. The apostles, the twelve kings of England's succession, martyrs, and confessors met him at the entrance to Cheapside and delivered to him leaves of silver mingled with wafers of bread as wine spouted from the conduit, "in order to receive him with bread and wine as Melchizedek did Abraham." At the cross in Cheapside, a castle had been constructed that bore the legend "Gloriosa dicta sunt de te, civitas dei" and the coats of arms of Saint George, the king, the emperor, and the nobles of the realm. From the castle issued a choir of beautiful maidens singing "as if to welcome another David," as from its top beautiful young boys showered the King with golden coins and leaves of laurel. Finally, at

89. Christ's entry into Jerusalem on Palm Sunday is, of course, the most important model for processional drama, and both the author of Henry's procession and Kempe invest the entries of their protagonists into London with references to that event. For further remarks on civic ritual in relation to the Corpus Christi drama, particularly the staging of the entry into Jerusalem, see pages 184–88.

Saint Paul's, Henry was greeted by maidens bearing golden chalices from which floated round leaves of gold upon the King and by a resplendent archangel, everyone praising God for the victory. Hailed as triumphant deliverer, as sacramental body, greeted with bounty, Henry, alone, in the midst of such splendor and such throngs, wore the purple of royalty and mourning and, accompanied only by a few trusted friends, rode slowly to Westminster Abbey and, from there, to his palace at Westminster.

What was staged, of course, by both the city and the King was an elaborately thought-out ritual not only meant to link victory and prosperity with piety in princes and gratitude in citizens, but also to present an image of England as a corporate body united around and through a majesty conceived of as sacramental. The bread and wine, the figure of Melchizedek, the round wafers of gold, and the anthems hailed Henry's corporal presence using symbols frequently employed for civic celebrations of the *corpus Christi.*[90] Such a moment of civic festivity imaged history itself— both sacred and profane—as present in and through the "corporali presencia" of Henry. Furthermore, through a carefully conceived and worked-out ceremonial, like the one prepared for Henry's return, those images considered central to the concept of community could be used to express a mythology of national unity. The number of accounts of this particular ceremonial suggests its powerful exploitation of contemporary symbols and systems of meaning and underlines the degree to which the desire or need for a definition of community was bound up with the subject of authority.

Kempe creates a progress for Margery that is similarly rich in the topoi of community. Margery leaves from Calais, where she has experienced the kindness and hospitality of those who had never seen her before (241). When she lands in Dover, however, she is deserted by her fellow English and must awaken a "poor man" to ask him for his horse and his help in taking her to Canterbury. As Christ entered Jerusalem on a colt borrowed from strangers, Margery makes her way through England helped by those who do not know her and derided by those who do. From Canterbury, she goes to London, where she is greeted by a city that appears to turn itself out to proclaim her as a false hypocrite. Like the king before her, Margery's

90. For a discussion of these symbols and texts, see Rubin, *Corpus Christi,* chapter 4. For discussions of civic rituals, see MacAloon, ed., *Rite, Drama, Festival, Spectacle: Rehearsals toward a Theory of Cultural Performance,* introduction; Mills, "Religious Drama and Civic Ceremonial," in *Medieval Drama,* ed. Cawley, Jones, McDonald, and Mills. For a contemporary treatment of the feast, see John Lydgate's poem, "A Procession of Corpus Christi," in *Minor Poems of John Lydgate,* 35–43.

clothing sets her apart from the citizens, for she comes to London "clad in a cloth of canvas," bearing a covering over her face to hide herself until she can raise money to buy herself other clothing (243). Once she asserts herself as a voice preaching penance to the community, Margery moves from parish to parish throughout the city, surrounded by those who see God in her: "Mech of þe comown pepil magnifijd God in hir, hauyng good trost þat it was þe goodnes of God whech wrowt þat hy grace in hir sowle" (245). Though Margery is rejected by the "curatys & preistys of þe chirchis in London," she nonetheless finds a following among those who appear to need such a witness to God's grace. Where Henry came as triumphant king, Margery comes to London as rejected flesh ("þu fals flesch"), providing the worldly and gossipy city with an image of the divine that has nothing to do with worldly victory or power. That Henry himself felt the real power of civic ritual is clear from his own choice of dress as well as his demeanor— the author of the *Gesta* says that Henry walked as though he gave thanks and glory alone to God—for he entered London not as a warrior but as a petitioner, making his way to Westminster Abbey and the threshholds ("limina") of the apostles Peter and Paul. Henry's progress ended at West-minster Abbey, symbol for the English cult of kingship; afterwards, he went home, to his palace. Kempe suggests her own understanding of the uses of topography by having Margery leave London for Shene.

The Carthusian Abbey of Shene and its sisterhouse, the Brigittine Abbey of Syon cannot be dissociated from the figure of Henry V, who in the second year of his reign founded these two abbeys on the banks of the Thames near Richmond, along with a nearby abbey which did not survive.[91] As Jeremy Catto notes, the three were planned as a group and intended to be palace monasteries, consequently placing the monarchy at the center of English religious life.[92] The houses themselves were famous for the strictness of their rules, for their emphasis upon the devotional life, and for their dissemination of vernacular devotional texts.[93] Though Kempe describes Margery as going to Shene on her way to Lynn, she

91. See Thompson, ed. and trans., *Chronicon*, 124, 305; Kingsford, ed., *The First English Life of King Henry the Fifth*, 19; Galbraith, ed., *The St. Albans Chronicle*, 82; Taylor and Roskell, eds. and trans., *Gesta*, 186–87. For other contemporary praise of Henry as a benefactor of the English church, see "Versus Rhythmici in Laudem Regis Henrici Quinti," in Cole, ed., *Memorials of Henry the Fifth* (1858).

92. Catto, "Religious Change under Henry V," in Harriss, *Henry V: The Practice of Kingship*, 110–11.

93. For an account of the library at Syon, which she suggests functioned as a "lending library," see Bateson, *Catalogue of the Library of Syon Monastery*.

must, in fact, go slightly out of her way to do so. The abbeys of Shene and Syon are south and west of London, whereas Lynn is almost directly north. Kempe locates Margery in Shene on Lammas Day, August 1, the feast of Saint Peter in Chains, a day on which rents were traditionally collected; a day associated with agricultural harvest; and a day that commemorated Peter's freedom from his prison chains, and thus our liberation from the "chains" of sin. By placing Margery in such a place on such a day, Kempe draws together what is a royal cult (implicitly a national one) with those themes of imminent justice—both agricultural and personal—inherent in Lammastide.[94] Margery, as any Christian should, goes to purchase her pardon; she ends by gaining yet another convert and by discovering her old guide from Lynn who helps her return to her own city.

The fiction of Margery's final journey, from Lynn to Ipswich, to Norway, to Germany, to France, to Dover, Canterbury, London, Shene, and back to Lynn is the story of England's own recent history of involvement in foreign conflict and in trade, of its effort to create and maintain an image of community, and of its attempt to erect figures and foundations that embody that image. Though Thomas Polton's words at the Council of Constance defining England as a nation in its own right owed their genesis to England's anti-French policies, they nonetheless evince a sense that nations must be defined in terms of their distinctions:

> Whether a nation be understood as a race, relationship, and habit of unity, separate from others, or as a difference of language, which by divine and human law is the greatest and most authentic mark of a nation and the essence of it, as explained below, or whether it be understood, as it should be, as an equality of territory . . . in all these respects the renowned nation of England or Britain is one of the four or five nations that compose the papal obedience.[95]

94. It is surely coincidental, but in his account of the events of 1420, Thomas Walsingham plays upon the theme of harvest, suggesting how poor a harvest Henry created in England by his need for money to support an army overseas. He juxtaposes these remarks to his description of Henry's royal entry into Paris that year. See Galbraith, ed., *The St. Albans Chronicle,* 126.

95. The passage is from Cardinal Fillastris' diary in *The Council of Constance,* ed. Mundy and Woody, trans. Loomis, 344. The passage is also quoted by Maurice Keen in *English Society in the Later Middle Ages,* 302. My thanks to Professor Keen for his help in locating and identifying the passage.

Polton here argues that nations can be understood only in terms of what is held in common, or, put another way, in terms of what is excluded from common usage.

Those issues that preoccupy Kempe throughout the *Book*—translation, use of the vernacular, ideas of conformity, and authority—underline the ways in which she intended her scrutiny of the English to serve as an exploration of the nation's terms of community. Through Margery's conflicts with her fellow English, Kempe neither narrates a myth of the founding of a "new Israel," nor an instance of national Pentecostal unity, but, instead, a series of episodes that dramatize the divisions of a people whose concern for signs of worldly status and power renders them incapable of speaking to one another in a single language. The details of Margery's final journey, which itself offers a kind of foil and implicit challenge to the primacy of the official and authorized "map" of Lancastrian England, adumbrate a symbolic progression away from worldly power by evoking more worldly progresses and triumphs as well as Christ's own final journey through Jerusalem to sacrifice. Kempe thereby provides another series of national criteria, or distinctions, in Margery, who disdains the tokens of privilege held sacred by her contemporaries, but gathers around herself a "nation" of folk who likewise define community in terms of language, relationship, and habit of unity. However, the language—English—is a medium of true communication among otherwise unlike people; the relationships are based upon spiritual kinship not upon networks of power; and the unity is embodied in a figure of authority who, like Margery herself, came poor and despised, the body through whom all are joined. By translating the Gospel into England's own mother tongue, Kempe presents new terms for the ongoing debate about the foundations of community.

Conclusion:
Fictions of Community

 If *The Book of Margery Kempe* is a fiction, which I believe it to be, it is a fiction that attempts to create a social reality and to examine that reality in relation to a single individual. By situating Margery squarely within the topography, social structures, and ideological conflicts of England during the first third of the fifteenth century, Kempe avoids both the limitations of the jeremiad and the possible penalties incurred by its author. *The Book of Margery Kempe* bears eloquent testimony to Kempe's ability to employ the conventions of her day in ways that allow her to assess the foundations of English Christian society through narrative prose. Social commentary is implicit in other medieval prose narratives like *Mandeville's Travels,* but Kempe's persistent focus upon the development of a single individual increases the number of issues she can address and thus expands the possibilities of what she can achieve. Those very conventions, or conventional modes, she uses to such good effect provide her with a language at once precise and ambiguous enough to explore some of the more important and explosive topics of her day. Though the *Book* certainly has affinities with more explicitly heterodox works of the early fifteenth century, it makes most sense when juxtaposed with poems like *Piers Plowman* or the *Canterbury Tales* or to later medieval works like the mystery cycles. The *Book* shares with those works an episodic structure, a tendency to destabilize the meanings it supposedly affirms and to hint at an overarching internal structure that is never allowed to predominate, and a sophisti-

cated use of words to convey and confuse meaning. What I am describing, of course, is artistry, the ability to evolve a strategy that meets the complex demands that will be placed upon it.

One of the most strenuous of these demands is bound up with Kempe's ability to establish Margery in the realm of the actual. Kempe certainly displays her understanding of the conventions of sacred biography, with its corresponding emphasis upon the social context for sanctity, but she does more than sketch in a background for her depiction of the holy. The "background" is integral to her purpose in the *Book*, which has a specificity and wealth of detail that point to Kempe's scrutiny of social structures. The intensity of Kempe's focus upon the nature of social structures and institutions is particularly evident if we juxtapose the *Book* to texts like the *Revelations of St. Elizabeth of Hungary* or the *Revelations of St. Bridget*.[1] Kempe describes both of these works as among those read to Margery, thus implicitly assimilating Margery to the tradition of married sanctity expressed through the lives of these women. Her references to Saint Elizabeth's tears and to some of the details of Saint Bridget's life are intended to validate Margery's emotive piety and secular holiness. However, by underlining the antecedents for the *Book*, they also point up the ways in which it is fundamentally unlike those literary godmothers to whom Kempe nods. For example, echoes of Saint Elizabeth's conversations with the Virgin, with John the Evangelist, and with Jesus can certainly be found in the *Book*, but the short text of the *Revelations of St. Elizabeth* does not prepare us for the full-blown fiction with its careful attention to detail that Kempe achieves. The texts of the revelations of other female devotees are composed as transcripts of private conversations between the visionary and figures of mystic authority. In her account of Margery's experience, Kempe uses references to these texts, along with those to Margery's various scribes and spiritual fathers, as ways of placing her account of Margery in the narrative foreground. If Margery serves as a screen for Kempe's analysis of communal codes and bonds, Kempe's allusions to these texts provide a convenient, safe, and conventional disguise for the *Book* that defines it by ignoring most of it.

1. For my remarks about the congruences between the *Revelations of St. Elizabeth of Hungary* and the *Book,* I am indebted to Sarah McNamer's introduction of her forthcoming edition of the *Revelations* from Cambridge University Library MS. Hh.1.11, which, along with her text, she was kind enough to share with me. For Saint Bridget, see Ellis, " 'Flores ad Fabricandam . . . Coronam': An Investigation into the Uses of the Revelations of St. Bridget of Sweden in Fifteenth-Century England."

The very background that Kempe composes for Margery's experience is one with important implications for an English reader. Her attention both to time and place suggests her interest in exploring the subject of secular and spiritual authority, since she locates the action during a period of anti-Lollard activity and in places that were particular hotbeds of Lollardy. She also peppers the narrative with names of real people, figures of the English church such as Philip Repingdon, Thomas Arundel, or Henry Bowet or of key individuals like the Duke of Bedford, who were active in supporting orthodoxy as a manifestation of nationalism. In fact, Kempe's verisimilitude can prevent us from looking more closely at the outlines of her fiction. If we take the *Book* as a sort of oral diary, composed through a scribe and at once artless and artful, we will be most concerned with examining Margery's struggles to achieve selfhood or with verifying Kempe's account of Margery's eventful life. Here, we are more than likely to be disappointed. We can use the episodes such as Margery's interviews with Philip Repingdon, Bishop of Lincoln, and Thomas Arundel, Archbishop of Canterbury, about a private ceremony of clothing to establish a chronological reference point for the action she recounts, but we cannot so simply use the *Book* as a guide to episcopal activities during the period. Similarly, Kempe describes Margery as being brought to trial in Leicester during what Meech conjectures is the late summer of 1417 (see 112–17). She describes the trial as a public one in which Margery was examined about her faith in the Church of All Hallows, where "þer was so meche pepyl þat þei stodyn vp-on stolys for to beheldyn hir & wonderyn vp-on hir" (114). However, neither the *Records of the Borough of Leicester* nor *The Register of Bishop Philip Repingdon* mention any such event.[2] Kempe's account in the final pages of the *Book* of Margery going from parish to parish in London and preaching against the excesses of the day, which must have "occured" in the summer of 1434, is not referred to in any contemporary source that I have seen. This, despite the fact that the *Register of Henry Chichele* (Chichele was Archbishop of Canterbury from 1414 to 1443) is extraordinarily rich in the details of local life, and Chichele's interest in maintaining the English church in orthodoxy and order certainly led him to inquire into anything that might have smacked of Lollardy. Though E. F. Jacob describes Chichele as a humane and beloved leader of the English church, an estimate I would not wish to challenge, reading his register leaves an overpowering

---

2. Archer, ed., *The Register of Bishop Philip Repingdon*; Bateson, *Records of the Borough of Leicester*.

impression of ecclesiastical surveillance and regulation of what to a twentieth-century American are the details of private life.[3] A woman derided by the London priesthood who nonetheless to all intents and purposes preached her way through the city followed and esteemed by the common people might be expected to excite a certain amount of official concern at a time when Lollard trials were not yet a distant memory.

Although some version of the events in the *Book* may well have happened, we do her a disservice as a writer not to inquire into the fictional reality she creates in the *Book*. The picture she presents of England is neither homogeneous nor orderly. The Leicestershire that challenged Margery for her beliefs was also the location for a good deal of Lollard activity during the late fourteenth and early fifteenth centuries, as, of course, was Margery's own East Anglia, or Bristol where Margery is also arrested.[4] By locating Margery in places associated with heterodoxy, Kempe raises the specter of dissent, and by raising it implicitly dissents from more official views of the English as bound together in a single and unified body. Kempe may or may not be portraying what happened to her; she is, however, portraying what she sees.

Her appraisal of her countrymen and -women has a good deal in common with other cultural documents that we have. The Parliament Rolls, for example, provide a fascinating glimpse into some of the tensions of the first third of the fifteenth century. First, the statement or sermon that opened Parliament not only underlined what were government concerns for any specific year but served as an expression of official views about government and, hence, about the relationship of any individual to the government, which, for the Middle Ages, was embodied in the figure of the king.[5] These opening statements seem especially interesting when they are read in relation to the sorts of concerns that are voiced by the Commons. Thus, Henry IV is imaged as a figure of counsel, law, equity, and justice. He is praised for his ability to call upon wisdom, for his willingness to take counsel, and for his honor; England is twice described as a body that can only function well if all parts agree to function as a whole. The uneasiness of the reign of Henry IV stands in contrast to this official emphasis upon order and justice. That there was a sharpening

---

3. See Jacob, ed., *The Register of Henry Chichele, Archbishop of Canterbury 1414–1443*.

4. See Crompton, "Leicestershire Lollards"; Plumb, "The Social and Economic Spread of Rural Lollardy: A Reappraisal"; Tanner, ed., *Heresy Trials*.

5. I am here referring to the *Rot. Parl.* from the accession of Henry IV in 1399 through the 1430s.

awareness of an individual's relationship to that whole is suggested by such requests as Commons brought in 1402 that any brief for felony or treason should specify not only the name of the individual, but also the names of his or her town and county. The request was brought to clear up the confusion resulting from similar names and surnames, revealing a concern for one's own "good name," particularly as that name might be falsely impugned by association. The request also suggests the growing awareness that written information could serve as well as gossip to destroy public images and expresses the ways in which identity was tied to locale. Kempe's description of Margery as equally careful to defend herself by saying that she is John Burnham's daughter of Lynn, implicitly not a traitor, evinces her own understanding of the need to define individual identity by reference to the group. Similarly, she describes Margery as persecuted by means of slander or "banning," forms of vilification that were anticipated by Lollard preachers and that reflect the contemporary dread of any act that severed a person from his or her community.[6]

In other entries that concern the need for public order, the Commons signify their dissent from the more official view of England's fundamental and divinely appointed order. Though the opening statements for the reigns of Henry V and Henry VI continue to play upon the theme of good government, the antiphonal role played by Commons undercuts any sense of a univocal nation. Where the voices of the Crown and the Church unite in decrying Lollards as traitors and, in some cases, linking them to common felons as promulgators of civic unrest, the voices of Commons more usually complain of excess taxation, petition against civic violence or for equitable solutions to economic or mercantile dilemmas, or bring up civic or ecclesiastical lapses. For example, in 1425 they raise the issue of the nonresidence of parsons and vicars, saying that people die without the care of the clergy; burials are delayed; and in some parish churches there are scarcely three Masses a week. In that same year, they ask that persons arrested for treason, felony, or Lollardy not be allowed to remain in prison for up to two years before being brought to trial, saying that such persons not only cost "the king" a good deal but place their "kepers" in great peril and fear.[7] In 1429, the chancellor chastises England for its

---

6. See for example, Hudson and Gradon, eds., *English Wycliffite Sermons*, 2:327. In general, the Lollard sermons on the Beatitudes describe persecution as some form of communal detraction.

7. See *Rot. Parl.*, vol. 4, III Hen. VI, nos. 38, 46, pp. 290, 292. Interestingly enough, both entries are in English.

infidelity, for error and heresy, obstinancy, and perversity, and raises the specter of the destruction of Jerusalem. Juxtaposed to what is a general moral warning linking national prosperity and stability to the obedience of subjects, are parliamentary petitions involving such issues as trespassing, protection of English sailing interests, the dangers to public order posed by fugitive felons and the burning of houses, in addition to the usual concern for trade, the Staple, and franchises. In 1433, the opening statement reiterated the model of the three estates, suggesting those duties owed by each: from prelates and magnates are expected peace, unity, and concord; from knights and the "medriocribus" are expected equity and the administration of justice; and from the vulgar and inferior orders, obedience to the will of the king and his laws are expected; they are also enjoined to avoid perjury and murmuring.[8] Though England's growing involvement in mercantile concerns is allowed for by the term "medriocribus," the reference hardly acknowledges what the Parliament Rolls themselves proclaim, that most of the business of Parliament centered around the need to regulate an increasingly complicated profit-oriented economy.

Kempe's treatment of her contemporaries is less an account of that world than a reading of it that dissents from more official or authoritative glosses upon the state of the body politic. The many techniques Kempe employs work against any simple understanding of the nature of that body. The episodic nature of the *Book* effectively fragments the experience of reading it and forces us into a process by which we establish meaning at the very moment when that meaning is likely to be qualified by or collapsed into the next episode.[9] Hence good confessors succeed bad confessors; John Kempe seems at times to threaten Margery's vocation and at others to support it; bishops are at once accessible and intractable; and Margery seems profound in one incident, banal in the next. Strategically, this sort of technique gives Kempe a good deal of latitude; her narrative cannot be judged as an explicit critique of contemporary institutions because she continually shifts the grounds whereby we judge the meaning of events. However, the combined effect of such shifts powerfully suggests that we read as fragmentary and irresolute the very community that official documents would have us believe is unified and definitive. Furthermore, by focusing upon Margery, whom she situates in a particular histori-

---

8. See *Rot. Parl.*, vol. 4, 8 Hen. VI, p. 335; 11 Hen. VI, p. 419.
9. For a description of episodic structure, see Middleton, "Narration and the Invention of Experience," 121.

cal context, Kempe can achieve a more delicately subversive image than she could if she merely offered a satiric description of Margery's world.

Her deployment of the topoi and language of gender is a case in point. By drawing upon the conventions of the holy woman, Kempe suggests the inadequacies of the contemporary Church since it too often excludes what Margery is. She also suggests its inability to control the feminine; Margery triumphs despite the powers vested in and wielded by a male hegemony. Margery's growing ability to evade those powers is, of course, rooted in the conventions of gender comedy that cultural historians have taught us to see as evidence of a broader social concern with order.[10] But where the comedy of gender frequently contains riot even as it depicts it, Kempe does not so conveniently dispose of Margery.[11] Most of the events described in the first section of the *Book* occur during the reign of Henry V, who even after his death in 1422 continued to be hailed for his manly strength, forcefulness, and heroism.[12] Praise for Henry was not limited to blazoning what can be described as his virility; he was also credited with upholding the true religion against the attacks of the Lollards. The "sotellete" introducing the second course of the infant Henry VI's coronation banquet lauded precisely these activities, and the opening statement of Henry VI's first Parliament praised his father as a perfect paragon of kingly rectitude and virtue.[13] Kempe's emphasis upon gender conflict in her accounts of episodes that most concern topics dear to the hearts of representatives of Henry's administration offers a subtle comment upon the ineffectiveness of such a power structure. Margery may be perceived as threatening the stabilities of the family, of the town, and of the country, and consequently is called to account in Leicester, in York, and in Bristol. However, she triumphs over such obstacles as the "men" of England place in her way and goes on to outlive the King himself. Kempe can thereby use one woman to do the work of several men. Just as the *Book*'s testimonies to Margery's sanctity at once provide an image of holiness and comment upon the society that will not recognize what is in its midst, so

10. See N. Z. Davis, "Woman on Top," in her *Society and Culture in Early Modern France*.

11. My remarks here owe much to Patterson's comments about the Wife of Bath. See *Chaucer and the Subject of History*, 281–83.

12. The *Libelle of Englysche Polycye* (1436), part of which recalls England's past mastery of the sea, provides an intentionally "masculine" image of Henry V as a shipbuilder, praising him for his magnificence, courage, wisdom, prudence, audacity, fortitude, justice, agility, and discretion, all traits that allowed him to dominate the sea (52).

13. Gairdner, *Historical Collections of a Citizen of London in the Fifteenth Century*, 148; *Rot. Parl.*, 4:169.

Kempe's emphasis on the gender of her protagonist—and thus upon gender conflict—gives her the scope to glance at the foundations of both spiritual and civil authority.

Even more pointed is her refusal to reintegrate Margery into prevailing structures. The *Book,* as we have seen, traces Margery's growing disengagement from the control of husbands, confessors, and all other figures of authority. Moreover, both parts of the *Book* conclude with depictions of Margery as having attained a necessary and objective distance from her world. The first part ends with a picture of Margery who is now, by choice, physically separated from the citizens of Lynn, since she is more usually to be found in her room with her writer. Kempe thereby concludes a narrative that chronicles spiritual growth as a species of conflict with neighbors, family, churchmen, and local officials with a picture that deliberately evokes an image of dissociation or of objectification. The second part ends with Margery's return to Lynn, after she has broken her word to her confessor, traveled to Germany and back, and progressed from London to Shene. Like many a wife before her, she endures "scharp wordys" but gets "as good loue of hym & of oþer frendys aftyr as sche had be-forn" (247). Kempe is vague about Margery's means of achieving such peace, but, as she implies, Margery's meekness conceals triumph. The communal and priestly pressure to which Margery nods at the *Book*'s end has nowhere near the force for her that it has at the beginning of her call to vocation. The *Book*'s final section of intercessory prayers can also be read as a powerful statement of disengagement that gives Margery herself the indisputably last word.

The layout of the manuscript of the *Book* suggests that the scribe who copied it was alive to the formal implications of ending with a selection of prayers. The second part of the *Book* ends only nine lines into the first leaf of folio 120. After the final words, "worschepyd be God," which are closed by a period, is the word "Amen." A decorative "Amen" is repeated in red ink on the same line, suggesting that, for one late medieval reader, at least, the narrative portion of the *Book* has concluded. The scribe then left the remainder of the page blank and began the prayers on the verso side of folio 120, using a large capital *T* ("Thys creatur, of whom is tretyd be-forn") to indicate the beginning of what is a separate section of the manuscript. Visually, the prayers appear as a section distinct from the *Book* itself, perhaps to be copied separately or committed to memory, and underline the scribe's awareness of the ways in which the prayers of the holy were used to feed the private devotional lives of late medieval men and women.[14] The scribe thus signified his sense of the prayers as generically distinct from the narrative portion of the manuscript. For him, though Margery's life justifies or authorizes the prayers, they can be used in ways the *Book* cannot, since they can be internalized and transformed by anyone who takes them as models for devotion.

On the other hand, the written prayer, like the written life, begs to be read as a composed text. There is no compelling reason to think that the person who wrote the *Book* did not also write the prayers and did not wish them to appear where they do in the manuscript.[15] They must therefore be understood within the context of the life they conclude. The prayers are further evidence of Kempe's innovative use of models that are at once spiritual and literary. The most obvious of these models is Saint Bridget of Sweden (c. 1302–73), whose example and Rule was memorialized by Henry V in the royal foundation at Syon, where Margery visits at the end of the narrative section of the *Book* on Lammas Day, a day the Pope had set aside for special pardon to pilgrims who honored Bridget by visiting the abbey.[16] As Gibson has pointed out, Saint Bridget seems to have had a special importance to the spiritual lives of East Anglians, and, at times, Kempe seems to be writing a "competitive" version of Saint Bridget's own eventful and important life.[17] Bridget was a wife and mother, a counsellor to the mighty, a prophet, a social critic, an international traveler, and a powerful example of sanctity; moreover, her prayers, *The Fifteen O's*, on the Passion of Christ were enormously popular in England well into the sixteenth century.[18] Just as the narrative of Margery's life is

14. See the notes by Allen to this section of the *Book*. Allen remarks that the prayers of a number of German holy women were composed for circulation. For remarks about private devotion in the late Middle Ages, see Gray, "Popular Religion and late Medieval English Literature"; Mertes, *The English Noble Household*, chapter 5.

15. On this subject, see Meech, ed., *The Book of Margery Kempe*, 349.

16. On the importance of Lammas to the cult of Saint Bridget, see the poem in her honor by John Audelay in Cumming, ed., *The Revelations*, introduction, xxxiii. On Saint Bridget of Sweden, see also Hollaway, ed. and trans., *Saint Bride and Her Book*; Kieckhefer, *Unquiet Souls*.

17. Gibson, *Theater of Devotion*, 20–21, 97–98. See also Lochrie, *Margery Kempe and Translations of the Flesh*, 76–88, for illuminating remarks about the relationship between the *Book* and the *Revelations* of Saint Bridget. There is even a curious parallel between the experiences of Margery and of Bridget in the deaths of their sons. As Cumming notes in his edition of *The Revelations*, 128 n. 117, when Bridget's son Charles became the lover of Joanna, queen of Naples, Bridget prayed to heaven for assistance and was "rewarded" by her son's death. Margery, of course, is similarly rewarded when her eldest son's lechery is punished by disease, which, in turn, inspires him to a holy life. Some years later, she takes comfort in his death, since he died a pious man.

18. See Cumming, ed., *The Revelations of Saint Birgitta*, introduction, xxxvii.

rooted in the literary conventions of sacred biography, Margery's prayers are designed to provide further evidence of her importance as a figure of English holiness.

The prayers image Margery as a singular figure of intercession. Here, Kempe may be deliberately recalling the powers accorded to Bridget of Sweden. For example, the 1531 edition of the *Horae Beatae Virginis* according to the Use of Sarum printed the *Fifteen O's* and promised that anyone who said them faithfully for a year could deliver fifteen of his kindred out of purgatory, convert fifteen others to good life, and help another fifteen persevere in a good life.[19] After requesting mercy for herself, Margery therefore requests mercy for others—her confessors; all members of the Church; the King and all members of government; all outsiders, Jews, Saracens, and heathens; and all of her fellow human beings. The requests, like the special prayers offered during the Mass, present a hierarchical view of society, and by their very conventionality implicitly suggest that Margery herself has the means to do what her own spiritual fathers do not. Though the concept of intercessory prayer is as old as the Church itself, the effect of ending the *Book* with a section of prayers has the effect of highlighting Margery at the expense of more obvious figures of authority and intercession. In so doing, Kempe specifically juxtaposes Margery to a world whose need for Margery is acute. Like Thomas of Cantimpré or Jacques de Vitry or Bridget of Sweden, Kempe locates sanctity in the context of worldliness.

This final depiction of Margery is paradoxical, since the prayers suggest that Margery's detachment from the world is a manifestation of her profound attachment to it. In introducing the prayers, Kempe is careful to situate Margery within the community of the Church:

> Thys creatur, of whom is tretyd be-forn, vysd many ȝerys to be-gynnyn hir preyerys on þis maner. First whan sche cam to chirche, knelyng be-forn þe Sacrament in þe worschep of þe blissyd Trinite (Fadir, Sone, & Holy Gost, oo God & iij Personys), of þat gloryows Virgine, Qwen of Mercy, owr Lady Seynt Mary, & of þe xij apostelys, sche seyd þis holy ympne "Veni creator spiritus" wyth alle þe versys longyng þerto, þat God xulde illumynyn hir sowle, as he dede hys apostelys on Pentecost Day, & induyn hir wyth þe ȝyftys of þe Holy Gost þat sche myth han grace to

19. Cumming, ed., *The Revelations of Saint Birgitta*, introduction, xxxvii.

vndirstondyn hys wil & parformyn it in werkyng, & þat sche myth han grace to wythstondyn þe temptacyons of hir gostly enmijs & enchewyn al maner synne & wikkydnes. (248)

The scene Kempe describes would have been familiar to any fifteenth-century reader, for the physical experience of churchgoing was then far different from what it is now. First, the interior architecture of the church compartmentalized it into separate sections. The elaborate rood screens of the late Middle Ages were designed to screen the sacrament and the ministrations of the Mass from those who stood or kneeled on the other side. Since the Mass was also celebrated in Latin, which few persons could understand, the laity was further distanced from the mysteries being enacted at the altar. The experience of the Mass was therefore concentrated in the act of viewing the sacrament when it was elevated and in acts of private devotion. Works like the *Lay Folks Mass Book*, along with private missals and books of hours, bear witness to efforts to provide focus or direction for the experience of private prayer. Thus, while the priest and his attendants celebrated in Latin a sacrament of salvific sacrifice at the altar, the very placement of which defined sacred space, those on the other side of the screen watched and, perhaps, engaged in vernacular devotions that were meant to open up the meaning of that which they came to observe.[20]

The experience was, as John Bossy has analyzed it, at once communal and private. Such practices as the distribution of holy bread (the unchanged but blessed bread) to a laity that did not normally participate in communion more than once or twice a year were meant to reinforce an idea of community as unity in the faith.[21] As Rosamund Faith has demonstrated, such rituals could also express ideas of anticlerical unity.[22] In the *Gesta Abbatum* Walsingham recounts a long dispute between the Abbey of Saint Albans and its local tenants over ancient rights, a dispute that culminated in an act meant both to underscore the tenants' rebellion against clerical privilege and to signify their own solidarity. The dispute concerned the peasants'

20. See Brooke, "Religious Sentiment and Church Design in the Later Middle Ages." On private devotion in relation to the Mass, see, for example, Brilioth, *Eucharistic Faith and Practice,* 80–81; Driver, "Pictures in Print"; Hoskins, ed., *Horae Beatae Mariae Virginis or Sarum and York Primers;* Simmons, ed., *Lay Folks Mass Book.*

21. See Rubin, *Corpus Christi,* 73–74; Thomas, *Religion and the Decline of Magic,* 29–30.

22. Faith, " 'The Great Rumour' of 1377 and Peasant Ideology," 63. For another discussion of this incident, see Middleton, "William Langland's 'Kynde Name,' " 70.

assertion of their right to use their own handmills rather than the abbey's, for which they must pay. The peasants lost the dispute and their mills were confiscated and set into the floor of the abbey parlor; but they later rebelled and on Corpus Christi Day, 1381, reclaimed their own: "They took the stones outside and handed them over to the commons, breaking them into little pieces and giving a piece to each person, just as the consecrated bread is customarily broken and distributed in the parish churches on Sundays, so that the people, seeing these pieces, would know themselves to be avenged against the abbey in that cause."[23] Walsingham's simile ("ut panis benedictus Dominicis diebus partiri et conferri in ecclesiis parochialibus consuivit") communicates his sense of outrage, which, in turn, reflects his own firm belief in hierarchical ordering. His language also emphasizes his feeling that ritual itself had been violated by this act of ritualized antiritual, which mimicked the community founded upon faith and ordered by estates. Not only is the unsanctified distributed among the rebels, but they serve one another in the priestly act of parting and distributing (*partiri et conferri*). In the act of composing a community, they have, to use a later reformist term, become their own advocates.

Kempe's description of Margery positions her at the focal point of the community of the Body of Christ. She describes Margery as kneeling before the sacrament, obediently assuming the place and the space assigned to her, where she prays as one of Christ's disciples for pentecostal power. The "prayers of thys creatur" follow her repetition of the verses of the Pentecostal hymn, "Veni creator." Implicitly, the prayers are the embodiment of the Holy Spirit's power in Margery, who, like the Church of the faithful, is quickened by the gift of the spirit. Whereas earlier in the *Book* Kempe describes Margery as a figure like Ecclesia, whose gift of tongues allows her to communicate with those who do not speak English but who love Christ, now she presents Margery as the medium through which the word comes to us and is returned to God. Present in this Church is no figure of priestly advocacy, but only Margery, whose prayer can be read as a "reading" of her world and thus of her relationship to it. Most obviously, the prayer evinces her detachment from that world; the ability to pray for, like the ability to write about, testifies to a process of objectification, an assertion of control over what is thereby constituted.

Margery thus describes herself as the means through which her world

---

23. The translation is Faith's (" 'The Great Rumour' of 1377 and Peasant Ideology," 63). For the original, see Walsingham, *Gesta Abbatum*, 3:309.

can apprehend God. In a startling sentence she asks, "And I prey þe, Soueryn Lord Crist Ihesu, þat as many men mote be turnyd be my crying & my wepyng as me han scornyd þerfor er xal scornyn in-to þe werdys ende & many mo yf it be ȝowr wille" (249). What Kempe signals here is her sense that the *Book* is as open to misinterpretation as the life it recounts, since those who may scorn Margery "in-to þe werdys ende" can only be those who read the text of her life. Kempe thereby implies that Margery functions as a sort of cipher for the meaning of Ecclesia, going on to emphasize her importance as a figure of mediation, whose powers transcend even those of the priesthood: "Lord, make my gostly fadirs for to dredyn þe in me & for to louyn þe in me" (249). Implicitly, "gostly fadirs," like mayors, fellow townspeople, and future readers need special help in recognizing the outlines of sanctity; recognition must then be a mark of grace.

If Kempe uses the prayer to establish Margery's singular position, she also uses it to compose a world. That world is not described in the conventional language of estates theory but rather in the language of the spirit, where the concept of sin has far more currency than the claims of wealth or status. Her presentation of society begins innocently enough, with prayers for the Pope and other ministers of the church, for the King of England, and the "lordys & ladijs þat arn in þis world" (250). However, Margery goes on to ask for such "gouernawnce" for these so that they may be lords and ladies in heaven and to pray that all rich men may learn the proper use of goods. She follows her prayer for rich men with one for "Iewys, & Saraȝinys, & alle hethen pepil," for heretics, "mysbeleuarys," false tithers, thieves, adulterers, prostitutes, and "mischievous" livers. She moves from these to all her friends and her enemies and, finally, to the community of the dead, the souls in purgatory.[24] The prayer does more than demonstrate Margery's charity toward all. By creating a catalogue whereby rich men, Jews, adulterers, heretics, false tithers, and loose livers are grouped indiscriminately together, Kempe destroys any sense of a social hierarchy based upon outward signs of status. What, finally, is the difference between a rich man who lives only for himself and a Jew, or between an adulterer and a prostitute, except that the one is an accepted part of the community and the other is excluded from it? If lords

---

24. On the prayers for the dead as invoking a vast community made up of both the living and the dead, see Burgess, "A fond thing vainly invented." On intercessory prayer and the metaphors of spiritual exchange, see Rosenthal, *The Purchase of Paradise*.

and ladies may *not* be lords and ladies in the court of heaven and if many a saint began as a heathen (250), how may we make social distinctions? What Kempe composes here is a community of the spirit, the true Church, whose members are bound together not by any ideology of commercial profit but by their hopes for spiritual gain, that is, in ways precluded by social hierarchies. What is imaged here is a unity achieved through Margery, the scorned and outcast member of society. In the final portion of her prayer she thus claims kinship with the holy dead who form one vast contingent of the Body of Christ.

By blurring the distinctions among various parts of society and between the secular and the sacred, Kempe, like the authors of the mystery cycles, adumbrates the process of composing a community. This is a process that goes on throughout the mystery cycles, but here I would like to touch briefly on the effect of two of the more obviously communal pageants, the Entry into Jerusalem and Pentecost, both of which are relevant to Kempe's handling of the relationship between Margery and the community. The plays are some of our most important "civic artifacts" from the late Middle Ages and are particularly valuable guides to secular and civic ideology and piety. As Lawrence Clopper has most recently emphasized, there is very little evidence that clergy of any kind were involved in the creation of secular drama; he describes them as the products of the city.[25] They can therefore tell us a good deal about the ways in which civic governments saw themselves as having a certain responsibility for public morality and religious education.[26] They also testify to a certain preoccupation with the process by which the community itself comes into existence. The plays that dramatize Christ's entry into Jerusalem are especially interesting in this regard; they embody that process as a moment when a community that is, for a brief moment, nonhierarchical is focused around that figure whose entry into the city is the first movement of the Passion. The Entry plays thus—either explicitly or implicitly—define the one community as antithetical to what is an existing civic structure. In so doing, the plays hint at a certain amount of anticlericalism, since Jerusalem is governed by the "Bishops" Caiphas and Annas and by Pilate, the representative of the Emperor, who is easily swayed by these self-serving figures of prelatical dominion.

Of the three extant cycles that have Entry plays—York, Chester, and N-Town—York is the most well-developed example of civic ceremony

25. Clopper, "Lay and Clerical Impact on Civic Religious Drama and Ceremony," 112.
26. Clopper, "Lay and Clerical Impact on Civic Religious Drama and Ceremony," 128.

and celebration.[27] However, in the very act of celebrating the idea of community and of locating that idea in York itself, the playwright suggests the differences between the community that coalesces around Christ and that in which his actors and audience lived.[28] The York Entry uses the procession as the pretext for imaging the community. Whereas actual medieval processions were composed according to strict rules of social hierarchy and reflected the participants' acute sense of the value they vested in degree, wealth, and social power, the York procession can almost be described as a "happening."[29] After the first 100 lines, which elaborate upon the biblical account of Christ sending Peter and Philip to borrow the ass, the playwright gives the play to Janitor, the porter who has loaned the beast to the disciples. Consequently, before we see Christ riding toward Jerusalem, we watch Janitor's progress toward the city where he spreads the news of Christ's coming. Around him appear citizens who bear witness to Jesus' ministry, to the prophets' description of his coming, and to their mutual love for him. What we see is a brief moment of civic harmony wherein each citizen is bound to all the others through adoration of the figure who is described as riding toward them. When Jesus actually appears, he moves through a city that at once hails him and manifests its need for him. As he goes, he heals the sick, gives sight to the blind, and cleanses the spiritual disease of men like Zaccheus, whose god has been the god of merchandizing. The play ends by encapsulating the fundamental tension between ideal and actuality. First, when Jesus sees Jerusalem, he does not salute it but mourns its coming destruction. It will "forsake" and "trespass against" its king, and its "game" and its "gle" will be taken from it.[30] In contrast to Jesus' lament,

27. Martin Stevens has written eloquently on this play; see his *Four Middle English Mystery Cycles*, 50–87.

28. Stevens, in *Four Middle English Mystery Cycles*, applies a Bakhtinian approach to the York cycle, pointing out that Christ comes riding toward the city as a sort of King of Fools. That same city, or York, will crucify him as vociferously as it hailed him. See 77–87 for a discussion of the social commentary embedded in the cycle. For further discussion of the relationship between the figure of Christ and the idea of the community, see Travis, "The Social Body of the Dramatic Christ in Medieval England."

29. On medieval civic processions much has been written. See Clopper, "Lay and Clerical Impact on Civic Religious Drama," 125; James, "Ritual, Drama and Social Body in the Late Medieval English Town"; Mills, "Religious Drama and Civic Ceremonial"; Phythian-Adams, "Ceremony and the Citizen"; Rubin, *Corpus Christi*, 233, 266–68; idem, "Small Groups," 143–45; Stevens, *Four Middle English Mystery Cycles*, 50ff. For the text of the York Entry, see Beadle, ed., *The York Plays*.

30. Beadle, ed., *The York Plays*, "The Entry into Jerusalem," lines 470–80.

the citizens of York end the play with eight separate speeches hailing his entry. The eighth and final speech suggests that they unknowingly hail their own coming desolation:

> Hayll domysman dredful, þat all schall deme,
> Hayll þat all quyk and dede schall lowte,
> Hayll whom worschippe moste will seme,
> Hayll whom all thyng schall drede and dowte.
> We welcome þe.
> Hayll and welcome of all abowte,
> To owre ceté.[31]

They hail Christ as conqueror and as judge, seemingly unaware that the very "ceté" into which they welcome him cannot sustain the scrutiny of that moment of judgment. That city may figuratively be Jerusalem, but literally it is York, whose civic government like that of Jerusalem was inextricably bound up with the privileges and powers accorded Ecclesia.[32] The playwright thereby dramatizes a moment of epiphanal paradox at which the shout of acclamation is, ironically, also an admission of incomprehension.

Both the N-Town and Chester cycles incorporate the Entry into other plays. The Chester cycle treats it in a sequence that begins with Jesus' visit to Bethany and to the house of Simon the Leper, where Mary Magdalene anoints Jesus with the costly ointment that so offends Judas's sense of economy. From there, the play moves back to Jerusalem with the entry and closes with Christ's cleansing of the Temple and Judas's conspiracy with Caiphas and Annas.[33] In the N-Town cycle, the entry is one part of the first Passion play, which opens with a speech by Satan and a prologue by John the Baptist, and then goes on to present in a parallel fashion the events of the conspiracy and those of the entry. Both these plays underline the difference between two notions of community by their emphasis upon opposing power groups. The power imaged in Christ that binds his followers together in a community of faith is not power in an earthly

---

31. Beadle, ed., *The York Plays*, "The Entry into Jerusalem," lines 538–44.

32. See Stevens, *Four Middle English Mystery Cycles*, 81–82, for an account of the ways in which the many ecclesiastical foundations in and around York affected the administration of civic justice.

33. For a searching discussion of this play that emphasizes its handling of the nature of Christ, see Travis, *Dramatic Design in the Chester Cycle*, 163–66.

sense, since it has nothing in common with the structures of communities. The power of the earthly city we can more easily comprehend. It is the power of the marketplace, of the ecclesiastical court, of reigning social groups. Furthermore, Jesus' entry directly threatens the community composed of hierarchies rooted in earthly power, as the inclusion of the Temple Cleansing at this point in the Chester play makes all too clear. The playwright's emphasis upon merchandizing, which makes it seem as if Christ is destroying a contemporary fair, locates the scene, less in the Temple than in local space: Christ does not scourge Jews from the Temple, but "merchants" from their tables. Thus, against the highly structured and self-consciously powerful members of Jerusalem's oligarchy, the playwrights image another community organized *around* a single figure who disdains social—and hence vertical—manifestations of power.

Within the contexts of the plays themselves, such images of spiritual community are shattered by the Crucifixion and tentatively reconstructed in the Pentecost plays. However, where the dramatizations of Christ's entry into Jerusalem present community as a manifestation of faith and consequently as far less hierarchically ordered than the city that produces and watches the pageant, treatments of Pentecost emphasize the composition of the community of the Church in terms of apostolic succession. Since the second chapter of Acts specifies that only the disciples received the gifts of the Holy Spirit, thus providing precedent for an understanding of the priesthood as sacramental and therefore distinct, medieval playwrights inevitably figure that community as organized in ways that more clearly resemble this world. For example, the treatment of Pentecost in the Chester cycle opens with the disciples choosing by lot a successor to Judas's empty "office." When the lot falls on Matthew, Peter is the one to "name" him an apostle.[34] The dramatization of the descent of the Holy Spirit that follows locates power, knowledge, and faith in the twelve, each of whom has a part to say. What they testify to is a faith that is expressed in credal form.[35] The play thus replaces the more spontaneous acclamations of the citizens hailing Christ's Entry into Jerusalem with pictures of the apostles receiving what is a religious education; it also presents ecclesi-

34. Lumiansky and Mills, eds., *The Chester Mystery Cycle*, "Pentecost," lines 46, 59–60. The scene is described in Acts 1 and directly preceeds the Descent. However, where the Bible simply says that the lot fell on Matthew, and he was numbered with the twelve, the playwright emphasizes what is a line of succession validated by and through Peter.

35. On credal design in the entire cycle, see Travis, *Dramatic Design in the Chester Cycle*, 192–217.

astical hierarchy as an expression of Pentecostal power, since the apostles' newly acquired and catechistically formulated knowledge of the divine authorizes them as guides to the holy. While both the York and N-Town Pentecost plays seem to make a greater effort to capture the dizzying effervesence of the Descent, they also epitomize revelation as a sign of apostolic succession or power. The N-Town Pentecost, for all its brevity, has a special brilliance; it captures the unity of the twelve by presenting them as speaking antiphonally of what they have seen. No speaker can claim any single sentence for himself, so their responses to the divine embody that moment of reformed Babel that is Pentecost. The York Pentecost is perhaps the most concerned with capturing the rapture of the moment, taking special pains to exploit some of the onlookers' remarks that the disciples' Pentecostal fervor must be a sign of drunkenness. Both plays, however, present the world as polarized by that moment of rapture, employing a stereotypical community of Jewish elders and citizens as the scoffers at and enemies of this newly composed community. But as the Doomsday plays make all too clear, Christ will come not to divide Jew from Christian, but rather to separate Christian citizens from one another, and he will do so by judging their attitudes towards community ("As ye have done to the least of these . . .").

Where the playwrights invent dramatic action that, at times, comments ironically upon the communities that enact and witness the plays, Kempe employs the strategies of narrative prose to reflect upon that same process by which communities compose and define themselves. For example, the York Entry into Jerusalem sends Christ along the same route traced by royalty in their entries into York, thus juxtaposing spiritual to earthly kingship.[36] Kempe employs a processional pattern for Margery's return to England in the final chapters of the *Book* as a way of pointing up the weaknesses of regal power or ecclesiastical authority. The Margery who comes to London on a borrowed horse is intended to provoke both a secular and a spiritual response: she comes as simply to London as Christ to Jerusalem, certainly far more simply than Henry came to London after the triumph of Agincourt, who also came in monarchical imitation of Christ. However, Margery receives few accolades to ease her progress in a city Kempe describes as composed of the scornful rich and the common people who magnify God in her (see 243–45). Kempe also uses the topoi

36. Stevens, *Four Middle English Mystery Cycles,* 52–62. On the implications of processional routing, see Rubin, *Corpus Christi,* 268.

of Pentecost to underline the worldliness of the contemporary Church; it is in describing Margery's experiences in Rome, which seems a confused Babel of persons of different nationalities, that Kempe pays greatest attention to the subject of language. Margery herself, though she speaks only English, moves among and communicates with the various and disparate persons she encounters in that city. Kempe's account of the seat of Christendom thus ignores the physical city—its many relics and splendors—to focus on Margery's personal relationships, depicting the Church as composed of persons who can only be judged in terms of their attitudes toward the holy. Whereas Julian of Norwich compares the face she sees in her second "showing" to that imprinted on one of Rome's most venerated relics, the Vernicle, Kempe, who might be expected to mention the effect of such a potent relic on the impressionable Margery during her long stay in Rome, neglects it altogether.[37] Significantly, in these scenes in Rome it is Margery to whom Kempe ascribes true moral authority; she alone attempts to imitate the Christ whose spiritual power has been transmogrified into earthly status.

Kempe's handling of the topic of pilgrimage is also designed to point up the ambiguities inherent in the formalization of private acts of devotion. The very subject of pilgrimage was, of course, charged with associations of Lollardy, since the Lollards discussed pilgrimage as a manifestation of image worship, or idolatry.[38] In his *Examination,* Thorpe first defines the true pilgrim as any person earnestly seeking the bliss of heaven through virtuous living and then argues against pilgrimages in terms of the fundamental hypocrisy of most pilgrims:

> As their works shew, the most part of men or women that go now on pilgrimages have not these foresaid conditions. . . . For . . . examine . . . twenty of these pilgrims! and he shall not find three men or women that know surely of commandment of God, nor can say their *Pater noster* and *Ave Maria!* nor their *Credo,* readily in any manner of language. . . . All such pilgrims despise GOD and all His commandments and Saints. For the commandments of GOD

---

37. On contemporary attitudes toward the city of Rome, see Nichols, ed. and trans., *The Marvels of Rome. Mirabilia Urbis Romae.* For Julian of Norwich, see Colledge and Walsh, eds., *The Showings,* the Long Text, 328; introduction, 53–57.

38. See Cronin, "The Twelve Conclusions of the Lollards," 300–301; Hudson, ed., *English Wycliffite Writings,* 83–88.

they will neither know nor keep, nor conform them to live virtuously by example of CHRIST and of his Saints.[39]

Thorpe goes on to say that people go on pilgrimage more for the health of their bodies than of their souls, stressing the worldliness of most pilgrimages, which are too often accompanied by the lewd music of hired pipers. He especially mentions bagpipes. Thorpe thus draws a sharp distinction between two concepts of pilgrimage, one that is ultimately based on an Augustinian distinction between two sorts of societies. The one is composed of men and women helping one another toward heaven, the other is the various and complex society of the world that cannot but impede the progress of the soul to God. What the world calls pilgrimage is merely a replication of its own distraction and vanity.

Although it is tempting to say that Kempe's orthodoxy is confirmed by her persistent focus upon pilgrimage, her handling of the topic is not so easily categorized. It is true that much of the *Book* is taken up by the subject: Margery's pilgrimage to Jerusalem includes secondary trips to Rome and to Assisi; she later goes to Santiago and to Wilsnak, in addition to making other trips to shrines in her own country. As I pointed out in Chapter 2, however, Kempe's description of these journeys is less an account of *loci* of power and sanctification than it is a story of Margery's personal relations with her fellow pilgrims. The sites themselves function less as ends than as means to elucidate the nature of the pilgrim community and Margery's status within it. Kempe's account of Jerusalem is the most detailed (there is none at all of Santiago), but what is memorable about Margery's experience in the Holy Land is Margery's experience. Each thing she sees—Mount Calvary, the Sepulcher, the stone on which Christ's body was laid, the room of the Last Supper, the place of Pentecost, and the burial place of the Virgin—Kempe describes as triggering a response in Margery. Though Kempe records the experience as underlining Margery's submission to the rule of others, she also suggests that Margery's imaginative re-creation of Jesus' passion frees her from conventional obedience. Jesus says to her, "I am wel plesyd wyth þe, dowtyr, for þu stondist vndyr obedyens of Holy Cherch & þat þu wylt obey þi confessowr & folwyn hys cownsel"; but he emphasizes, "I am aboue al Holy Cherch & I xal gon [wyth þe] & kepyn þe rygth wel" (72–73). He

---

39. *Examination of Master William Thorpe,* in Pollard, ed., *Fifteenth Century Prose and Verse,* 139, 140.

speaks here of pilgrimage itself, telling her that she need not go for spiritual merit, for her sins were forgiven before she came; but he nonetheless commands her to go to Rome and Santiago, presumably for the very spiritual experience that Kempe's account of Jerusalem verifies. Though Kempe describes Jesus as supporting the authority of ecclesiastical figures of authority, he also offers himself as a higher authority and implicitly suggests that pilgrimage itself is only efficacious *if* it produces a private spiritual response. Not only here does Kempe fix our attention upon Margery and her subjective record of Jesus' command, but she also, albeit carefully, defines pilgrimage in ways Thorpe himself might allow.

She primarily defines it as a society united by an ostensibly common goal that can be attained through sound financial management and cooperation. Margery's way to Jerusalem is paved with contractual agreements—with her husband, with her fellow pilgrims, with the Saracens who lead her around the Holy Land, and with innkeepers. Furthermore, Kempe makes it clear that Margery's path is eased by her ability to pay. In fact, references to a cash economy recur throughout the first half of this first pilgrimage of Margery's. Not only is she free to go to Jerusalem because she agrees to pay her husband's debts, but "hir gold" is the occasion for trouble with her fellow pilgrims (see 62 and 64). Margery is able to proceed to Venice without her company because she can "reward" William Weaver for guiding her. Kempe's description of the business of getting to Jerusalem from Venice emphasizes that it is a business; words denoting commercial exchange dominate a passage of only about eighteen lines. The company must "buy" wine vessels and "ordain" a ship as well as bedding. Since they have failed to do so for her, Margery must "buy" and "purvey" and "ordain" for herself. She continues to display her abilities to negotiate the world once she is in Jerusalem, putting a "grote" in the hand of the Saracen who carries her to the top of Mount Quarentine (74). That the nature of Margery's pilgrimage changes radically when in Rome Christ commands her to give away all her money says much about Kempe's appraisal of pilgrimages. Clearly, though all of the company go to Jerusalem, not all can be described as pilgrims. By defining pilgrimage as a company made up of persons with a single goal and of a relatively similar social status, Kempe at once assimilates the pilgrim community to the world and presents the world as opposed to spiritual gain. Though her depiction has its roots in the actual— ships and bedding must be purveyed and gold must be somehow carried along—it is finally a fiction meant to be understood in relation to Margery, whose journey is increasingly inward. By carefully selecting the details by which she describes Margery's world, Kempe suggests the fundamental weaknesses of communities held together by values as flimsy as the covenants that bind both guildsmen and pilgrims.

In her effort to understand the nature or foundations of community, Kempe ultimately chooses to place her greatest emphasis upon relationships. It is therefore not the places Margery visits that stand out in the *Book*, for they serve as stations marking her own private response to holiness, but the people she encounters and the conversations she has that claim our greatest attention. Kempe uses the reactions of Margery's fellows to her admittedly uncomfortable spirituality as the means of gauging the values of the community she composes around Margery. She also uses Margery's relations with her fellows as a way of devaluing the very pilgrimages on which Margery so earnestly embarks. What the Lollards castigate in the contemporary institution of pilgrimage Kempe transforms into dramatic narrative. Take, for example, Kempe's account of Margery's last pilgrimage, a journey to see the Blood of Wilsnak. Kempe's account epitomizes the pilgrimage world as merely a replication of the world itself, where relations between England and Germany are polarized by mercantile concerns, and spiritual devotion is scorned in favor of good company by the way (see 232–35).[40] In contrast to the rich descriptions of Margery's unfortunate adventures, Kempe's account of the object of the pilgrimage is terse; "þus what wyth wel & wyth woo thorw þe help of owr Lord sche was browt to Wilsnak & saw þat Precyows Blod whech be myracle cam owt of þe blisful Sacrament of þe Awtere" (234–35). From Wilsnak, Margery goes to Aachen where she stays for ten or eleven days until Saint Margaret's Day, when the Virgin's smock is displayed. If we didn't know how seriously relics were taken during the late Middle Ages, we might accuse Kempe of parody: her account of Margery's final trip seems at times to transform Margery into a sort of vagabond whose encounters with others—merchants, worldly women, poor folk, pilgrims robbed of their money, thirsty friars, scornful monks—are finally the point of the narrative. In those encounters, Kempe presents an image of fifteenth-century society whose fundamental disorder is the manifestation of its factionalization.

The very society Kempe constitutes is the society she deconstructs; she presents Margery as at once the representative of that society and as its

---

40. On the international situation at the time of this final journey, see Meech, ed., *The Book of Margery Kempe*, 344–45.

remedy. Her needs for status, for goods, and for spiritual gratification can be detected in countless human documents of the late Middle Ages.[41] The social and religious rituals that helped to define individual life in relation to the community serve to bind Margery to her world even as they become her means of escape from its strictures. Thus, in describing the details of such annual celebrations as Purification Day (see 198) or Palm Sunday (see 184), Kempe locates Margery among "þe pepyl" as one who goes in procession with others or bears a candle in church, one member of a common body. But for Margery these communal rituals are catalytic in the sense that Kempe describes her as using them as means of entry into a more vividly experienced private world. Furthermore, the society that celebrates its faith in such rituals is one whose institutions implicitly do not satisfy Margery's yearnings for spiritual fulfillment and can only reject Margery for her individualistic expressions of faith.

Kempe, like Chaucer, employs pilgrimage as a means of presenting a highly selective picture of society that serves as an exploration of the inadequacies of contemporary institutions. She also uses it to suggest a new way of conceiving of community. She accomplishes this through Margery, whose liminality allows her to move freely in and around the stratifications of late medieval society. By presenting Margery's experience as a series of conversations or personal encounters with a wide variety of persons, Kempe provides the narrative with vignettes that, when taken together, begin to suggest ways in which the holy might be located in areas where we are not usually prepared to find it.[42] I would thus like to end my own exploration of Kempe's *Book* by focusing on two separate but ultimately related incidents that underscore her profoundly radical investigation into the core of human social existence.

The first of these incidents, which I have already touched on in Chapter 2, is the account in chapter 17 of Margery's interview with Richard Caistyr, the Vicar of Saint Stephen's in Norwich, to whom Christ bids her

---

41. For a discussion of some of these documents, see Gibson, *Theater of Devotion,* chapters 1 and 2. As Gibson has emphasized, late medieval wills provide eloquent testimony of the needs of late medieval men and women. For discussions of these, see, for example, Driver, "Pictures in Print"; Gray, "Popular Religion and Late Medieval English Literature"; Harrod, "Extracts from Early Wills in the Norwich Registries"; Perrow, "The Last Will and Testament as a Form of Literature"; Post, "The Obsequies of John of Gaunt"; Tanner, *The Church in Late Medieval Norwich;* Vale, *Piety, Charity, and Literacy Among the Yorkshire Gentry, 1370–1480.* See also the wills recorded in the registers of Bishop Repingdon and Archbishop Chichele.

42. In her discussion of the fifteenth century's complicated use of images, Gibson applies the phrase, "incarnational esthetic" as a way of describing the insistence on the concrete.

go. Kempe's choice of Richard Caistyr is itself significant, for he had a reputation for erudition, for sanctity, and for piety. He was even praised by John Bale, who suggested Caistyr was secretly sympathetic to Lollardy, for his dislike of clerical excess and abuses.[43] Kempe's decision to include Caistyr in the *Book* as a figure Christ himself recommends to Margery was thus probably not coincidental; she thereby signifies her approbation for a certain type of clerical figure, whose authority derives from holiness rather than from administrative power. Margery's interview with Caistyr is even more significant. She enters his church on a Thursday, a little before noon, and finds him walking up and down with another priest. Margery approaches Caistyr and asks to speak with him for an hour or two about the love of God sometime in the afternoon after he had eaten. Caistyr is at once amazed ("What cowd a woman ocupyn an owyr er tweyn owyrs in þe lofe of owyr Lord?") and receptive, for he says he will not eat until he hears such a marvel:

> þan he sett hym down in þe chirche. Sche, syttyng a lytyl be-syde, schewyd hym all þe wordys whech God had reuelyd to hyr in hyr sowl[e]. Sythen sche schewyd hym al hyr maner of levyng fro hyr chyldhod as ny as it wolde come to hir mende, —how vnkynd sche had ben a-geyn owyr Lord Ihesu Crist, how prowde & veyne sche had ben in hir aport, how obstynat a-geyns þe lawes of God, & how envyows a-geyn hir euyn-cristen, sythen, whan it plesyd owyr Lord Crist Ihesu, how sche was chastysed wyth many tribulacyons & horrybyl temptacyons, & aftyrward how sche was fed and com-fortyd wyth holy medytacyons & specyl in þe mende of owyr Lordys Passyon. (38–39)

This passage, taken together with Kempe's preceding description of Margery's approach to Caistyr, captures much about her sure sense of technique as well as her interest in relocating the holy in what is, finally, homely space. Here, as elsewhere throughout the *Book,* Kempe is specific about time and place. Thus, she is careful to indicate when Margery found Caistyr (on a Thursday, a little before noon) and where (walking up and down his church with his own confessor). She then, as few medieval authors do, provides us with a dramatization of the process of confession that underlines its status as conversation between two persons. As John

43. See Meech, ed., *The Book of Margery Kempe,* 276 n. 38; 320 n. 142.

Bossy puts it, "Medieval confession, we need to remember, was a face-to-face encounter between two people who would probably have known each other pretty well; we may also remember that it occurred, normally speaking, once a year, in the not-so-remote presence of a large number of neighbours, and more or less at the time (Maundy Thursday) set aside for the reconciliation to the community of public penitents in the pre-scholastic sense."[44] Kempe's account, however, though located in the realm of the actual, uses what is conventional as a screen for a more probing interest in the subject of confession: by confessing to Caistyr—the two of them sitting there in the church of Saint Stephen's—Margery effectively introduces herself to him.

She does so by "showing" herself to him. Kempe consistently uses the verb "schew," meaning to disclose or to make oneself known, to describe Margery's acts of confession. Since it was commonly employed in that context, Kempe's usage of *schew* is at once utterly conventional and point-edly reflexive. Presenting herself as a text upon which God has inscribed words, Margery first "shows" to Caistyr "all þe wordys whech God had reuelyd to hyr in hyr sowl[e]." The syntax seems to suggest that Caistyr is intended to function as the reader or interpreter. However, Margery next images herself as her own exegete, for she "shows" him the events of her life but does so by glossing or analyzing them in terms of pride or vanity or envy. She goes on to tell him of her revelations, which she describes as a text indebted to none ("neyþyr Hyltons boke, ne [B]ridis boke, ne Stimulus Amoris, ne Incendium Amoris"). Kempe's language throughout the passage makes it clear that the act of showing involves far more than disclosure; it is also an interpretative act, one meant to validate the shower's self-awareness. Margery is both the text and its most astute translator.

Finally, Margery's act of confession focuses attention upon the compli-cated relationship between the individual and the community. Not only is it located in communal space with Caistyr's fellow priest, presumably, somewhere nearby, but she sits talking with a fellow human being, whom she can see and whose reactions she can gauge. In addition, Margery confesses to sins that impinge upon the well-being of the social body—pride, vanity, and envy—presenting what is individual in the analytical

44. John Bossy, "The Social History of Confession in the Age of the Reformation," 24. For the standard study see Lea, *A History of Auricular Confession*. See also Murray, "Confession as a Historical Source."

and communal language with which the Church describes sin.[45] Kempe also suggests something about her own process of selection in the *Book,* for Caistyr is privy to information we, the readers of this other text, do not have. Caistyr begins by "reading" an account of her childhood; we begin by reading an account of her marriage. Kempe thus evinces her awareness of fictional order, that the beginning of a text may help to shape its end. The text that Margery discloses and interprets to Caistyr is vaguely Augustinian; it begins in the heedlessness of childhood and proceeds to an account of a life described as displaying a classic pattern of sin. Chastisement, conversion, comfort, and revelation follow. What Kempe adumbrates here is a process of growing spiritual self-awareness; the Margery who both shows and glosses is master of her own text and apparently fully capable of constituting her public by the way she shapes her text. She therefore ends the chapter by stressing Caistyr's continual advocacy of her in the face of her later troubles with the authorities. What is private is thus brought into public view and presented as available and usable, but the process of publicizing is personal, individual, and suited to a specific circumstance (on a Thursday, a little before noon) and a particular person. Though Caistyr reads the beginning of a text we pick up a third of the way through, his encounter with Margery is incorporated into the text we read. He may know the beginning, but we know somewhat more of the end. I am not being entirely fanciful here; Kempe's account of this confession makes it clear that she, like Chaucer, thought of confession as a process of self-conscious narration at once subjective and social, as a moment when the individual locates the self in the context of community.[46] Kempe's account of Margery's experience with Richard Caistyr is but one instance among many of her ability to use a particular moment, which she describes in a highly particular way, as a means of expressing the true nature of community. In the *Book* the community of the spirit is not an entity but a process that is continually and mysteriously unfolding.

One of the most mysterious and evocative of these instances is the nonverbal "conversation" between Margery and a poor woman in Rome (see 94). It begins, "An-oþer tyme ryth as sche cam be a powr womanys hows, þe powr woman clepyd hir in-to hir hows & dede hir sytten be hir lytyl fyer, ȝeuyng hir wyn to drynke in a cuppe of ston." What Kempe

---

45. See Bossy, "The Social History of Confession," and idem, *Christianity in the West,* chapter 4, for the ways in which the Church focused on the social implications of sin.

46. On this subject, see also Patterson, *Chaucer and the Subject of History,* chapter 8.

here sketches in is a moment at once rooted in time and timeless. The poor woman who welcomes the holy into her house figures in the Old Testament stories of Elijah and Elisha, in New Testament stories of Jesus and the apostles: in her loving and generous response to what she does not fully understand, she stands as a signifier of our more sophisticated and culpable lack of charity and generosity. But Kempe anchors this particular moment to a place in time by her judicious use of details—the "lytyl fyer" and the wine offered in a "cuppe of ston." Such trappings of communion serve as the preamble to Margery's private experience of Christ's Passion: the woman's young son, who runs from the breast of his mother, who sits "ful of sorwe and sadnes," to Margery, causes Margery to "see" the Virgin and her son *in tyme of his Passyon* and to have other holy thoughts, which Kempe does not divulge. The sight, then, of the toddler calls to mind, not pictures of Mary and the baby Jesus, but images of that sacrifice enacted at the altar, the body broken and yet one. Kempe ends the scene with words that any writer would be proud to own, "þan owr Lord Ihesu Crist seyd to þe creatur, 'Thys place is holy.' And þan sche ros up & went forth in Rome & sey meche pouerte a-mong þe pepyl."

Kempe thus depicts a moment wherein community and communion are joined through the salvific image that Margery herself superimposes upon it.[47] She thereby hints at the very process of communal joining effected by the Mass, and though the stone cup holds no consecrated wine, it nonetheless is invested with symbolic power that derives from those very practices that were peripheral to the medieval Mass. The chalice was withdrawn from the laity during the thirteenth century, but at the annual Communion the entire population theoretically took at Easter unsanctified wine was normally offered to the communicant after he or she had received the Host. Like the blessed but unsanctified bread distributed on other Sundays among Mass-goers, the wine at once signified the distinctions of medieval society and the existence of a community of the faithful.[48] In the scene Kempe describes, Christ's words, "This place is holy," serve as a private version of "Ite, Missa est," providing the scene between the two women who barely speak with one another but who truly communicate with a moment of closure. The next sentence, "And

47. Bossy also plays with the associations between the two words; see *Christianity in the West,* 168.
48. See Bossy, "The Mass as a Social Institution," 53–54, for a description of this practice. See Rubin, *Corpus Christi,* 70, for an account of the Church's decision to withdraw the chalice from the laity.

þan sche ros up & went forth in Rome," joins Margery to the great mass of the poor who await her outside the private moment of revelation and communication. Significantly, the rest of chapter 39 describes Margery's reentry into her company; those who had despised and excluded her now make "hir ryth good cher & weryn rith glad of hir comyng" (94). Though the picture of communal unity is later fragmented once again, Kempe's handling of the passage underlines that the relationship among individuals in a community reflects a more profound joining embodied in moments of extraordinary and, strictly speaking, unsanctified meaning.

I am not suggesting here that Kempe is a Protestant or a Leveler, but simply that she consistently probes the foundations of our need for or belief in community. She tends to find the strongest evidence for the possibility of unity in individual moments of charity that are truly instances, to use a term she uses to describe various and diverging situations, of *comownyng*. The word itself encompassed several related meanings: it was used to describe the acts of sharing or of dividing into parts, of conforming, of associating, of having sexual intercourse, of communicating or telling stories, and of receiving Communion.[49] Kempe's persistent use of the words *comownyn* and *medelyn* to describe activities associated with what are human attempts at unity (sexual, social, or spiritual) is a sign of her self-conscious and highly strategic use of language as a means of suggesting both similarity and difference. What distinguishes the true moment of joining from the false or superficial is the charity that transcends the barriers of sex, language, or age and makes of two one through love of Christ. As Kempe repeatedly makes clear, the text of Margery's life contains far more instances of missed communication than of true communion, lapses that, more often than not, occur within the confines of the sanctioned institutions of the late medieval world. Margery's life is a protracted process of "showing" that only the few are prepared to understand or affirm. The place that is holy is more likely to be the spot beside a poor woman's fire or at the dinner table of a friend or wherever two can talk as if reading a single text.

Finally, what Pentecost confers is power, the power of the word and power over the word. It is a power Kempe assigns to Margery, through

---

49. Ellis ("The Merchant's Wife's Tale," 605) also mentions the various meanings of the verb *comowne,* seeing these as an instance of what she calls "social meanings" that in themselves indicate social confusion. In contrast, I see Kempe as consciously and meaningfully exploiting the richness of Middle English.

whom the Christ is manifest to her world. The prayers that end the *Book* are thus a sign of the Descent; Margery is described as reliving that Pentecostal moment and as going on to join the concerns of the world through her intercession. In the power with which Kempe invests her protagonist, we may find her diagnosis of an ecclesiastical and secular society whose claims to power are empty because, in lacking charity, they do not join but fragment. Kempe, unlike so many medieval authors, does not allude to or mention the "body politic"; instead, she provides a picture of parts whose momentary and ephemeral joining occurs around a figure whose dissociation is at once discomfort and release.

Works Cited

Primary Texts

Anonymous Pilgrims I–VIII (eleventh and twelfth centuries). Trans. Aubrey Stewart, Palestine Pilgrim's Text Society, 6, no. 1. London, 1894.

Archer, Margaret, ed. *The Register of Bishop Philip Repingdon.* 3 vols. Hereford: Lincoln Record Society, 1963–82.

Bateson, Mary. *Catalogue of the Library of Syon Monastery.* Cambridge: Cambridge University Press, 1898.

———. *Records of the Borough of Leicester.* 3 vols. London: C. J. Clay and Sons, 1899–1905.

Beadle, Richard. *The York Plays.* York Medieval Texts. London: Edward Arnold, 1982.

Benson, Larry D., ed. *The Riverside Chaucer.* 3d ed. Boston: Houghton Mifflin, 1987.

Blunt, J. H., ed. *The Mirror of Our Lady.* EETS, e.s. 19. London: Oxford University Press, 1873.

Bokenham, Osbern. *Legendys of Hooly Wummen.* Ed. Mary S. Serjeantson. EETS 206. London: Oxford University Press, 1938.

Brie, W. D., ed. *The Brut or The Chronicles of England.* EETS 136. London: Oxford University Press, 1908.

Bühler, Curt F. "A Lollard Tract: On Translating the Bible into English." *Medium Ævum* 7 (1938): 167–83.

Capgrave, John. *Abbreuiacion of Cronicles.* Ed. Peter J. Lucas. EETS 285. London: Oxford University Press, 1983.

Cassian, John. *Conferences.* Trans. Colm Luibheid. Intro. Owen Chadwick. New York: Paulist Press, 1985.

Christine de Pisan. *The Treasure of the City of Ladies.* Trans. Sarah Lawson. London: Penguin, 1985.

———. *The Book of the City of Ladies.* Trans. Earl Jeffrey Richards. New York: Persea, 1982.

Cole, C. A., ed. *Memorials of Henry the Fifth*. London: Longman, Brown, Green, Longmans, and Roberts, 1858.

Colledge, Edmund, and Romana Guarnieri. "The Glosses by 'M.N.' and Richard Methley to 'The Mirror of Simple Souls.'" *Archivio Italiano per la Storia della Pietà* 5 (1968): 357–82.

Colledge, Edmund, and James Walsh, eds. *A Book of Showings to the Anchoress Julian of Norwich*. 2 vols. Toronto: University of Toronto Press, 1978.

Collins, A. Jefferies, ed. *Manuale ad Vsum Percelebris Ecclesie Sarisburiensis*. Henry Bradshaw Society, vol. 91. Chicester: Moore and Tillyer, 1958.

Compston, H. F. B. "The Thirty-Seven Conclusions of the Lollards." *EHR* 26 (1911): 738–49.

Cronin, H. S., ed. "The Twelve Conclusions of the Lollards." *EHR* 22 (1907): 290–304.

Cumming, William Patterson, ed. *The Revelations of Saint Birgitta*. EETS 178. London, 1929; repr., Kraus, 1987.

Doiron, Marilyn. "Margaret Porete: 'The Mirror of Simple Souls': A Middle English Translation." *Archivio Italiano per la Storia della Pietà* 5 (1968): 241–355.

Ellis, Roger. *The Liber Celestis of St. Bridget of Sweden*. EETS 291. London: Oxford University Press, 1987.

The Examination of Master William Thorpe. In *Fifteenth Century Prose and Verse,* ed. Alfred W. Pollard. Westminster: Archibald Constable, 1903. 90–174.

Fisher, J. H., M. Richardson, and J. L. Fisher. *An Anthology of Chancery English*. Knoxville: University of Tennessee Press, 1984.

Forshall, Josiah, and Sir Frederic Madden, eds. *The Holy Bible containing the Old and New Testaments, with the Apocryphal Books in the Earliest English Versions made from the Latin Vulgate by John Wycliffe and his Followers*. 4 vols. Oxford: Oxford University Press, 1850; repr., AMS Press, 1982.

Fortescue, Sir John. *The Governance of England. A revised text*. Ed. Charles Plummer. Oxford: Clarendon Press, 1885.

Frere, Walter Howard, ed. *The Use of Sarum*. 2 vols. Cambridge: Cambridge University Press, 1898, 1901.

Gairdner, James, ed. *Historical Collections of a Citizen of London in the Fifteenth Century*. Camden Society, n.s. 17. London, 1876.

Galbraith, V. H., ed. *The St. Albans Chronicle, 1406–1420*. Oxford: Clarendon Press, 1937.

Genet, J. P., ed. *Four English Political Tracts of the Later Middle Ages*. Camden Society, 4th ser., 18. London: Royal Historical Society, 1977.

Glossa Ordinaria. PL 113, PL 114.

Guide-book to Palestine (c. 1350). Trans. J. H. Bernard. Palestine Pilgrim's Text Society, 6, no. 3. London, 1894.

Harrod, Henry. "Extracts from Early Wills in the Norwich Register." *Norfolk Archaeology* 4 (1855): 317–39.

Hildegard of Bingen. *Scivias*. PL 197.

———. *Scivias*. Trans. Francesca Maria Steele. In *Medieval Women's Visionary Literature,* ed. Elizabeth Alvilda Petroff. New York, 1986.

Hingeston, Francis Charles, ed. *Johannis Capgrave Liber de Illustribus Henricis*. Rolls Series no. 7. London: Longman, Brown, Green, Longmans, and Roberts, 1858.

Hodgson, Phyllis, and Gabriel M. Leegey, eds. *The Orcherd of Syon*. EETS 258. London: Oxford University Press, 1966.

Hollaway, Julia Bolton, ed. and trans. *Saint Bride and Her Book*. Focus Library of Medieval Women. Newburyport, Mass.: Focus Texts, 1992.

Horstmann, C., ed. *Lives of Women Saints*. EETS 86. Millwood, N.Y., 1987.

Horstmann, Karl, ed. *Prosalegenden. Anglia* 7–8 (1884–85): 102–96.

Hoskins, Edgar, ed. *Horae Beatae Mariae Virginis or Sarum and York Primers With Kindred Books and Primers of the Reformed Roman Use*. London: Longmans, Green, 1901.

Hudson, Anne, ed. *Selections from English Wycliffite Writings*. Cambridge: Cambridge University Press, 1978.

———, and Pamela Gradon, eds. *English Wycliffite Sermons*. 3 vols. Oxford: Clarendon Press, 1988–90.

Jacob, E. F., ed. *The Register of Henry Chichele, Archbishop of Canterbury, 1414-1443*. 4 vols. Canterbury and York Series. Oxford: Oxford University Press, 1943.

Jacques de Vitry. *The Life of Marie d'Oignies*. Trans. Margot H. King. Saskatoon, Canada: Peregrina, 1986.

———. *Vita Maria Oigniacensis*. In *Acta Sanctorum . . . editio novissima*, ed. J. Carnandet et al. (Paris, 1863–), 23 June (1867) 5: 42–572.

John Poloner's Description of the Holy Land (c. 1421). Trans. A. Stewart. Palestine Pilgrim's Text Society, 6, no. 4. London, 1894.

Johnston, Alexandra F., and Margaret Rogerson, eds. *York*. 2 vols. Records of Early English Drama Series. Toronto: University of Toronto Press, 1979.

Kingsford, Charles Lithbridge, ed. *The First English Life of King Henry the Fifth*. Oxford: Clarendon Press, 1911.

London B. L. Additional MS. 41175 (Wycliffite *Glossed Gospels*, Matthew and Mark).

Love, Nicholas. *The Mirrour of the Blessed Lyf of Jesu Christ*. Ed. Lawrence Powell. Oxford: Clarendon Press, 1908.

Lozar, Paula. "The 'Prologue' to the Ordinances of the York Corpus Christi Guild." *Allegorica* 1 (1976): 94–113.

Ludolph von Suchem. *Description of the Holy Land (1350)*. Trans. A. Stewart. Palestine Pilgrim's Text Society, 12, no. 3. London, 1895.

Luminasky, R. M., and David Mills, eds. *The Chester Mystery Cycle*. 2 vols. EETS, s.s. 3, no. 9. Oxford: Oxford University Press, 1974, 1986.

MacCracken, Henry Noble, ed. *Minor Poems of John Lydgate*. EETS 107. London: Oxford University Press, 1911.

Matthews, F. D., ed. *The English Works of Wyclif hitherto unprinted*. EETS 74. London: Oxford University Press, 1880.

McNamer, Sarah, ed. *The Revelations of St. Elizabeth of Hungary*. Heidelberg: Middle English Texts, forthcoming.

Meech, Sanford Brown, ed. *The Book of Margery Kempe*. EETS 212. London: Oxford University Press, 1940; repr., 1961.

Menner, Robert J., ed. *Purity, A Middle English Poem*. Yale Studies in English, vol. 61. (1920); repr., Archon Books, 1970.

Mundy, John Hine, and Kennerly M. Woody, eds. Trans. Louise Ropes Loomis. *The Council of Constance: The Unification of the Church*. New York: Columbia University Press, 1961.

Nichols, Francis Morgan, ed. and trans. *The Marvels of Rome. Mirabilia Urbis Romae*. 2d ed. Intro. Eileen Gardiner. New York: Italica, 1986.

Owen, Nancy H. "Thomas Wimbledon's Sermon: 'Redde racionem villicacionis tue.' " *Medieval Studies* 28 (1966): 176–97.

Oxford Bodleian MS Bodley 243 (Wycliffite *Glossed Gospels*, Luke and John).

Petroff, Elizabeth Alvilda. *Medieval Women's Visionary Literature*. Oxford: Oxford University Press, 1986.

Putnam, Bertha H., ed. *Proceedings before the Justices of the Peace in the Fourteenth and Fifteenth Centuries*. London: Spottiswoode, Ballantyne, 1938.

Ragusa, Isa, and Rosalie Green, eds. and trans. *Meditations on the Life of Christ: An Illustrated Manuscript of the Fourteenth Century*. Princeton: Princeton University Press, 1961.

Riley, Henry Thomas, ed. *Memorials of London and London Life*. London: Longmans, Green, 1868.

Roth, F. W. E., ed. *Die Visionen der hl. Elisabeth und die Schriften der Aebte Ekbert und Emecho von Schönau*. Studien aus dem Benedictiner- und Cistercienser-Orden. Brünn: 1884.

Rotuli Parliamentarum. 6 vols. London, 1783.

Sargent, Michael G., ed. *Nicholas Love's "Mirror of the Blessed Life of Jesus Christ."* New York: Garland, 1992.

Shirley, Walter Waddington, ed. *Fasciculi Zizaniorum Magistri Johannis Wyclif cum Tritico, ascribed to Thomas Netter of Walden*. Rolls Series, vol. 5. Kraus Reprint, 1965.

Simmons, Thomas Frederick, ed. *Lay Folks Mass Book*. EETS 71–72. London: Oxford University Press, 1879.

Skaife, H., ed. *The Register of the Guild of Corpus Christi in the City of York*. Durham, England: Surtees Society, 1872. 1–9.

Spector, Stephen, ed. *The N-Town Play, Cotton MS Vespasian D.8*. 2 vols. EETS, s.s. 11 and 12. Oxford: Oxford University Press, 1991.

Statutes of the Realm. 2 vols. London, 1816; repr., 1963.

Swenburn, L. M., ed. *The Lanterne of Light*. EETS 151. London: Oxford University Press, 1917.

Talbot, C. H., ed. and trans. *The Life of Christina of Markyate: A Twelfth Century Recluse*. Oxford: 1959.

Tanner, N. P., ed. *Heresy Trials in the Diocese of Norwich, 1428–31*. Camden Society, 4th ser., vol. 20. London: Royal Historical Society, 1977.

Taylor, Frank, and John S. Roskell, eds. and trans. *Gesta Henrici Quinti: The Deeds of Henry the Fifth*. Oxford: Clarendon Press, 1975.

Taylor, Richard. *Index Monasticus; or, The Abbeys and Other Monasteries, Alien Priories, Friaries, Colleges, Collegiate Churches, and Hospitals with Their Dependencies formerly Established in the Diocese of Norwich and the Ancient Kingdom of East Anglia*. London: Richard and Arthur Taylor, 1821.

Thomas of Cantimpré. *The Life of Christina of Saint Trond*. Trans. Margot H. King. Saskatoon, Canada: Peregrina, 1986.

———. *Vita Christinae Mirabilis*. In *Acta Sanctorum . . . editio novissima*, ed. J. Carnandet et al. (Paris, 1863–), (24 July) 5 (1868): 637–60.

Thompson, Sir Edward Maunde, ed. and trans. *Chronicon Adae de Usk, 1377–1421*. London: Henry Frowde, 1904.

Trevisa, John. *Dialogue between a Lord and a Clerk upon Translation*. In *Fifteenth Century Prose and Verse*, ed. Alfred W. Pollard. Westminster: Archibald Constable, 1903. 203–8.

Waldron, Ronald. "Trevisa's Original Prefaces on Translation: A Critical Edition." In *Medieval English Studies Presented to George Kane*, ed. Edward Donald Kennedy, Ronald Waldron, and Joseph Wittig. Wolfeboro, N.H.: D.S. Brewer, 1988. 285–300.

Walsingham, Thomas. *Gesta Abbatum Monasterii Sancti Albani*. 3 vols. Ed. Henry Thomas Riley. Rolls Series. Kraus Reprint, 1965.

Warner, Sir George, ed. *The Libelle of Englysche Polycye. A Poem on the Use of Sea-Power, 1436*. Oxford: Clarendon Press, 1926.

Wilkins, David, ed. *Concilia Magnae Britanniae et Hiberniae*. 4 vols. London, 1737.

Secondary Studies

Abram, Alice. "Women Traders in Medieval London." *Economic Journal* 28 (1916): 276–85.

Aers, David. *Community, Gender and Individual Identity: English Writing 1360–1430*. London: Routledge, 1988.

———. "Criseyde: Woman in Medieval Society." *Chaucer Review* 13 (1978–79): 177–200.

———. "*Piers Plowman* and Problems in the Perception of Poverty: A Culture in Transition." *Leeds Studies in English* 14 (1983): 5–25.

———. "Rewriting the Middle Ages: Some Suggestions." *Journal of Medieval and Renaissance Studies* 18 (1988): 221–40.

Anderson, Bonnie S., and Judith Zinsser. *A History of Their Own*. 2 vols. New York: Harper and Row, 1988.

Ashley, Kathleen, and Pamela Sheingorn, eds. *Interpreting Cultural Symbols: Saint Anne in Late Medieval Society*. Athens: University of Georgia Press, 1990.

Aston, Margaret. " 'Caim's Castles': Poverty, Politics, and Disendowment." In *The Church, Politics, and Patronage in the Fifteenth Century*, ed. Barrie Dobson. New York: St. Martin's, 1984. 45–81.

——— . *England's Iconoclasts*. Oxford: Clarendon Press, 1988.

———. *Lollards and Reformers: Images and Literacy in Late Medieval Religion*. London: Hambledon, 1984.

———. "Lollardy and Sedition, 1381–1431." *Past and Present* 17 (1960): 1–44.

Atkinson, Clarissa. *Mystic and Pilgrim: The Book and the World of Margery Kempe*. Ithaca: Cornell University Press, 1983.

———, Constance H. Buchanan, and Margaret R. Miles, eds. *Immaculate and Powerful: The Female in Sacred Image and Social Reality*. Harvard Women's Studies in Religion Series. Boston, 1985.

Baldwin, John W. *Masters, Princes and Merchants: The Social Views of Peter the Chanter and His Circle*. 2 vols. Princeton: Princeton University Press, 1970.

Bäuml, Franz H. "Medieval Texts and the Two Theories of Oral Formulaic Composition: A Proposal for a Third Theory." *New Literary History* 16 (1984): 31–50.

———. "Varieties and Consequences of Medieval Literacy and Illiteracy." *Speculum* 55 (1980): 237–65.

Baym, Nina. "The Madwoman and Her Language: Why I Don't Do Feminist Literary Theory." In *Feminist Issues in Literary Scholarship*, ed. Sheri Benstock. Bloomington: Indiana University Press, 1987. 45–61.

Beckwith, Sarah. "A Very Material Mysticism: The Medieval Mysticism of Margery Kempe." In *Medieval Literature: Criticism, Ideology, and History*, ed. David Aers. New York: St. Martin's, 1986. 34–57.

———. "Problems of Authority in Late Medieval English Mysticism: Language,

Agency, and Authority in *The Book of Margery Kempe*." *Exemplaria* 4 (1992): 171–200.

Bellamy, John. *Crime and Public Order in the Later Middle Ages*. London: Routledge and Kegan Paul, 1973.

Bennett, H. S. "The Production and Dissemination of Vernacular Manuscripts in the Fifteenth Century." *The Library*, 5th ser., 1 (1946–47): 167–77.

Bennett, Judith M. *Women in the Medieval English Countryside*. New York: Oxford University Press, 1987.

Bennett, Michael J. *Community, Class and Careerism: Cheshire and Lancashire Society in the Age of "Sir Gawain and the Green Knight."* London: Cambridge University Press, 1983.

Black, Antony. *Guilds and Civil Society in European Political Thought from the Twelfth Century to the Present*. Ithaca: Cornell University Press, 1984.

Blake, N. F. *The Textual Tradition of the Canterbury Tales*. London: Edward Arnold, 1985.

Bloch, R. Howard. *Medieval French Literature and Law*. Berkeley and Los Angeles: University of California Press, 1977.

———. "Wasteland and Round Table: The Historical Significance of Myths of Dearth and Plenty in Old French Romance." *New Literary History* 11 (1980): 255–76.

Bossy, John. *Christianity in the West, 1400–1700*. Oxford: Oxford University Press, 1987.

———. "Holiness and Society." review article, *Past and Present* 75 (1977): 119–37.

———. "The Mass as a Social Institution." *Past and Present* 81 (1983): 29–61.

———. "The Social History of Confession in the Age of the Reformation." *Transactions of the Royal Historical Society* 25 (1975): 21–38.

Brilioth, Y. *Eucharistic Faith and Practice*. London: SPCK, 1930; repr., 1965.

Brooke, C. N. L. "Religious Sentiment and Church Design in the Later Middle Ages." *Bulletin of the John Rylands Library* 50 (1967–68): 13–33.

Brown, Elizabeth A. R. "Philip V, Charles IV, and the Jews of France: The Alleged Expulsion of 1322." *Speculum* 66 (1991): 294–329.

Brown, Peter. *Augustine of Hippo*. Berkeley and Los Angeles: University of California Press, 1969.

———. *The Body and Society: Men, Women and Sexual Renunciation in Early Christianity*. New York: Columbia University Press, 1988.

———. *The Making of Late Antiquity*. Cambridge: Harvard University Press, 1978.

———. *Society and the Holy in Late Antiquity*. Berkeley and Los Angeles: University of California Press, 1982.

Brundage, J. A. *Law, Sex, and Christian Society in Medieval Europe*. Chicago: University of Chicago Press, 1987.

Bugge, John. *Virginitas. An Essay in the History of a Medieval Ideal*. The Hague: Martinus Nijhoff, 1976.

Burgess, Clive. " 'A fond thing vainly invented': An Essay on Purgatory and Pious Motive in Late Medieval England." In *Parish, Church and People: Local Studies in Lay Religion, 1350–1750*, ed. S. J. Wright. London: Hutchinson, 1988. 56–84.

Bynum, Caroline Walker. *Holy Feast and Holy Fast: The Religious Significance of Food to Medieval Women*. Berkeley and Los Angeles: University of California Press, 1987.

———. *Jesus as Mother: Studies in the Spirituality of the High Middle Ages*. Berkeley and Los Angeles: University of California Press, 1982.

———. "Women Mystics and Eucharistic Devotion in the Thirteenth Century." *Women's Studies* 11 (1984): 179–214.

————. "Women's Stories, Women's Symbols: A Critique of Victor Turner's Theory of Liminality." In *Anthropology and the Study of Religion,* ed. Frank Reynolds and Robert Moore. Chicago, 1984. 105–25.

Carruthers, Mary J. *The Book of Memory: A Study of Memory in Medieval Culture.* Cambridge: Cambridge University Press, 1990.

Castelli, Elizabeth. "Virginity and Its Meaning for Women's Sexuality in Early Christianity." *Journal of Feminist Studies in Religion* 2 (1986): 61–88.

Catto, Jeremy. "Religious Change under Henry V." In *Henry V: The Practice of Kingship,* ed. G. L. Harriss. New York: Oxford University Press, 1985. 97–115.

Clanchy, Michael T. "Looking Back from the Invention of Printing." In *Literacy in Historical Perspective,* ed. Daniel P. Resnick. Washington, D.C., 1983. 7–22.

Clopper, Lawrence M. "Lay and Clerical Impact on Civic Religious Drama and Ceremony." In *Contexts for Early English Drama,* ed. Marianne G. Briscoe and John C. Coldeway. Bloomington: Indiana University Press, 1989. 102–36.

Cockburn, J. S., H. P. F. King, and K. G. T. McDonnell. *A History of the County of Middlesex.* 3 vols. Oxford: Oxford University Press, 1969.

Cohen, Jeremy. *The Friars and the Jews: The Evolution of Medieval Anti-Judaism.* Ithaca: Cornell University Press, 1982.

————. "The Jews as Killers of Christ in the Latin Tradition, from Augustine to the Friars." *Traditio* 39 (1983): 1–27.

Cohen, Ralph. "History of Genre." *New Literary History* 17 (1986): 203–18.

Coleman, Janet. *Medieval Readers and Writers, 1350–1400.* New York: Columbia University Press, 1981.

Coletti, Theresa. "Biblical Wisdom: Chaucer's *Shipman's Tale* and the *Mulier Fortis.*" In *Chaucer and Scriptural Tradition,* ed. David Lyle Jeffrey. Ottawa: University of Ottawa Press, 1984. 171–82.

————. "A Feminist Approach to the Corpus Christi Cycles." In *Approaches to Teaching Medieval English Drama,* ed. Richard Emmerson. New York: Modern Language Association of America, 1990. 79–89.

————. "Reading REED: History and the Records of Early English Drama." In *Literary Practice and Social Change in Britain, 1380–1530,* ed. Lee Patterson. Berkeley and Los Angeles: University of California Press, 1990. 248–84.

Colish, Marcia, *The Mirror of Language.* Rev. ed. Lincoln: University of Nebraska Press, 1983.

Copeland, Rita. "Lollardy, Literalism, and the Vernacular: Margery Baxter's Deposition in the Norwich Heresy Trials." Paper delivered at the 27th International Congress on Medieval Studies, 1992.

————. "Rhetoric and Vernacular Translation in the Middle Ages." *Studies in the Age of Chaucer* 9 (1987): 41–76.

————. *Rhetoric, Hermeneutics, and Translation in the Middle Ages: Academic Traditions and Vernacular Texts.* Cambridge: Cambridge University Press, 1991.

————. "Why Women Can't Read: Medieval Hermeneutics, Statutory Law, and the Lollard Trials." In *Law, Literature, and Feminism,* ed. Susan Heinzelman, et al. Durham: Duke University Press, 1994.

Cosman, Madeline Pelner. *Fabulous Feasts: Medieval Cookery and Ceremony.* New York: George Braziller, 1976.

Crompton, James. "Leicestershire Lollards." *Transactions of the Leicestershire Archaeological and Historical Society* 44 (1968–69): 11–44.

Cross, Claire. " 'Great Reasoners in Scripture': The Activities of Women Lollards." In

Medieval Women: Essays Dedicated and Presented to Professor Rosalind M. T. Hill, ed. Derek Baker. Oxford: Basil Blackwell, 1978. 359–80.

Curtius, Ernst Robert. *European Literature and the Latin Middle Ages.* Trans. Willard R. Trask. New York, 1953; reissued, 1963.

Davies, W. J. Frank. *Teaching Reading in Early England.* London, 1973.

Davis, Natalie Zemon. "Gender and Genre: Women as Historical Writers, 1400–1820." In *Beyond Their Sex: Learned Women of the European Past,* ed. Patricia H. LaBalme. New York: New York University Press, 1980. 153–82.

———. *Society and Culture in Early Modern France.* Stanford: Stanford University Press, 1975.

Davis, Virginia. "The Rule of St. Paul, the First Hermit, in Late Medieval England." In *Monks, Hermits, and the Ascetic Tradition,* ed. W. J. Sheils. Oxford: Basil Blackwell, 1985. 203–14.

de Roover, Florence E. "The Scriptorium." In *The Medieval Library,* ed. James W. Thompson. Chicago, 1939. 591–612.

Deanesly, Margaret. *The Lollard Bible and Other Medieval Biblical Versions.* Cambridge: Cambridge University Press, 1920.

———. *The Significance of the Lollard Bible.* London: Athlone, 1951.

Delany, Sheila. "Sexual Economics, Chaucer's Wife of Bath and *The Book of Margery Kempe*." *Minnesota Review* 5 (1975): 104–15.

Denley, Marie. "Elementary Teaching Techniques and Middle English Religious Didactic Writing." In *Langland, The Mystics, and the Medieval English Religious Tradition,* ed. Helen Phillips. Cambridge: D. S. Brewer, 1990. 223–42.

Dickens, A. G. *Lollards and Protestants in the Diocese of York, 1509–1558.* Oxford, 1959; repr., London: Hambledon, 1982.

Dickman, Susan. "Margery Kempe and the Continental Tradition of the Pious Woman." In *The Medieval Mystical Tradition in England,* ed. Marion Glasscoe. Cambridge: D. S. Brewer, 1984. 150–68.

———. "Margery Kempe and the English Devotional Tradition." In *The Medieval Mystical Tradition in England,* ed. Marion Glasscoe. Exeter: Exeter University Press, 1980. 156–72.

Dinshaw, Carolyn. *Chaucer's Sexual Politics.* Madison: University of Wisconsin Press, 1989.

Dobson, R. "The Jews of Medieval York and the Massacre of March 1190." Borthwick Papers, no. 45. York, 1974.

Douglas, Mary. *Purity and Danger: An Analysis of Concepts of Pollution and Taboo.* New York, 1966; repr., Penguin, 1970.

Driver, Martha W. "Pictures in Print: Late Fifteenth- and Early Sixteenth-Century English Religious Books for Lay Readers." In *De Cella in Seculum,* ed. Michael G. Sargent. Cambridge: D. S. Brewer, 1989. 229–44.

Dronke, Peter. *Women Writers of the Middle Ages. A Critical Study of Texts from Perpetua (+ 203) to Marguerite Porete (+ 1310).* Cambridge: Cambridge University Press, 1984.

Du Boulay, F. R. H. *An Age of Ambition: English Society in the Late Middle Ages.* London: Thomas Nelson and Sons, 1970.

———. *The England of "Piers Plowman."* Cambridge: D. S. Brewer, 1991.

Duby, George. *Medieval Marriage. Two Models from Twelfth-Century France.* Baltimore: Johns Hopkins University Press, 1978.

———. *The Three Orders: Feudal Society Imagined.* Trans. Arthur Goldhammer. Chicago: University of Chicago Press, 1980.

Dyer, Christopher. *Standards of Living in the Later Middle Ages: Social Change in England c. 1200–1520*. Cambridge: Cambridge University Press, 1989.

Ellis, Deborah S. "The Merchant's Wife's Tale: Language, Sex, and Commerce in Margery Kempe and in Chaucer." *Exemplaria* 2 (1990): 595–626.

Ellis, Roger. " 'Flores ad Fabricandam . . . Coronam': An Investigation into the Uses of the Revelations of St. Bridget of Sweden in Fifteenth-Century England." *Medium Ævum* 51 (1982): 163–86.

———. "Margery Kempe's Scribe and the Miraculous Books." In *Langland, the Mystics, and the Medieval English Religious Tradition*, ed. Helen Phillips. Cambridge: D. S. Brewer, 1990. 161–76.

Emmerson, Richard, ed. *Approaches to Teaching Medieval English Drama*. New York: Modern Language Association of America, 1990.

Faith, Rosamond. " 'The Great Rumour' of 1377 and Peasant Ideology." In *The English Rising of 1381*, ed. R. H. Hilton and T. H. Aston. Cambridge: Cambridge University Press, 1984. 43–73.

Feinberg, Nona. "Thematics of Value in *The Book of Margery Kempe*." *Modern Philology* 87 (1989): 132–41.

Ferguson, Chris D. "Autobiography as Therapy: Guibert de Nogent, Peter Abelard, and the Making of Medieval Autobiography." *Journal of Medieval and Renaissance Studies* 13 (1983): 187–212.

Fisher, J. H. "Chancery and the Emergence of Standard Written English in the Fifteenth Century." *Speculum* 52 (1977): 869–99.

Flandrin, Jean-Louis. "Sex in Married Life in the Early Middle Ages: The Church's Teaching and Behavioral Reality." In *Western Sexuality: Practice and Precept in Past and Present Times*, ed. P. Ariès and A. Béjin. Trans. Anthony Forster. Oxford: Basil Blackwell, 1985. 114–29.

Fleming, P. W. "Charity, Faith, and the Gentry of Kent 1422–1529." In *Property and Politics: Essays in Later Medieval English History*, ed. Tony Pollard. Gloucester: Alan Sutton, 1984. 36–58.

Frugoni, Chiara. *A Distant City: Images of Urban Experience in the Medieval World*. Trans. William McCuaig. Princeton: Princeton University Press, 1991.

Gellrich, Jesse M. *The Idea of the Book in the Middle Ages: Language, Theory, Mythology, and Fiction*. Ithaca: Cornell University Press, 1985.

Georgianna, Linda. *The Solitary Self: Individuality in the Ancrene Wisse*. Cambridge: Harvard University Press, 1981.

Gibson, Gail McMurray. "Saint Anne and the Religion of Childbed: Some East Anglian Texts and Talismans." In *Interpreting Cultural Symbols: Saint Anne in Late Medieval Society*, ed. Kathleen Ashley and Pamela Sheingorn. Athens: University of Georgia Press, 1990. 95–110.

———. *The Theater of Devotion: East Anglian Drama and Society in the Late Middle Ages*. Chicago: University of Chicago Press, 1989.

Given-Wilson, Chris. *The English Nobility in the Late Middle Ages*. New York: Routledge and Kegan Paul, 1987.

Goodich, Michael. "The Contours of Female Piety in Later Medieval Hagiography." *Church History* 50 (1981): 20–32.

Goodman, Anthony. "The Piety of John Brunham's Daughter of Lynn." In *Medieval Women: Essays Dedicated and Presented to Professor Rosalind M. T. Hill*, ed. Derek Baker. Oxford: Basil Blackwell, 1978. 347–58.

Goody, Jack. *The Development of the Family and Marriage in Europe*. Cambridge: Cambridge University Press, 1983.

Gottfried, Robert S. *Bury St. Edmunds and the Urban Crisis, 1290–1539*. Princeton: Princeton University Press, 1982.

Gray, Douglas. "Popular Religion and Late Medieval English Literature." In *Religion in the Poetry and Drama of the Late Middle Ages in England,* ed. Piero Boitani and Anna Torti. Cambridge: D. S. Brewer, 1990. 1–28.

Green, Alice Stopford. *Town Life in the Fifteenth Century*. Boston, 1984; reissued, New York, 1971.

Griffiths, J. J., and D. A. Pearsall. *Book Production and Publishing in Britain, 1375–1475*. Cambridge: Cambridge University Press, 1989.

Gurenvich, Aaron J. "Oral and Written Culture of the Middle Ages: Two 'Peasant Visions' of the Late Twelfth–Early Thirteenth Centuries." *New Literary History* 16 (1984): 51–66.

Haines, Roy. "Church, Society and Politics in the Early Fifteenth Century as Viewed from an English Pulpit." *Studies in Church History* 12 (1975): 143–57.

———. *Ecclesia Anglicana*. Toronto: University of Toronto Press, 1989.

———. " 'Our Master Mariner, Our Sovereign Lord': A Contemporary View of Henry V." *Medieval Studies* 38 (1976): 85–96.

———. " 'Wilde Wittes and Wilfulnes': John Swetstock's Attack on those 'Poyswunmongeres,' the Lollards." *Studies in Church History* 8 (1971): 143–53.

Hanawalt, Barbara A. *The Ties That Bound: Peasant Families in Medieval England*. Oxford, 1986.

Hanna, Ralph, III. "The Difficulty of Ricardian Prose Translation: The Case of the Lollards." *Modern Language Quarterly* 50 (1990): 319–40.

———. "Sir Thomas Berkeley and His Patronage." *Speculum* 64 (1989): 878–916.

Hansen, Elaine Tuttle. *Chaucer and the Fictions of Gender*. Berkeley and Los Angeles: University of California Press, 1992.

Hargreaves, Henry. "Popularizing Biblical Scholarship: The Role of the Wycliffite Glossed Gospels." In *The Bible and Medieval Culture,* ed. W. Lourdaux and D. Verhelst. Louvain: Louvain University Press, 1979. 171–89.

Heffernan, Thomas J. *Sacred Biography: Saints and Their Biographers in the Middle Ages*. New York: Oxford University Press, 1988.

Hillen, Henry J. *History of the Borough of King's Lynn*. 2 vols. Norwich, 1907.

Hilton, Rodney H. *Class Conflict and the Crisis of Feudalism. Essays in Medieval Social History*. London: Hambledon, 1985.

———. "Women Traders in Medieval England." *Women's Studies* 11 (1984): 139–55.

Hindman, Sandra L. *Christine de Pizan's "Epistre Othéa": Painting and Politics at the Court of Charles VI*. Studies and Texts, no. 77. Toronto: University of Toronto Press, 1986.

Hirsch, John C. *The Revelations of Margery Kempe: Paramystical Practices in Late Medieval England*. Leiden: E. J. Brill, 1989.

Holbrook, Sue Ellen. "Margery Kempe and Wynkyn de Worde." In *The Medieval Mystical Tradition in England,* ed. Marion Glasscoe. Exeter Symposium IV. Cambridge: D. S. Brewer, 1987. 27–46.

Howell, Martha C. *Women, Production, and Patriarchy in Late Medieval Cities*. Chicago: University of Chicago Press, 1986.

Hudson, Anne. *Lollards and Their Books*. London: Hambledon, 1985.

———. "Lollardy: The English Heresy?" *Studies in Church History* 18 (1982): 261–83.

———. *The Premature Reformation: Wycliffite Texts and Lollard History*. Oxford: Clarendon Press, 1988.

———. "Wyclif and the English Language." In *Wyclif in His Times,* ed. Anthony Kenny. Oxford: Clarendon Press, 1986. 85–103.

Hughes, Jonathan. *Pastors and Visionaries: Religion and Secular Life in Late Medieval Yorkshire.* Wolfeboro, N.H.: Boydell and Brewer, 1988.

Jacob, E. F. *Archbishop Henry Chichele.* London: Thomas Nelson, 1967.

———. *Essays in the Conciliar Epoch.* Manchester: Manchester University Press, 1943.

———. *The Fifteenth Century.* Oxford: Clarendon Press, 1961.

James, Mervyn. "Ritual Drama and Social Body in the Late Medieval English Town." *Past and Present* 98 (1983): 3–29.

Janson, Tore. *Latin Prose Prefaces: Studies in Literary Conventions.* Studia Latina Stockholmiensia, no. 13. Stockholm, 1964.

Jauss, Hans Robert. *Toward an Aesthetic of Reception.* Trans. Timothy Bahti. Intro. Paul de Man. Minneapolis: University of Minnesota Press, 1982.

Jeffrey, David Lyle. "Chaucer and Wyclif: Biblical Hermeneutic and Literary Theory in the XIVth Century." In *Chaucer and Scriptural Tradition,* ed. David Lyle Jeffrey. Ottawa: University of Ottawa Press, 1984. 109–40.

Johnson, Lynn Staley. "Chaucer's Tale of the Second Nun and the Strategies of Dissent." *Studies in Philology* 89 (1992): 314–33.

———. "Inverse Counsel: Contexts for the *Melibee.*" *Studies in Philology* 87 (1990): 137–55.

———. *"The Shepheardes Calender": An Introduction.* University Park: The Pennsylvania State University Press, 1990.

Jones, W. R. "The English Church and Royal Propaganda during the Hundred Years' War." *Journal of British Studies* 19 (1979–80): 18–30.

Jordan, William Chester. *The French Monarchy and the Jews.* Philadelphia: University of Pennsylvania Press, 1989.

Kaske, R. E. " 'Clericus Adam' and Chaucer's 'Adam Scriveyn.' " In *Chaucerian Problems and Perspectives: Essays Presented to Paul E. Beichner, C.S.C.,* ed. E. Vasta and Z. P. Thundy. Notre Dame, Ind.: Notre Dame University Press, 1979. 114–18.

Keen, Maurice. *English Society in the Later Middle Ages.* London: Penguin, 1990.

———. "Wyclif, the Bible, and Transubstantiation." In *Wyclif in His Times,* ed. Anthony Kenny. Oxford: Clarendon Press, 1986. 1–16.

Kendall, Ritchie D. *The Drama of Dissent: The Radical Poetics of Nonconformity, 1380–1590.* Chapel Hill: University of North Carolina Press, 1986.

Kennedy, Elspeth. "The Scribe as Editor." In *Mélanges de langue et de littérature du Moyen Age et de la Renaissance offerts à Jean Frappier.* Geneva, 1970. 523–31.

Kieckhefer, Richard. *Unquiet Souls: Fourteenth-Century Saints and Their Religious Milieu.* Chicago: University of Chicago Press, 1984.

King, John N. *English Reformation Literature: The Tudor Origins of the Protestant Tradition.* Princeton: Princeton University Press, 1982.

Knapp, Peggy. *Chaucer and the Social Contest.* New York: Routledge, 1990.

Knowles, David. *The English Mystical Tradition.* London: Burns and Oates, 1961.

Köhler, Erich. "Les Troubadours et La Jalousie." In *Mélanges de langue et de littérature du Moyen Age et de la Renaissance offerts à Jean Frappier.* Geneva: Droz, 1970. 543–59.

Kolve, V. A. "Chaucer's Second Nun and the Iconography of Saint Cecilia." In *New Perspectives on Chaucer Criticism,* ed. Donald M. Rose. Norman, Okla.: Pilgrim, 1981. 137–76.

Kristeva, Julia. "Stabat Mater." *Poetics Today* 6 (1985): 133–52.

Kurtz, Patricia Deery. "Mary of Oigniés, Christine the Marvelous, and Medieval Heresy." *Mystics Quarterly* 14 (1988): 186–96.

Ladurie, Emmanuel Le Roy. *Montaillou.* Trans. Barbara Bray. New York: George Braziller, 1978.

Lea, H. C. *A History of Auricular Confession and Indulgences in the Latin Church.* 3 vols. Philadelphia, 1896.

Leff, Gordon. *Heresy in the Later Middle Ages.* 2 vols. New York: Barnes and Noble, 1967.

Lerer, Seth. "Textual Criticism and Literary Theory." *Exemplaria* 2 (1990): 329–45.

Lerner, Robert E. *The Heresy of the Free Spirit in the Later Middle Ages.* Berkeley and Los Angeles: University of California Press, 1972.

Lipman, V. *The Jews of Medieval Norwich.* London: Jewish Historical Society of England, 1967.

Little, Lester K. *Religious Poverty and the Profit Economy in Medieval Europe.* Ithaca: Cornell University Press, 1978.

Lochrie, Karma. "*The Book of Margery Kempe:* The Marginal Woman's Quest for Literary Authority." *Journal of Medieval and Renaissance Studies* 16 (1986): 33–55.

———. *Margery Kempe and Translations of the Flesh.* Philadelphia: University of Pennsylvania Press, 1991.

Lucas, Peter J. "John Capgrave, O.S.A. (1393–1464), Scribe and 'Publisher.' " *Transaction of the Cambridge Bibliographical Society* 5 (1969): 1–35.

MacAloon, John J., ed. *Rite, Drama, Festival, Spectacle: Rehearsals toward a Theory of Cultural Performance.* Philadelphia: ISHI, 1984.

Mann, Jill. *Chaucer and Medieval Estates Satire.* Cambridge: Cambridge University Press, 1973.

Martin, Jeanne S. "Character as Emblem: Generic Transformations in the Middle English Saint's Life." *Mosaic* 8 (1975): 47–60.

McFarlane, K. B. *John Wycliffe and the Beginnings of English Nonconformity.* London, 1952; New York, 1953.

———. *Lancastrian Kings and Lollard Knights.* Oxford: Clarendon Press, 1972.

McHardy, A. K. "Liturgy and Propaganda in the Diocese of Lincoln During the Hundred Years War." *Studies in Church History* 18 (1982): 15–27.

McKenna, J. W. "Popular Canonization as Political Propaganda: The Case of Archbishop Scrope." *Speculum* 45 (1970): 608–23.

McKisack, May. *The Fourteenth Century, 1307–1399.* Oxford: Oxford University Press, 1959.

McNiven, Peter. *Heresy and Politics in the Reign of Henry IV.* Woodbridge, Suffolk: Boydell Press, 1987.

McRee, Ben R. "Religious Gilds and Civic Order: The Case of Norwich in the Late Middle Ages." *Speculum* 67 (1992): 69–97.

———. "Religious Gilds and Regulation of Behavior in Late Medieval Towns." In *People, Politics, and Community in the Later Middle Ages,* ed. J. T. Rosenthal and C. Richmond. Gloucester, 1987. 108–22.

Mertes, Kate. *The English Noble Household, 1250–1600: Good Governance and Politic Rule.* Oxford: Basil Blackwell, 1988.

Middleton, Anne. "The Audience and Public of *Piers Plowman.*" In *Middle English Alliterative Poetry and Its Literary Background,* ed. D. A. Lawton. Cambridge: D. S. Brewer, 1982. 101–23.

———. "Narration and the Invention of Experience: Episodic Form in *Piers Plowman.*" In *The Wisdom of Poetry: Essays in Early English Literature in Honor of*

Morton W. Bloomfield, ed. Larry D. Benson and Siegfried Wenzel. Kalamazoo, Mich.: The Medieval Institute, 1982. 91–122.

———. "William Langland's 'Kynde Name': Authorial Signature and Social Identity in Late Fourteenth-Century England." In *Literary Practice and Social Change in Britain, 1380–1530,* ed. Lee Patterson. Berkeley and Los Angeles: University of California Press, 1990. 15–82.

Mills, David. "Religious Drama and Civic Ceremonial." In *Medieval Drama,* ed. A. C. Cawley, Marion Jones, Peter F. McDonald, and David Mills. *The Revels History of Drama in English.* London: Methuen, 1983. 152–206.

Mollat, Michel. *The Poor in the Middle Ages. An Essay in Social History.* Trans. Arthur Goldhammer. New Haven: Yale University Press, 1986.

Moran, Jo Ann Hoeppner. *The Growth of English Schooling, 1340–1548: Learning, Literacy, and Laicization in Pre-Reformation York Diocese.* Princeton: Princeton University Press, 1985.

Mueller, Janel M. "Autobiography of a New 'Creatur': Female Spirituality, Selfhood, and Authorship in *The Book of Margery Kempe.*" In *Women in the Middle Ages and Renaissance,* ed. Mary Beth Rose. Syracuse: Syracuse University Press, 1986. 155–72.

Murray, A. "Confession as a Historical Source in the Thirteenth Century." In *The Writing of History in the Middle Ages: Essays Presented to Richard William Southern,* ed. R. H. C. Davis and J. M. Wallace-Hadrill. Oxford: Oxford University Press, 1981. 275–322.

Nelson, Alan H. "On Recovering the Lost Norwich Corpus Christi Cycle." *Comparative Drama* 4 (1970–71): 241–52.

Newman, Barbara. *Sister of Wisdom. St. Hildegard's Theology of the Feminine.* Berkeley and Los Angeles: University of California Press, 1987.

Olsen, Glenn. "The Idea of the *Ecclesia Primitiva* in the Writings of the Twelfth-Century Canonists." *Traditio* 25 (1969): 61–86.

Owen, Nancy H. "Thomas Wimbledon." *Medieval Studies* 24 (1962): 377–81.

Owst, G. R. *Literature and Pulpit in Medieval England.* 2d ed. Oxford: Basil Blackwell, 1966.

Parker, Vanessa. *The Making of King's Lynn.* London: Phillimore, 1971.

Parkes, M. B. "The Influence of the Concepts of *Ordinatio* and *Compilatio* on the Development of the Book." In *Medieval Learning and Literature: Essays Presented to R. W. Hunt,* ed. J. J. G. Alexander and M. T. Gibson. Oxford, 1976. 115–141.

Parkes, Malcolm, and Andrew G. Watson, eds. *Medieval Scribes, Manuscripts, and Libraries: Essays Presented to N. R. Ker.* London: Scolar Press, 1978.

Partner, Nancy F. "Reading the Book of Margery Kempe." *Exemplaria* 3 (1991): 29–66.

Patterson, Lee W. "Ambiguity and Interpretation: A Fifteenth-Century Reading of *Troilus and Criseyde.*" *Speculum* 54 (1979): 297–330.

———. *Chaucer and the Subject of History.* Madison: University of Wisconsin Press, 1992.

———. "Court Politics and the Invention of Literature: The Case of Sir John Clanvowe." In *Culture and History, 1380–1450,* ed. David Aers. London: Harvester, 1992. 7–41.

———. "The Historiography of Romance and the Alliterative *Morte Arthure.*" *Journal of Medieval and Renaissance Studies* 13 (1983): 1–32.

———. "Making Identities in Fifteenth Century England: John Lydgate and Henry V." In *New Historical Literary Study: Essays on Reproducing Texts, Representing*

History, ed. Jeffrey N. Cox and Larry J. Reynolds. Princeton: Princeton University Press, 1993.

———. *Negotiating the Past.* Madison: University of Wisconsin Press, 1987.

———. "On the Margin: Postmodernism, Ironic History, and Medieval Studies." *Speculum* 65 (1990): 87–108.

Peck, Russell A. "Public Dreams and Private Myths: Perspectives in Middle English Literature." *PMLA* 90 (1975): 461–68.

———. "Social Conscience and the Poets." In *Social Unrest in the Late Middle Ages,* ed. Francis X. Newman. Binghamton, N.Y.: Center for Medieval and Early Renaissance Studies, 1986. 113–48.

Pelphrey, Brant. *Love Was His Meaning: The Theology and Mysticism of Julian of Norwich.* Salzburg Studies in English Literature. Salzburg: Universität Salzburg, 1982.

Perrow, Eber Carle. "The Last Will and Testament as a Form of Literature." *Transactions of the Wisconsin Academy of Sciences, Arts, and Letters* 17, no. 1 (1914): 682–753.

Platt, Colin. *The English Medieval Town.* London, 1976.

Plumb, Derek. "The Social and Economic Spread of Rural Lollardy: A Reappraisal." *Studies in Church History* 23 (1986): 111–29.

Post, J. B. "The Obsequies of John of Gaunt." *Guildhall Studies in London History* 5 (1981): 1–11.

Pythian-Adams, Charles. "Ceremony and the Citizen: The Communal Year at Coventry, 1450–1550." In *The Early Modern Town,* ed. Peter Clark. London: Longman, 1976. 106–28.

Quilligan, Maureen. *The Allegory of Female Authority: Christine de Pizan's "Cité des Dames."* Ithaca: Cornell University Press, 1991.

Rembaum, J. "The Talmud and the Popes: Reflections on the Talmud Trials of the 1240's." *Viator* 13 (1982): 203–21.

Reynolds, Susan. *An Introduction to the History of English Medieval Towns.* Oxford: Clarendon Press, 1977.

———. *Kingdoms and Communities in Western Europe, 900–1300.* Oxford: Clarendon Press, 1984.

Richards, P. *The Medieval Leper and His Northern Heir.* Cambridge: D. S. Brewer, 1977.

Riehle, Wolfgang. *The Middle English Mystics.* London, 1981.

Robbins, Rossell Hope. "Dissent in Middle English Literature: The Spirit of (Thirteen) Seventy-Six." *Medievalia et Humanistica* 9 (1979): 25–51.

Robertson, D. W., Jr. *Chaucer's London.* New York: John Wiley and Sons, 1968.

Rosenthal, Joel T. *The Purchase of Paradise: Gift Giving and the Aristocracy, 1307–1485.* London: Routledge and Kegan Paul, 1972.

Rossiaud, Jacques. *Medieval Prostitution.* Trans. Lydia G. Cochrane. Oxford: Basil Blackwell, 1988.

———. "Prostitution, Sex and Society in French Towns in the Fifteenth Century." In *Western Sexuality: Practice and Precept in Past and Present Times,* ed. P. Ariès and A. Béjin. Trans. Anthony Forster. Oxford: Basil Blackwell, 1985. 76–94.

Rubin, Miri. "Corpus Christi Fraternities and Late Medieval Piety." *Studies in Church History* 23 (1986): 97–110.

———. *Corpus Christi: The Eucharist in Late Medieval Culture.* Cambridge: Cambridge University Press, 1991.

———. "Small Groups: Identity and Solidarity in the Late Middle Ages." In *Enter-*

prise and Individuals in Fifteenth-Century England, ed. Jennifer Kermode. Wolfboro Falls, N.H.: Alan Sutton, 1991. 132–50.

Saenger, Paul. "Silent Reading: Its Impact on Late Medieval Script and Society." *Viator* 13 (1982): 367–414.

Salter, Elizabeth Zeeman. "Continuity and Change in Middle English Versions of *Meditationes Vitae Christi.*" *Medium Ævum* 26 (1957): 25–31.

———. "Nicholas Love—A Fifteenth Century Translator." *Review of English Studies* 6 (1955): 113–27.

———. *Nicholas Love's "Myrrour of the Blessed Lyf of Jesu Crist." Analecta Carthusiana,* no. 10. Salzburg, 1974.

Scase, Wendy. *"Piers Plowman" and the New Anticlericalism.* Cambridge: Cambridge University Press, 1989.

Schultz, James H. "Medieval Adolescence: The Claims of History and the Silence of German Narrative." *Speculum* 66 (1991): 519–39.

Simpson, James. "The Constraints of Satire in 'Piers Plowman' and 'Mum and the Sothsegger.'" In *Langland, The Mystics and the Medieval English Religious Tradition,* ed. Helen Phillips. Cambridge: D. S. Brewer, 1990. 11–30.

Staley, Lynn. See Johnson, Lynn Staley.

Stanbury, Sarah. "Feminist Film Theory: Seeing Chrétien's *Enide.*" *Literature and Psychology* 36 (1990): 47–66.

———. "The Virgin's Gaze: Spectacle and Transgression in Middle English Lyrics of the Passion." *PMLA* 106 (1991): 1083–93.

Stenton, F. M. "The Road System of Medieval England." *Economic History Review* 7 (1936): 1–21.

Stevens, Martin. *Four Middle English Mystery Cycles: Textual, Contextual, and Critical Interpretations.* Princeton: Princeton University Press, 1987.

Stock, Brian. *The Implications of Literacy.* Princeton: Princeton University Press, 1983.

———. "Medieval Literacy, Linguistic Theory, and Social Organization." *New Literary History* 16 (1984): 13–30.

Strayer, Joseph R. *The Albigensians.* New York: Dial Press, 1971.

Strohm, Paul. "Chaucer's Fifteenth-Century Audience and the Narrowing of the Chaucer Tradition." *Studies in the Age of Chaucer* 4 (1982): 3–32.

Stuard, Susan. "The Dominion of Gender: Women's Fortune's in the High Middle Ages." In *Becoming Visible: Women in European History,* ed. Renate Bridenthal, et al. Boston: Houghton Mifflin, 1987. 154–72.

Swanson, R. N. *Church and Society in Late Medieval England.* Oxford: Basil Blackwell, 1989.

Synan, Edward A. *The Popes and the Jews in the Middle Ages.* New York: MacMillan, 1965.

Tanner, Norman P. *The Church in Late Medieval Norwich, 1370–1532.* Toronto: Pontifical Institute of Medieval Studies, 1984.

Taylor, John. *The "Universal Chronicle" of Ranulf Higden.* Oxford: Clarendon Press, 1966.

Thomas, Keith. *Religion and the Decline of Magic.* New York: Charles Scribner, 1971.

Thompson, James Westfall. *The Literacy of the Laity in the Middle Ages.* University of California Publications in Education. Berkeley and Los Angeles, 1939; repr., New York, 1963.

Thrupp, Sylvia. *The Merchant Class of Medieval London, 1300–1500.* Ann Arbor: University of Michigan Press, 1948; repr., 1989.

Travis, Peter. *Dramatic Design in the Chester Cycle*. Chicago: University of Chicago Press, 1982.

———. "The Social Body of the Dramatic Christ in Medieval England." In *Early Drama to 1600,* ed. Albert H. Tricomi. *Acta* 13 (1987): 17–36.

Tuck, J. Anthony. "Carthusian Monks and Lollard Knights: Religious Attitudes at the Court of Richard II." *Studies in the Age of Chaucer. Proceedings* (1985): 149–61.

Vale, M. G. A. *Piety, Charity, and Literacy Among the Yorkshire Gentry, 1370–1480.* Borthwick Papers, no. 50. York, 1976.

Vance, Eugene. "Augustine's *Confessions* and the Grammar of Selfhood." *Genre* (1973): 1–28.

Walker, Simon. *The Lancastrian Affinity, 1361–1399*. Oxford: Clarendon Press, 1990.

Wallace, David. "Mystics and Followers in Sienna and East Anglia: A Study in Taxonomy, Class and Cultural Mediation." In *The Medieval Mystical Tradition in England,* ed. Marion Glasscoe. Cambridge: D. S. Brewer, 1984. 169–91.

Wawn, Andrew. "Truth-telling and the Tradition of *Mum and the Sothsegger*." *Yearbook of English Studies* 13 (1983): 270–87.

White, Hayden. "The Value of Narrativity in the Representation of Reality." In his *The Content of the Form: Narrative Discourse and Historical Representation*. Baltimore: Johns Hopkins University Press, 1987. 1–25.

Willard, Charity Cannon. *Christine de Pizan: Her Life and Works*. New York, 1984.

Windeatt, B. A. "Julian of Norwich and Her Audience." *Review of English Studies* 28 (1977): 1–17.

———. "The Scribes as Chaucer's Early Critics." *Studies in the Age of Chaucer* 1 (1979): 119–41.

Withington, Robert. *English Pageantry*. 2 vols. Cambridge: Harvard University Press, 1918.

Woolf, Rosemary. *The English Religious Lyric in the Middle Ages*. Oxford: Clarendon Press, 1968.

Index